MW00965220

mySAP CRM Interaction Center

 **PRESS**

SAP PRESS is issued by
Bernhard Hochlehnert, SAP AG

SAP PRESS is a joint initiative of SAP and Galileo Press. The know-how offered by SAP specialists combined with the expertise of the publishing house Galileo Press offers the reader expert books in the field. SAP PRESS features first-hand information and expert advice, and provides useful skills for professional decision-making.

SAP PRESS offers a variety of books on technical and business related topics for the SAP user. For further information, please visit our website: *www.sap-press.com*.

S. Karch, L. Heilig, C. Bernhardt, A. Hardt, F. Heidfeld, R. Pfennig
SAP NetWeaver Roadmap
2005, 312 pp., ISBN 1-59229-041-8

R. Buck-Emden, P. Zencke
mySAP CRM
The Official Guidebook to SAP CRM 4.0
2004, 462 pp., ISBN 1-59229-029-9

M. Missbach, P. Gibbels, J. Karnstädt, J. Stelzel, T. Wagenblast
Adaptive Hardware Infrastructures for SAP
2005, 534 pp., ISBN 1-59229-035-3

H. Keller
The Official ABAP Reference
2-volume set with 3 CDs
2nd Ed. 2005, 1216 pp., ISBN 1-59229-039-6

Thorsten Wewers, Tim Bolte

mySAP CRM
Interaction Center

SAP PRESS

First Edition 2006
© 2006 by Galileo Press
SAP PRESS is an imprint of Galileo Press,
Fort Lee (NJ), USA
Bonn (Germany)

All rights reserved. Neither this publication
nor any part of it may be copied or reprodu-
ced in any form or by any means or translated
into another language, without the prior
consent of Galileo Press, Rheinwerkallee 4,
53227 Bonn, Germany.

Galileo Press makes no warranties or representations with respect to the content hereof
and specifically disclaims any implied warranties of merchantability or fitness for any particular purpose. Galileo Press assumes no re-
sponsibility for any errors that may appear in
this publication.

Translation Lemoine International, Inc.,
Salt Lake City, UT
Copy Editor John Parker, UCG, Inc.,
Boston, MA
Cover Design Silke Braun
Printed in Germany

All of the screenshots and graphics reprodu-
ced in this book are subject to copyright
© SAP AG, Dietmar-Hopp-Allee 16,
69190 Walldorf, Germany.

SAP, the SAP logo, mySAP, SAP NetWeaver,
mySAP Business Suite, mySAP.com, SAP R/3,
SAP R/2, SAP B2B, SAPtronic, SAPscript, SAP
BW, SAP CRM, SAP EarlyWatch, SAP Archive-
Link, SAP GUI, SAP Business Workflow, SAP
Business Engineer, SAP Business Navigator,
SAP Business Framework, SAP Business Infor-
mation Warehouse, SAP inter-enterprise solu-
tions, SAP APO, AcceleratedSAP, InterSAP,
SAPoffice, SAPfind, SAPfile, SAPtime, SAPmail,
SAPaccess, SAP-EDI, R/3 Retail, Accelerated
HR, Accelerated HiTech, Accelerated Consu-
mer Products, ABAP, ABAP/4, ALE/WEB,
BAPI, Business Framework, BW Explorer,
EnjoySAP, mySAP.com e-business platform,
mySAP Enterprise Portals, RIVA, SAPPHIRE,
TeamSAP, Webflow and SAP PRESS registered
or unregistered trademarks of SAP AG, Walldorf, Germany.

All other products mentioned in this book are
registered or unregistered trademarks of their
respective companies.

ISBN 1-59229-067-1

Contents

4 Selected Customization and Extension Options 105

5   Selected Examples From Customer Projects   195

Preface

Interaction centers are the key area through which enterprises work directly with their customers; the customer, in turn, expects to receive support regarding all issues across all the business areas of the enterprise. This can happen only if an interaction center can be integrated with other applications and individually adapted and extended to user processes.

The solution mySAP CRM Interaction Center fulfills these requirements. Our intention with this book is to provide consultants, project managers, and decision makers in SAP customer enterprises with comprehensive insight into ways for meeting project-specific requirements, beyond the information provided by the SAP help and standard documentation. At the same time, a less technical chapter presents numerous customer projects that illustrate the bandwidth of possible implementations of this solution.

This book could not have been published as you see it without committed support from many people. We would like to thank our colleagues at ecenta AG, who helped us compile the extension options of SAP CRM Interaction Center and in processing the examples from customer projects: Christian Matz, Jens Höfer, Jörg Hopmann, Dr. Johann von Saldern, and Dr. Klemen Cas. Without their text contributions and ABAP programs, this book would not have come into existence. The "heart and soul" of this project, who kept together all files, graphics, formats, and pieces of paper, was Katrin Willnat, who even managed to decipher our handwriting.

For excellent care and support from the publishing and editorial sides, we would like to thank Stefan Proksch, Florian Zimniak, and John Parker of SAP PRESS.

In particular, special thanks go to our wives Laura and Dagmar, who showed patience and understanding for this book, despite the small amount of time we had left for our private lives even before this project.

Wiesloch, Germany
November 2005

Dr. Thorsten Wewers

Mannheim, Germany
November 2005

Dr. Tim Bolte

1   Introduction

*The interaction center is a key area within Customer Relation-
ship Management (CRM). This introduction describes the
intention and structure of this book.*

1.1   mySAP CRM and Interaction Centers

Within mySAP Business Suite, mySAP CRM is dedicated to business scenarios and processes related to the customer. With mySAP CRM, you
have many options for providing marketing, sales, and service processes
via various channels. Precise analyses of these processes form the basis of
target-oriented decisions. However, the focus of this solution is not limited to classic CRM processes. Especially when developing long-term,
profitable customer relationships, an integrated view of business processes across systems or departments is indispensable. You only get the
"complete picture" of a customer if you can access information from the
logistics or financial-accounting areas. On the other hand, CRM information such as forecasts of future sales closures can be used for optimizing
downstream planning.

Business processes vary between industries. Therefore, mySAP CRM not
only provides industry-specific marketing, sales, and service processes
but also offers integration with industry solutions for downstream processes. By using the integration technologies of SAP NetWeaver, SAP's
open technology and integration platform, which is already used with
mySAP CRM today, you have many additional options for integrating
data and processes with virtually any other system—even between enterprises.

An interaction center covers far more than just processing telephone calls
in a traditional call center. As a matter of fact, it means the central provi-
sion of interactive services, with or without product reference, for internal or external customers. Newer technical terms like "customer interaction hub" or "customer service hub" should be considered in this context.
Although numerous processes become relevant in the interaction center
at some stage, most of the processes don't start or end there. This means
that, especially in an interaction center, an integrative view on business
processes in an enterprise is required. This requirement can hardly be met
by a standalone application that focuses on contact management. Thus,
mySAP CRM Interaction Center is not only an integral part and key capa-

bility of the comprehensive mySAP CRM solution but uses the integration technologies of SAP NetWeaver.

In the standard version, mySAP CRM Interaction Center includes numerous processes that can be adapted to the specific project requirements through standard customizing. A multitude of successful interaction center projects have shown that mySAP CRM Interaction Center can be implemented easily and within very short project timeframes.

However, the complexity of the requirements in an interaction center project can sometimes go beyond what can practically be covered by standard Customizing. This may occur because it is necessary to integrate third-party systems and because customer-specific customization demands are diverse at the user interface, process, and possibly application levels. In both of these situations, the mySAP CRM Interaction Center concept and architecture provide excellent foundations. Instead of limiting the solution's flexibility to the functions available in standard Customizing, the open architecture provides extensive possibilities for meeting project-specific requirements. These possibilities cannot be described to a reasonable extent within the scope of the SAP help and standard documentation. For this reason, there is a natural gap between the full functionality of mySAP CRM Interaction Center and the features provided and described in the standard system.

This book is intended to fill this gap. It provides a concise introduction to the basics and enhancement options of mySAP CRM Interaction Center. The enhancement options are illustrated by real-life examples and described using selected sample projects in their business context.

The goal of this book is to provide consultants, project managers, and decision makers on the customer side with a comprehensive insight into the functionalities of mySAP CRM Interaction Center for meeting project-specific requirements in interaction center projects.

Many customers who have already implemented mySAP CRM Interaction Center use only some of the options provided. Considering the broad variety and the necessity of a focused implementation of this solution for special work areas in an enterprise, this is almost a matter of course. In today's fast-changing enterprise environment, however, new implementation options and work areas emerge, particularly for interaction centers. In this context, this book aims at presenting additional usage options to customers who are already using mySAP CRM Interaction Center.

1.2   Structure

This book's chapters are structured as follows. **Chapter 2** describes the basic concept and evolutionary paths of mySAP CRM Interaction Center. Since 1999, Interaction Center has been part of several SAP solutions. Therefore, this chapter begins with the different versions and shows how they found their way into mySAP CRM Interaction Center. We then briefly describe the CRM scenarios supported in Interaction Center as well as some special uses of Interaction Center, for instance within help desk processes. A description of the basic technical concept and of central technical components such as the framework, the process and master data integration, or the interfaces with communication management software, can be found at the end of Chapter 2. In particular, this part contains a list of the most important technical packages of SAP CRM Interaction Center.

Chapter 3 takes up the structure of the last part of Chapter 2 and describes the technical basics of mySAP CRM Interaction Center in greater detail. You must have a certain technical understanding and knowledge of the basic concepts behind customizing SAP products to understand this chapter fully. The chapter is divided into three main sections on Interaction Center WinClient, Interaction Center WebClient, and Interaction Center Management. The two front-end-specific sections (Agent Desktop) are divided into representations of the framework, the basic functions (the action box, for example), the process and master data integration, the integration of communication channels, and the supporting functions (such as Knowledge Search). Every section contains a list of the most important transactions and function groups as well as useful SAP Notes, which can be read in full detail from the SAP Support Portal in SAP Service Marketplace (*http://service.sap.com*); the descriptions are supported by numerous illustrations. The last section of Chapter 3 describes Interaction Center Management. It focuses on the Email Response Management System, the tools for operating the interaction center as well as the reporting functions of the interaction center. This section, too, contains numerous illustrations and helpful technical information, such as a list of available web reports about interaction statistics.

Chapter 4 aims at illustrating the flexibility of this solution using some selected customization and extension options of mySAP CRM Interaction Center. In addition, the examples shown contain sufficient detail for you to reproduce and possibly implement them immediately in a profitable way in an interaction-center project. In order to achieve this, some knowledge of ABAP programming and ABAP Objects is necessary. The structure of this chapter corresponds to that of the two preceding chapters: Examples of workspaces and hidden components illustrate the framework and architecture of the interaction center. The action box or the transaction launcher are basic functions. Master data integration is dealt with by extensions of the business-partner workspace or view set, respectively, and of the customer fact sheet. The work item execution in the interaction center focuses on process integration. Extensions of the agent inbox illustrate the possibilities within the communication channels. The chapter ends with the development of customer-specific alerts in a marketing scenario.

While Chapter 4 focuses on the technical side of the options in mySAP CRM Interaction Center, **Chapter 5** contains six examples of customer projects. In selecting these examples, we tried to map a comprehensive range of industries, business processes, and company sizes. The first two sections of this chapter present a complete scenario of a service process—including analytics in a Business Information Warehouse. After that, you'll find an example from the consumer-goods area in which the connection is made between after sales and marketing. The fourth section deals with an Employee Interaction Center that was implemented by a medium-size HR outsourcing company within a short project timeframe. An internal sales support process of an IT service provider is the subject of the fifth section. The last section of the chapter describes a customer-specific solution of a logistics-service provider that integrated mySAP CRM Interaction Center with a third-party computer-telephony-integration (CTI) software.

The book concludes in **Chapter 6** with a summary and a look into the future.

2   Concept and Evolution

Since 1999, Interaction Center has been an integral part of mySAP CRM. This chapter briefly describes the development history of the solution. We also will explain business scenarios and processes of the standard solution, as well as the technical concept of Interaction Center.

2.1   History of Current Applications in mySAP CRM Interaction Center

Almost every company offers its customers interaction options via media such as telephone or email. Many companies also use these media to contact their customers proactively. What is so special about these interaction options is that—in contrast to automated interaction methods (Web self-services, voice portals)—you need to provide staff to process the interactions. Even so, the interaction methods can be used easily without first making an appointment as in face-to-face or field sales activities.

Active contact

As is normal for incoming contacts in interaction centers, the content of the interaction is more or less unknown to the employee in the interaction center (interaction center agent) before he or she accepts the contact. For the customer, the interaction is a central experience, a "moment of truth" in his or her relationship with a company. This situation creates strict demands on the informational qualities and process competence of the interaction center agent. And this, in turn, leads to special demands on the information and process provisioning at the agents' workplace, quite aside from the qualifications required of the staff themselves. Especially in the case of synchronous communication, for instance in interactions over the telephone, the customer's request cannot be forwarded arbitrarily to several experts without the customer perceiving this as a lapse in service quality.

It is not only in the customers' interest to quickly receive appropriate answers to their requests. A tedious process involving several resources is associated with unacceptable costs for the company. Instead, employees are to be provided with tools which enable them to process customer requests effectively and efficiently. While at first the main reason for considering a software solution for their interaction center organizations was improvement in service quality, during recent years there has been a growing tendency to also look for improvement of the cost equation.

Improvement of service quality and cost

mySAP CRM Interaction Center stands at the crossroads of conflicting requirements for both excellent service quality and cost efficiency. The development history of the product is tightly connected with the change of requirements that interaction center organizations have been facing in recent years.

First interaction center solution

The foundation of the SAP solution was laid with R/3 Release 4.5B. In this release, a customer interaction center was provided for the first time (see Figure 2.1). With this solution, information about the caller could be retrieved and displayed automatically via a central user interface on the basis of the caller's telephone number. Additionally, there was the option to jump to a variety of business processes mapped in the R/3 system and made available to the interaction center agent. For the purpose of information retrieval, intranet pages could be integrated or displayed. This customer interaction center then was provided and extended in industry solutions as well, for example in those designed for utility and telecommunication companies.

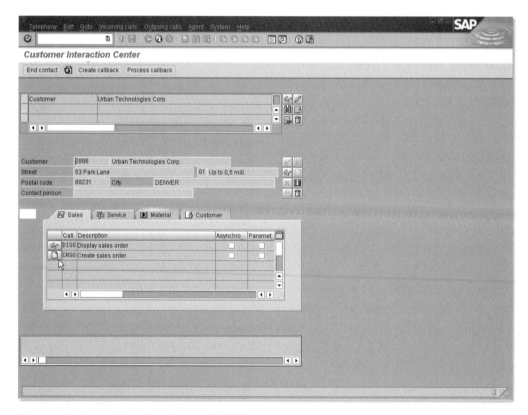

Figure 2.1 Customer Interaction Center in SAP R/3

With the introduction of mySAP Business Suite, these basic features were integrated into mySAP CRM, where the range of solutions for interaction centers was further extended then. With mySAP CRM 2.0, the interaction center was delivered for the first time as an integral part of a comprehensive CRM solution, and its functions were from then on continuously enhanced. With this solution—today's Interaction Center WinClient (IC WinClient)—an interaction center can be integrated with companywide marketing, sales, and service processes within a holistic customer relationship management (see Figure 2.2).

Interaction Center WinClient

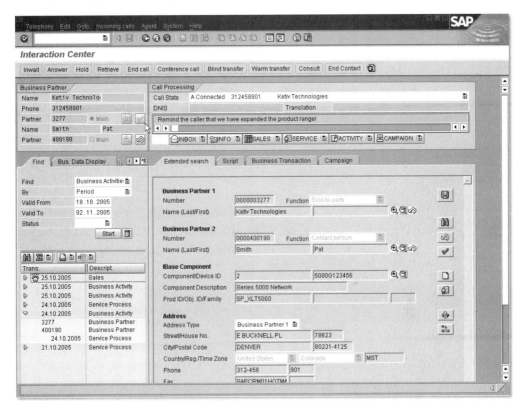

Figure 2.2 Interaction Center WinClient

After identifying the customer, the agent is provided with a complete overview of all interactions between the customer with the company. Active telemarketing can be supported by call lists and integration with comprehensive campaign management. In telesales processes, functions like automated product proposals as well as cross-selling and up-selling can be integrated. Additionally, the agents can take advantage of a knowledge-based search function (Knowledge Search) which allows for entering user-defined text and is integrated tightly with the email channel for convenient email editing. Thus, the informational qualities and process competence of the agent can be improved, and a higher rate of successfully completed customer interactions can be achieved. Interactive scripts support a consistent service quality, while rule-based alerts point out particularities during the interaction. In this context, and in combination with the option to seamlessly jump from interactions into business processes that are mapped, for example, in SAP R/3 or ERP, IC WinClient supports effective and efficient interaction processing. It is implemented by many interaction-center organizations around the world.

Interaction Center WebClient The generally increasing cost pressure on companies, combined with the development of new technologies in SAP Web Application Server (SAP Web AS) has made advisable and feasible an innovation called the Interaction Center WebClient (IC WebClient). With this browser-based thin client, a new software interaction design for the SAP CRM Interaction Center was implemented (see Figure 2.3).

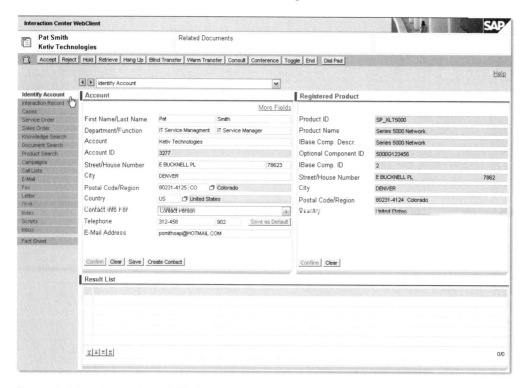

Figure 2.3 Interaction Center WebClient

This solution is intended particularly for those interaction-center organizations whose agents don't have any experience in handling business software such as SAP R/3. The intuitive user interface design enables short training periods. The thin-client architecture saves the local installation of a GUI; all you need is a browser. This Agent Desktop considerably enhances the options for adapting the interface to company-specific processes in the respective interaction-center organization. As of mySAP CRM Release 4.0, this solution is available in addition to IC WinClient.

Together with the offerings for interaction-center agents, since Release 3.1 mySAP CRM Interaction Center has included its own enterprise portal content for the role of an interaction-center manager. Reporting and monitoring have always been of great significance in the interaction-center environment, especially for planning and controlling the capacity load of the interaction center: The mainly reactive service production process in an interaction center places high demands on capacity planning and on the continuous monitoring of the capacity load if customer-oriented service levels are to be maintained or guaranteed. Telephone systems, for example, offer an abundance of detailed information on call and wait times, numbers of calls and service levels achieved. The essential data that cannot be provided by these systems is information about call contents and thus about business processes that are triggered or executed during call processing.

Reporting and monitoring

Accessing such a reporting system is one core objective of interaction-center management content in mySAP CRM Interaction Center. Moreover, this portal role provides the option of an integrated view of the reporting system of the attached communication systems and access to administrative functions of mySAP CRM Interaction Center. One example of this is graphic modeling of interactive scripts or broadcast messaging (see Figure 2.4).

Portal content for interaction center management

Apart from the option of connecting integrated communication systems and thus supporting concepts like universal queuing and universal routing, mySAP CRM Interaction Center provides its own solution for email response management. This can be used for email and structured Web forms, and also for letters and faxes as communication media. In contrast to the telephony channel, the routing rules and the physical routing of incoming interactions are configured in SAP technology in this case. Since mySAP CRM Edition 2004, a user-friendly rule editor is available; SAP Business Workflow is used for routing. mySAP CRM Edition 2004 consists of several extensions to mySAP CRM 4.0 that can be implemented sepa-

Email Response Management System

rately. The most useful component for interaction centers is the *Service Industry Add-On* of mySAP CRM Edition 2004. Apart from email response management, it also contains the industry-specific versions of IC Web-Client for utility and telecommunication companies.

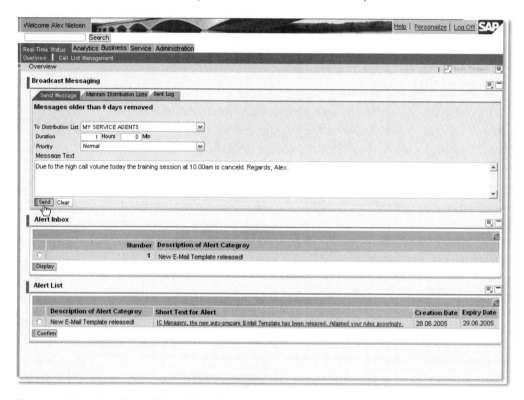

Figure 2.4 Interaction Center Manager Portal

Flexible enhancement options

Traditionally, the SAP training offers focus on the configuration of basic settings of SAP CRM Interaction Center as well as the configuration of the integrated functions and processes. The objective of this book is not to repeat these contents. It rather focuses on the possibilities resulting from the architecture of interaction-center applications to flexibly extend the functionality of the standard system with customized functions. Therefore, the following sections outline the functionality of the standard system from a business-related and process-oriented point of view. After that, we will work toward a basic understanding of the technical concept of SAP CRM Interaction Center, which enables the provisioning of standard processes and functions and forms the basis of customer-specific extensions of the solution.

2.2   Business Scenarios and Processes

2.2.1   Scenarios and Processes for CRM

Four scenarios

All SAP solutions are structured according to business scenarios and processes. Within mySAP CRM, the interaction center is a key capability that is mapped into four scenarios: Interaction Center Marketing, Interaction Center Sales, Interaction Center Service, and Interaction Center Management. The first three scenarios include operational processes for the interaction center according to the customer life cycle. The fourth scenario is dedicated to the administrative processes for managing the interaction center (see Table 2.1).

Scenario	Processes
Interaction Center Marketing	Customer information and feedback; lead management
Interaction Center Sales	Inbound telesales; outbound telesales
Interaction Center Service	Help desk; customer service and support; complaints and returns management
Interaction Center Management	Management and analysis of interaction center operation; email response management

Table 2.1 Scenarios and Processes

Modeling independent of technical implementation

Within the scenarios, processes are modeled accordingly and process-specific functions are mapped to business processes based on single process steps. These business scenarios and processes are initially modeled irrespective of their technical environments. This means that the modeling of operational processes applies to both IC WinClient and IC Web-Client.

SAP Solution Manager

The modeling is mapped in SAP Solution Manager, which is used for implementing and maintaining SAP software. Apart from flow charts of business processes, Solution Manager includes the software documentation and an introduction to the configuration. Thus, when implementing a specific business process, you can easily determine the documentation and configuration of technical functions relevant for this part. After defining business requirements through business processes, you obtain a focused view of the technical functionality and the corresponding configuration options of the software.

The following sections explicate the interaction center processes described in the scenarios and included in the standard system.

Interaction Center Marketing

Customer information and feedback The processes in the Interaction Center Marketing scenario are related to the early stage of the customer relationship. For example, the customer information and feedback process includes the qualification of prospect data, even based on purchased address lists. In addition to address qualification, functions for enhancing customer data are supported, for example with additional marketing attributes.

Lead management The substantiation of the business relationship is covered in the lead management process. This process includes the functions for a demand analysis and for forwarding qualified demands to the sales area. Apart from initiation of business relationships and individual contracts, these processes also address the continuation of business relationships beyond an individual deal. Using surveys and analyses of existing customers, for example, telemarketing campaigns can be produced to generate subsequent or complementary business.

In both processes, telemarketing functions such as manual or automated processing and maintenance of call lists, scheduling follow-ups, interactive scripts, and information provisioning for telemarketing campaigns are available.

Interaction Center Sales

Quote creation and order entry While complex initiation processes aimed at opportunity management can be integrated with the interaction center (with functions for project sales, team selling, mapping of buying contors and sales cycle analyses), telesales processes in the interaction center focus on quote creation and order entry. The inbound process starts with identifying the customer and then deals with the quote or order creation up to the interaction wrap-up. The outbound process starts with determining call appointments, for example based on typical contact periods for a regular release of individual orders through special customers. Within the scope of interaction preparation, customer selection includes an enhanced representation of corresponding information. After the interaction has started, quote- and order-creation functions are made available; the process ends with the interaction wrap-up. In both processes, telesales functions such as automated product proposals or cross-selling and up-selling can be accessed. Additionally, a manual product-search function and product details views optimized for the interaction center are included. The telesales agent can also handle situational prompts for the sales negotiation. The actual order functions, such as availability check or credit scoring, are available in the interaction center through integration with the sales functionality of mySAP Business Suite and use of the processes it contains.

Interaction Center Service

With its three processes, the Interaction Center Service scenario covers the general creation of interaction-related services for customers and prospects (help desk) as well as the integration with technical support (customer service and support). A separate process is dedicated to the special case of complaints and returns management, which can be used to address customer dissatisfaction—with or without product or delivery reference.

Creation of inter-action-related services

In these processes, customer requests can be initially documented and classified. In order to enable the highest possible completion rate of requests in the interaction center, you can use supportive functions such as a Knowledge Search function within a solution database or among already existing problem cases. Likewise, products used or components installed by customers can be identified and assigned to the customer request. On the other hand, it is possible to use functions like appointment planning for customer service technicians (customer service and support), assignment of requests to comprehensive problem cases or the issuing of credit memos (complaints and returns management) in the interaction center. If it isn't possible to conclude processing in the interaction center, you can use convenient forwarding functions, either manual, partially automated or fully automated. All processes include access to the interaction and service history of the customer and of all products used.

Documentation, classification, history

Interaction Center Management

The Interaction Center Management scenario contains a process in which basic administrative functions are mapped for an Interaction Center Manager. It enables monitoring and management of operations using functions for real-time monitoring of call lists and transaction processing as well as the current capacity load of the interaction center via a *Manager Dashboard*. In addition, tools for process modeling and knowledge management and access to the interaction-center reporting functions are provided.

Administrative functions, process modeling, knowledge management

Moreover, additional processes are integrated for the email response-management system which is a solution developed specifically for the interaction center. It allows you to handle emails (partially) automatically that are sent to central email addresses in a company.

Process Variants

Some processes have technical variants that can be selected during implementation. One example is the outbound telesales process, for which you decide during the implementation whether the process will be mapped using the order management in SAP CRM or using the R/3 order. Business modeling is neutral with regard to this option.

The help-desk process within the Interaction Center Service scenario is noteworthy. In addition to the Information Help Desk variant, which can be used for a classical information hotline, more variants are available. These allow for use of interaction center and CRM functions beyond the areas of a company that deal directly with the customer. The following section shows how interaction center and CRM functions can be used in other parts of a company.

2.2.2 Special Use of mySAP CRM Interaction Center

In administrative areas

Besides the implementation at the interface between company and customer, further possibilities of using mySAP CRM Interaction Center have proved to be useful. Many SAP customers use this solution in internal departments that provide interactive services for certain parts of a company or entire groups within a corporation. Particularly remarkable in this context is the use in an employee interaction center and in an internal IT help desk. The first is a central organizational unit that responds to staff-related questions from employees and managers of a company via communication media such as telephone or email. The latter is the central internal point of contact for IT-related issues and problems in the company technical infrastructure.

Administrative areas like these have been facing increasing cost sensitivity in recent years. At the same time, the demand for service quality and responsiveness is rising, driven in part by the optimization of service processes in areas close to the customer. Thus, it is almost inevitable even for administrative groups to consider the use of an interaction center as an efficient organizational structure for interactive, reactive business processes and to face up to the demand for guaranteed service quality and process standards. Against the background of a make-or-buy decision, this is also about achieving a competitive performance, which requires thinking about (internal) activity prices and profitability objectives. This also gives administrative groups the possibility to offer these services to other companies in the sense of business process outsourcing and thus to be able to contribute to increasing the company value.

As far as operation is concerned, these internal departments face similar challenges as do those that deal directly with the customer. On the one hand, requests from various interaction channels are to be processed in an integrated solution without integration gaps that are cost-critical and quality-critical. In this solution, structured trouble-ticketing processes and access to processes and sub-processes in other applications need to be mapped for the requests. Furthermore, transparency of business processes is called for. Besides short-term situational status overviews, transparency requires reporting that offers performance indicators about service quality, cost efficiency, and profitability and that thus forms a basis for decisions at strategic and tactical levels.

Similar challenges

Employee Interaction Center

Given both the range of services offered and the contact cost structure, an employee interaction center is positioned between the classical HR administration and the provisioning of staff-related processes in the form of self-services. This interesting central position allows for the mapping of more complex trouble-ticketing processes than would be possible via self-services. Compared to the classical administration, there is significant potential for cost reduction. In addition, an employee interaction center is usually even available when Web self-services cannot be accessed because an employee is not at his desk, or for some other reason.

Between administration and self-services

In an employee interaction center, an integrated work list can be accessed via mySAP CRM Interaction Center. This contains inbound emails as well as current, already qualified requests and pending work items from an HCM system (*Human Capital Management*). Employee data can be loaded from an HCM back-end system and is then available in the employee interaction center for an automated search. The particular request can be qualified and submitted to standardized processing. Staff-related processes can also be triggered or executed in the HCM system (see Figure 2.5). In combination with the mySAP HCM Employee and Manager self-services, there is the possibility for the user in the employee interaction center to execute these services as a substitute.

Usage of HCM data

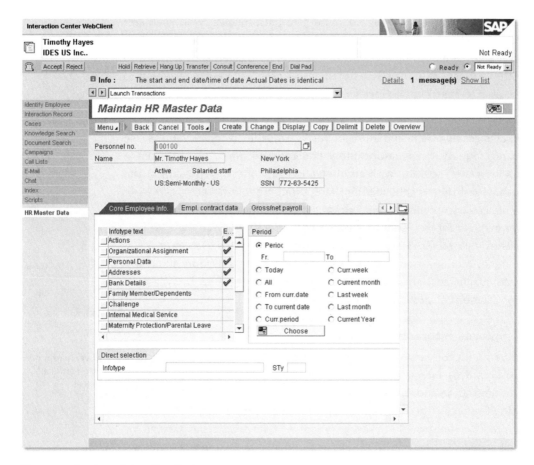

Figure 2.5 Employee Interaction Center

Since CRM Release 3.1, the employee interaction center is available as a packaged solution or as a project solution. With mySAP CRM 2005, the employee interaction center is included in mySAP CRM Interaction Center as a standard process. This standard process provides the option to operate the employee interaction center as *Business Process Outsourcer* (BPO). In order to ensure the highest data separation possible between BPO customers, different SAP system clients can be used for the employee interaction center processes of different companies. The system identifies the correct SAP client for each interaction and provides the agent with the business processes contained therein.

IT Help Desk

ITIL processes   According to the worldwide de facto standard ITIL (*Information Technology Infrastructure Library*), an IT help desk covers the central areas of incident and problem management in the sense of a service desk and enables an integration with other ITIL areas. These areas might include configuration management, for which technical configurations can be adopted or updated directly from an R/3 system or—via the SAP Exchange Infrastructure (XI)—from non-SAP systems.

With mySAP CRM Interaction Center, you can receive problem messages and user requests in an IT help desk via several interaction channels. The integration of the email response management and the integration of user-defined Web forms therein enable the automated processing and documentation of simple requests. In general, problem messages can be classified at multiple levels, related to technical components, and processed in a standardized manner via a specific user interface, the service ticket (see Figure 2.6).

Problem messages and user questions

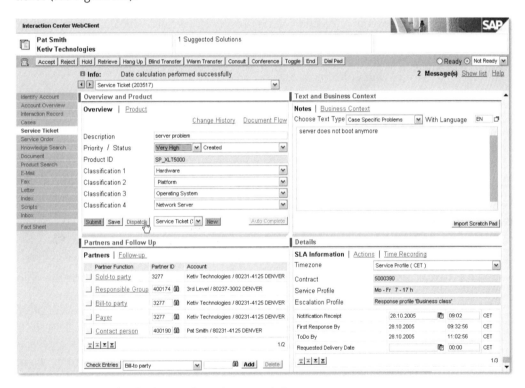

Figure 2.6 Service Ticket for the IT Help Desk in IC WebClient

Response and escalation times can be determined from service contracts and provided as *Service Level Agreements* for processing the various problem cases. Processing times can be recorded for every incident and used for further processing up to the invoicing of the service. Multilevel trouble-ticketing processes can be mapped using partially automated, rule-based forwarding. For maintaining these rules, you can use the same rule editor as for maintaining the rules for email routing. Alternatively, forwarding can be carried out using SAP Business Workflow. The integrated Case Management enables you to merge several problem messages (incidents) into one comprehensive problem case. Apart from interaction-centered and process-centered evaluations, reporting provides integrated performance indicators such as the average call time or the average interaction rate per problem category.

Since mySAP CRM Edition 2004, the IT help desk is included in mySAP CRM Interaction Center as a standard process.

2.3 Technical Concept and Components

In addition to the functional specialties within the scenarios and processes, the interaction center contains a technical concept which enables the mapping and integration of these processes and permits user-defined process combinations. The following sections describe the basic concept and central technical components.

2.3.1 Solution Concept

Components of the CRM server
Although IC WebClient and IC WinClient are implemented using different technologies, they are both based on the same concept: Both are components of the CRM server that can access the master and transaction data defined there and use the corresponding available functions. The core of both applications is made up of the framework and basic functions that provide for the integration with transactional processes and maintain the interaction context.

Framework

Integration of different application components
First and foremost, the framework enables you to integrate different application components. This configuration has to be defined in an *interaction center profile,* which in turn is mapped to an item of the organizational structure. In this way, it is possible to provide different agent groups with different IC profiles and thus provide functionalities with different characteristics. Profiles of the individual application components are assigned to an IC profile. Thereby, the characteristics of individual components can be differentiated for different agent groups.

Events
The interaction of the individual components within the framework is implemented via events. Individual components can subscribe to events or raise events by themselves. An event shows that at least one compo-

nent wants to run program logic. All components that want to respond to a certain event subscribe to that event and determine the functions to be executed when this event is raised. At the time an event is raised, all registered functions are started.

Basic Functions

Both Agent Desktop applications have a basic function to maintain the interaction context. In IC WinClient, this is the *Business Data Display* (BDD), in IC WebClient it is both the *Activity Clipboard* and the *Business Data Context* (BDC). At the beginning of an interaction, a data container is created that is populated at runtime with references to business objects, which are accessed during the interaction. After the interaction has been terminated, the objects in the container can be linked to each other via object links. After that the container is deleted. In both applications, you can configure which business objects are relevant to the container and thus to be linked using object links after the interaction has been closed.

Container concept

This container concept is tightly connected to a second basic functionality of both applications: the possibility of integrating with different transactional processes. In IC WinClient, this is mapped via the action box and the context menu, while in IC WebClient it is mapped via the transaction launcher and the navigation bar. In these components, you can determine which business objects you can access at runtime. Additionally, you can define the methods to use and the logical system in which they are contained. As a prerequisite, these objects have to come from the *Business Object Repository* (BOR) of the respective system. This configuration is then stored in a profile that is assigned to the IC profile. Apart from the simple call of a business object, you can also configure a bidirectional data flow. This means that in the course of the configuration, you can determine which data should be passed and which data should be transferred from this object back to the interaction center when the business object is called. For processing the data flow, the container concept applies: When an object is called, attribute values of the business objects referenced in the container can be transferred, and the data returned can be included in the container.

Process integration

Apart from the ability to integrate virtually any object from SAP systems with the SAP CRM Interaction Center, there is also the option of integrating with processes that are modeled in non-SAP systems. To this end, data could, for instance, be passed from the container to an HTML control and transferred from this control back to the container. Thus, virtually

Integration with non-SAP systems

any HTML-enabled application can be integrated with SAP CRM Interaction Center.

Process and Master Data Integration

Use of existing transaction data

The SAP CRM Interaction Center does not contain any process objects of its own. In fact, existing objects like CRM activity or CRM order are used in the CRM server and presented in a specific display for the interaction center. At runtime, the interaction center controls access to these objects and determines at the end of an interaction whether objects are to be linked to each other, and—if so—which objects are to be linked. In particular, it is decided at runtime which process is the one to document the interaction with the customer. This decision is made based on configuration information. It is possible to include a separate record for every interaction or to integrate the contact information in a superordinate record such as an order. This enables the mapping of different project-specific requirements with regard to the CRM process modeling without having to modify the data model.

Use of created master data

Likewise, the SAP CRM Interaction Center uses master data created in the CRM server. For a convenient search of this data, there are special functions which enable you to automatically identify a business partner on the basis of the telephone number or email address. Additionally, customers can be identified using their "installation," that is, a product they are using. To ensure an optimized usability, only central information on master data is displayed. You still can access information about a certain data record for master data defined in SAP CRM, SAP R/3, SAP BW or other systems.

Integrating Communication Channels

Use of server-side interfaces

SAP CRM Interaction Center permits the integration of communication channels via server-side interfaces. For asynchronous communication channels like emails, both Agent Desktop applications make it possible to receive inbound contacts in an *agent inbox*. For the integration, the following interfaces of the SAP Web AS are used:

▶ SAPphone

▶ SAPconnect

▶ SAP Archive Link (for inbound letters)

▶ Integrated Communication Interface (ICI)

Providers of communication-management software can certify for these interfaces. The current list of certified providers can be retrieved from *http://www.sap.com*; you also can implement a client-side integration on a project basis (see also Section 5.7).

The RFC-based (*Remote Function Call*) SAPphone interface (see Figure 2.7) includes various functionalities that are reflected in three different certification levels. In addition to the direct integration via RFC, Computer Telephony Integration (CTI) providers for the functionality of the first two levels can also integrate via TAPI (*Microsoft Telephony Application Interface*). In this case, the *SAPphone server* takes care of the translation from RFC to TAPI. The first certification level (*Basic Telephony*) includes soft-phone functions, typical telephone functions like answering or forwarding a call, or consultation calls can be carried out via an SAP front end. The second level (*Call Center Telephony*) includes further functions like logging on to a telephone server or handling call-attached data which are for instance used for voice data forwarding ("screen transfer"). The third certification level deals with the integration of automatic dialers and includes functions like uploading call lists to a dialer. In addition, SAPphone offers the option to integrate historical data from telephony into an SAP system (*Statistics interface*). The SAPphone interface is used in IC WinClient; it can be used in IC WebClient of the Release mySAP CRM 4.0 after installing an SAP note and is supported in standard as of mySAP CRM 2005.

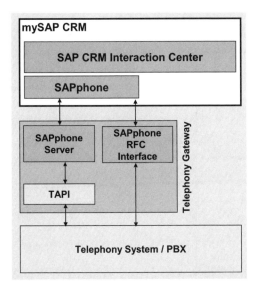

Figure 2.7 SAPphone Interface

SAPconnect   The SAPconnect interface is used for integrating asynchronous communication channels such as email or fax. Besides special interfaces for a number of mail systems, the integration via SMTP (*Simple Mail Transfer Protocol*) is also supported. This interface becomes relevant when inbound contacts (emails, or faxes) are to be directed using SAP Business Workflow to an inbox from which they are then available to individual agents or agent groups for processing (*pull mode*). It therefore represents an alternative to the uniform processing of all communication channels where all inbound contacts are signaled like telephone calls at the agents' workplace (*push mode*). The SAPconnect interface can be used in both Agent Desktop applications. In both cases, it is integrated in the existing agent-inbox component.

ICI   A uniform handling of calls, emails and Web chat is possible via the *Integrated Communication Interface* (ICI) (see Figure 2.8). This enables the implementation of universal routing or universal queuing concepts. Compared to SAPphone and SAPconnect, the ICI is a completely re-designed interface that is not connected via SAP-proprietary RFC technology but rather via XML/SOAP. Just like SAPphone, ICI does not interfere with the routing of the contacts, which has to be configured in the partner software to be integrated. The ICI functionality ranges from calling operational functions (such as initiating or accepting a contact), up to transferring a user's status (*work mode*, available, busy, at break etc). ICI is currently integrated in IC WebClient only. For a uniform handling of calls, emails, Web chat, etc. in IC WinClient, partner solutions can be integrated.

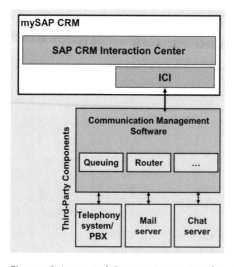

Figure 2.8 Integrated Communication Interface (ICI)

Supporting Functions

Besides the framework, the basic functions, and the integration interfaces, the SAP CRM Interaction Center provides supporting functions for the interaction center operation. These include alerts, interactive scripting, and broadcast messaging. Alerts are messages displayed on-screen that call the interaction center agent's attention to situational particularities during call processing. Interactive scripting refers to scripts with which standard call flows and sequences of functions to be executed can be modeled and made available to individual agent groups. Broadcast messaging is a tool for the communication between supervisor and agent. The supervisor can send messages to individual agents or agent groups, and these are then displayed in a banner in their Agent Desktop application. Using an integrated Knowledge Search function, the agent can access information stored in a solution database or other sources.

Alerts, interactive scripting, broadcast messaging

Manager Functions

The role of the Interaction Center Manager in the SAP Enterprise Portal allows access to functions that can be used for monitoring and managing the operation of an interaction center. Further, it enables access to functions that support knowledge management and process modeling in the interaction center. Special analytical content for this role is available in SAP BW (see Figure 2.9).

Monitoring, Knowledge management, process modeling

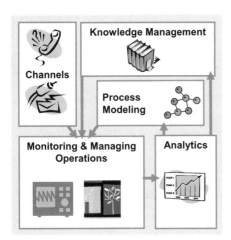

Figure 2.9 Interaction Center Manager

Operations monitoring can be carried out using the Manager Dashboard: This is where data from connected communication management software is displayed via the ICI interface. If call lists for active telemarketing are

Manager dashboard

used, the interaction-center manager can display the current processing status of these call lists in real time via a special user interface. On the same user interface, he or she can maintain the assignment of agents to lists or create new lists. The portal role also includes access to the broadcast-messaging tool.

In the knowledge-management area, the Interaction Center Manager can access the maintenance of problems and solutions for the solution database. Individual service tickets also can be merged to comprehensive cases. Additionally, templates and text modules for email processing can be created from scratch or customized. This is also where the classification hierarchies for transactions and email requests are maintained.

A graphical editor for the interactive scripts allows for modeling the processes relevant to the interaction center. There is another editor to create and revise rules for automated email processing and for the automated forwarding of processes.

2.3.2 Overview of Technical Components

When looking for technical information about individual applications within mySAP CRM Interaction Center, you can either check the SAP notes in the SAP Support Portal in the SAP Service Marketplace (*http://service.sap.com*) or take a look at the packages (development classes) of the applications. The following sections contain useful information about this search for IC WinClient, IC WebClient, and Interaction Center Manager.

Interaction Center WinClient

Parts and Components — The SAP *Online Service System* (OSS) is structured according to software components. Table 2.2 shows a correlation of the application components mapped therein to the basic components of IC WinClient described in Section 2.3.1.

Parts of IC WinClient	SAP application component
Framework	CRM-CIC-FRW
Basic functions	
▶ BDD, Action Box, Context menu	▶ CRM-CIC-ABO
▶ HTML control	▶ CRM-CIC-FRW

Table 2.2 OSS Components of IC WinClient

Parts of IC WinClient	SAP application component
Master-data integration	
▶ Business partner search	▶ CRM-CIC-BP-SEA
▶ Customer Fact Sheet	▶ CRM-CIC-HIS-CFA
▶ Processes	▶ CRM-CIC-BTX
Communication channels	
▶ CTI	▶ CRM-CIC-COM-TEL
▶ Agent inbox	▶ CRM-CIC-COM-EMA
Supporting functions	
▶ Alert modeler	▶ CRM-CIC-ALM
▶ Interactive scripting	▶ CRM-CIC-SCR
▶ Broadcast messaging	▶ CRM-CIC-BRO
▶ Knowledge Search	▶ CRM-CIC-KNO

Table 2.2 OSS Components of IC WinClient (cont.)

The SAP application packages can be displayed via Transaction SE80. The IC WinClient application is implemented in the packages shown in Table 2.3.

Package	Description
CCMA	Interaction center components
CCMB	Interaction center components
CICA	Interaction center
CICB	Interaction center
CRM_CIC_COMPONENTS	Interaction center components
CRM_CIC_FRAMEWORK	Interaction center framework
CRM_CIC_IBASE	IBASE objects within the IC
CRM_CIC_ORDER	One order in the IC

Table 2.3 Main Packages of IC WinClient

Interaction Center WebClient

Similar to the listing of application components for IC WinClient above, Table 2.4 shows the corresponding application components for IC Web-Client and maps them to the IC WebClient components described in Section 2.3.1.

Parts and Components

Parts of IC WebClient	SAP application component
Framework	CRM-IC-FRW
Basic functions ▶ BDC, Activity clipboard ▶ Transaction launcher ▶ Navigation bar	 ▶ CRM-IC-ACC ▶ CRM-IC-ABO ▶ CRM-IC-NVG

Master-data integration
 ▶ Business partner search
 ▶ Customer fact sheet
 ▶ Processes
	
	 ▶ CRM-IC-SEA
	 ▶ CRM-IC-CFA
	 ▶ CRM-IC-INR; CRM-IC-FOL;
	   CRM-IC-SLO; CRM-IC-SVO;
	   CRM-IC-SCO; CRM-IC-LEA

Communication channels ▶ CTI ▶ Agent inbox	 ▶ CRM-IC-CHA ▶ CRM-IC-UNI
Supporting functions ▶ Alert modeler ▶ Interactive scripting ▶ Broadcast messaging ▶ Knowledge-based search	 ▶ CRM-IC-ALT ▶ CRM-IC-SCR ▶ CRM-IC-BRO ▶ CRM-IC-SOL

Table 2.4 OSS Components of IC WebClient

Table 2.5 shows the packages of IC WebClient.

Package	Description
CRM_IC	CRM Interaction Center
CRM_BSP_IC_FRAMEWORK	UI framework for IC WebClient
CRM_IC_ERMS	ERMS component in IC WebClient
CRM_IC_MCM	Multichannel management
CRM_IC_SCRIPTING_RUNTIME	CRM IC interactive scripting runtime

Table 2.5 Main Packages of IC WebClient

IC WebClient Workbench

Since mySAP CRM Edition 2004, Transaction BSP_WD_WORKBENCH provides an overview of the application structure of IC WebClient in addition to the above lists of technical components and packages. Via the application structure, it is possible to navigate to the most important development objects of the application. Furthermore, you can call wizards for application extensions from this transaction.

Interaction Center Manager

The components of Interaction Center Manager do not have their own nodes in the component hierarchy of the SAP support system. Therefore, most components are listed several times in Table 2.6, since they are listed underneath the hierarchy nodes for both IC WinClient and IC Web-Client.

Parts and Components

Parts of Interaction Center Manager	SAP application component
Tools for operating the IC	
▶ Manager dashboard	▶ CRM-IC-MDB; CRM-CIC-MDB
▶ ERMS monitoring	▶ CRM-IC-EMS-MON
▶ Call list	▶ CRM-IC-CAL; CRM-CIC-CAM-CAL
▶ Broadcast Messenger	▶ CRM-IC-BRO; CRM-CIC-BRO
Knowledge management	
▶ Knowledge Search	▶ CRM-BF-SAF; CRM-BF-KNO
▶ Standard response	▶ CRM-BF-ML; CRM-IC-EMS
▶ Categorization	▶ CRM-IC-EMS-CAT
Process modeling	
▶ Interactive scripting	▶ CRM-CIC-SCR; CRM-IC-SCR
▶ ERMS and rule editor	▶ CRM-IC-EMS-RUL; CRM-IC-EMS-AUT
Analytical CRM in the IC	
▶ Logging of IC WinClient	▶ CRM-CIC-REP-LOG
▶ Evaluations of ERMS	▶ CRM-ANA-IC-EMS

Table 2.6 OSS Components of Interaction Center Manager

The concepts and technical components of mySAP Interaction Center introduced in Section 2.3 are dealt with in more detail in Chapter 3.

3 Technical Principles

mySAP CRM Interaction Center includes IC WinClient, IC WebClient, and processes for Interaction Center Manager. This chapter concisely describes the technical principles of these applications.

3.1 Preliminary Note

This chapter introduces the technical basics of Interaction Center WinClient, Interaction Center WebClient, and the functionality for the Interaction Center Manager role. Our goal here is to give you a foundation for understanding the enhancement options of the solution. Throughout this book, selected enhancements are described in detail using real-life examples (see Chapter 4) and the context of project descriptions (see Chapter 5).

In contrast to the descriptions in the system documentation, the Implementation and Installation Guides, the SAP Help Portal (*http://help.sap.com*), and the contents of SAP Solution Manager, this chapter points out certain central functions and provides technical details about these functional areas. As an additional source for further information, please refer to the *IC WebClient Cookbook*, the latest version of which can be found in the SAP Service Marketplace (*http://service.sap.com*) in the Installation Guides section.

In addition to descriptions of technical principles structured by main components, you will find at the end of each section lists or tables with technical information, including transactions or SAP notes relevant to the respective area.

3.2 Interaction Center WinClient

3.2.1 Framework and Architecture

The IC WinClient configuration begins with *framework customizing*. During this process, you will define the layout of the user interface and also assign individual areas of the layout (slots) to components. The standard system contains two L-shaped layouts, one with and one without a call state. The schematic structure of these are illustrated in the left-hand and right-hand parts of Figure 3.1.

Layout and component mapping

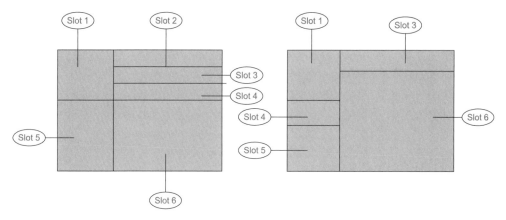

Figure 3.1 Schematic IC WinClient Layout With (Left) and Without (Right) Call State

Components and slot assignment

With SAP CRM Release 5.0, the additional vertical layout has been used in the standard version for the client switch functionality. The individual slots are assigned visible components, e.g. workspaces. Some slots are permanently assigned to certain components (1 = Business partner search, 5 = Navigation area, 6 = Application area), other components can be used flexibly in the remaining three slots (see Table 3.1).

Visible Component	L-Shaped With Call State	L-Shaped Without Call State
Broadcast messaging	2, 3, 4	3
Call state	2, 3, 4	–
Quick keys	2, 3, 4	3
Reminder scripting	2, 3, 4	3
Lean action box	2, 3, 4	4 (variant 0004 or 0005), 3

Table 3.1 Visible Components and Possible Slot Assignments

Visible and hidden components

One distinguishing feature of IC WinClient is that, apart from the visible components, there are hidden ones that are active in the background. Some visible components, like the action box, require an associated hidden component.

The functional characteristics of individual components are determined by the IC WinClient profile. One configuration profile can be associated to each component. An IC WinClient profile also references a particular framework. This means that through the IC WinClient profile, all configuration settings required to start the application with certain characteristics are known. This is effected via transaction code CIC0.

From a technical point of view, the application launch is carried out via the central function module CIC_START_FRAMEWORK, which is used for initiating all the necessary steps. The procedure within this function module is as follows:

Technical processes at application start

1. The function module CIC_INITIALIZE_FRAMEWORK is called, where the IC WinClient profile (function module CIC_GET_ORG_PROFILES) is determined first, then the framework layout and corresponding component profiles. The visible components are assigned to their slots, and the hidden ones are written to an internal table.

2. Components are created, components subscribe to events, receiver components for events are determined, and the functions to be executed are defined. The individual steps are carried out sequentially, first for the hidden, then for the visible components.

3. The framework itself subscribes to events.

4. The events for reading the components' configuration data (Event CO_ GLOBAL_CONFIG_MOD) are triggered.

5. All components are opened.

6. Visible components are enabled.

7. The framework screen is called.

8. Visible components are disabled.

9. All components are closed.

This procedure illustrates that the communication between individual components and the framework is carried out through events at runtime, after the application has been started.

Events

One special type of event is the OK code. This event is called by the framework, and all parts of the framework using OK code processing have to subscribe to this event. To make sure that the OK code event handlers of individual framework parts are called only when OK codes relevant to them are to be processed, they can register for specific OK codes.

The contents of the navigation and application areas (Slots 5 and 6) after application startup can be defined via a common profile for both areas (Customizing activity **Define Profile for Automatically Created Workspaces**, Transaction CRMC_CIC_WSP3). Both areas can be populated with several workspaces in the form of tabs. A list of all workspaces included in a standard system is available either via **F4** help or via Transaction CRMC_CIC_WSP0. This transaction also enables you to add cus-

Application and navigation areas

tomer-specific workspaces (see SAP note 516843 and Sections 4.2 and 4.3).

Assigning a toolbar The IC WinClient profile can be assigned a special profile for the application toolbar and thus a special toolbar configuration (GUI status) using Transactions CICU and CICN. For that purpose, the framework used must be assigned the obligatory hidden component CIC_TOOLBAR. An extended GUI status (PF777) has been available since mySAP CRM Edition 2004, which provides the choice of two additional pushbuttons for changing the presentation of the navigation and application areas at runtime: With one of the pushbuttons, you can toggle the application area between full screen and standard display; the other pushbutton enables you to expand the navigation area to full screen width. In order to enable these pushbuttons, the framework used must be assigned the hidden component LAYOUT_SWITCH.

Technical Information

Transaction	Description
CICO	Start the application
CICO	Define IC WinClient profiles
CRMC_CIC_FW_MAINTAIN	Define Framework ID and Parameters
CRMC_CIC_TITLE_TEXTS	Maintain Window Titles
CRMC_CIC_WSP3	Define Profiles for Automatically Created Workspaces
CRMC_CIC_WSP0	Define customer-specific workspaces
CICU and CICN	Define Toolbars and GUI Status

Table 3.2 Customizing Transactions of the Framework

Function Group/Class	Description	Package
CICO	CIC framework	CICA
CIC2	CIC framework customizing	CICA
CL_CCM_WORKSPACE_MANAGER1	CIC workspace manager	CCMA
CL_CRM_CIC_AREA_COMPONENT	CIC workspace display	CRM_CIC_COM-PONENTS

Table 3.3 Function Groups and Classes of the Framework

Function Group/Class	Description	Package
CL_CCM_WORKSPACE_FACTORY2	Factory for work-spaces	CCMA
CL_CCM_WORKSPACE2	Implementation of IF_CCM_Work-space	CCMA

Table 3.3 Function Groups and Classes of the Framework (cont.)

SAP Note	Description
516843	How to create a customer-specific workspace?

Table 3.4 SAP Note on the Framework

3.2.2 Basic Functions

The basic functions of IC WinClient are represented by the Action Box and Context Menu components and in the Business Data Display.

Business Data Display

The business data display can be represented as a tab in the navigation area. In this display, you can list all objects called during an interaction. For SAP CRM objects called with their IC WinClient standard screens, this listing in the business data display is carried out automatically. At the end of an interaction, the content of the business data display is deleted, and the objects listed therein are linked via the document flow to the interaction process documenting the interaction. In this way, all linked objects from the business data display are listed in the contact history underneath the interaction at the next call of the interaction.

Associating objects with the interaction process

Action Box

The action box is presented to the user as a pushbutton bar with sub-menus whose appearance and scope of functionality can be configured in a very flexible way. The three most important purposes of the action box are calling workspaces, calling BOR methods, and calling HTML pages. The scope of functionality of the action box is configured in the Customizing Transaction EWFC0.

Calling workspaces, BOR methods and HTML pages

If a workspace is called via the action box and if no tab exists for it yet, the workspace is added to the application area as another tab. If there already was a tab for the workspace, it will be placed in the foreground.

| Text | Content |

Calling objects from other systems The action box call of a BOR method provides a high degree of flexibility during configuration. With the BOR method, it is possible to access all BOR objects of SAP applications with their corresponding methods. For objects from other systems than SAP CRM, all you need to do is to store information about the target system for the 'jump', i.e. the Remote Function Call (RFC). This is carried out by maintaining the logical system, which is described in the SAP note 363097. In order to avoid that the user has to log on separately to the target system during processing, a *trusted RFC connection* is required between the CRM and the target system. It is possible to transfer data from the business data display and to return data to it after processing in the target system.

Calling the R/3 order with data forwarding For example, from IC WinClient, an R/3 order for the customer identified in IC WinClient can be created for order entry in the familiar R/3 interface, and the order number can then be returned into the business data display. For this purpose, the BOR object of the R/3 order, BUS2032, needs to be called with the CREATEWITHDIA method. Besides order type and data on the sales organization, the customer identified in IC WinClient can be transferred in the data flow as the ordering party. For this purpose, in the data flow for the document partner, the constant AG is transferred as the partner role, and the customer is set as follows (see also Figure 3.2):

`&<DESKOBJ>BUS1006005.CUSTOMERNO&.`

DESKOBJ means that an object is to be forwarded from the business data display. The CRM object BUS1006005 is a CRM object for the business partner and contains a mapping of the R/3 customer number.

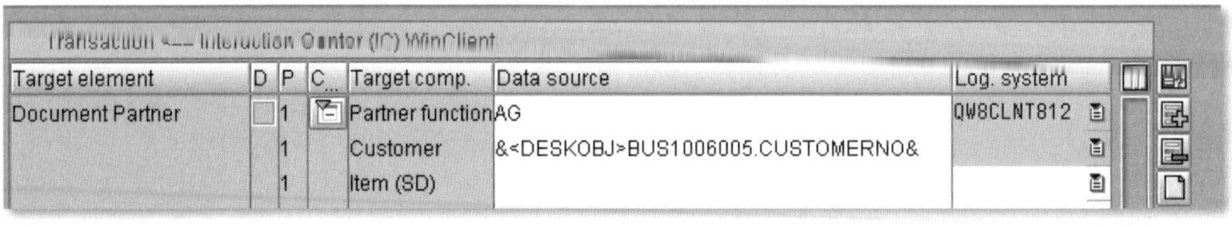

Target element	D	P	C	Target comp.	Data source	Log. system
Document Partner		1		Partner function	AG	QW8CLNT812
		1		Customer	&<DESKOBJ>BUS1006005.CUSTOMERNO&	
		1		Item (SD)		

Figure 3.2 Data Flow from IC WinClient to the Transaction

Data return For importing the document number in the business data display, the BOR object BUS2032 needs to be entered in the return data flow as target element, and &<*MAINOBJ*>& as data origin (see Figure 3.3). Thus, the R/3 document number is transferred to IC WinClient as a standard attribute of the BOR method used. Further methods of modeling the data flow are discussed in detail in SAP note 322517.

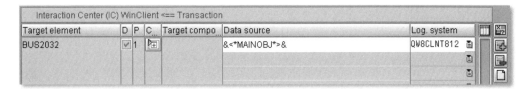

Figure 3.3 Data Flow from the Transaction to IC WinClient

One BOR object of special interest is the object TSTC. It enables calling every transaction from any SAP system. For this purpose, you need to select the EXECUTE method and maintain the transaction code in the data flow as a constant.

Calling SAP transactions

From the action box, you can call any HTML pages—intranet, Internet or even user-defined pages—and these are then displayed in a workspace in the application area. To this end, an entry has to be created in Transaction CICAM, which references the address of the HTML page. Additionally, browser options for the workspace can be determined there, and page call parameters to be transferred from IC WinClient (external parameters) can be maintained. From the HTML page, you also can start action box calls (internal parameters). For this purpose, you need to create a corresponding action box in Transaction EWFC1, and this requires programming in the HTML page.

Calling HTML pages

Context Menu

The context menu is used to enable calling of objects from the business data display. The maintenance of the context menu is similar to that of the action box in that they are using the same technology. For every object, you can define several methods that can be provided at runtime by means of a right-click. The context menu is used for purposes other than the business data display. The interaction history with the customer, which is assigned to the navigation area in the IC WinClient profiles of the standard Customizing, accesses the context menu as well. Thus, it is possible to jump from a customer's history to any objects listed in the business data display during a previous interaction with the customer.

Calling linked objects

Technical Information

Tables 3.5, 3.6, and 3.7 provide further background information on IC WinClient basic functions.

Transaction	Description
EWFC0	Action box profile
CRMC_CIC_COMP_ACTION	Define Context Menus
CICAM	HTML configuration
EWFC1	HTML action box

Table 3.5 Customizing Transactions for the Basic Functions

Function Group/Class	Description	Package
CCM2_HIDDEN_ACTION_BOX	Hidden action box	CCMA
CRM_CIC_SLIM_ACTION_BOX	Lean action box	CRM_CIC_COMPONENTS
EB*	Action box	CCMA&CCMB
EW*	Action box	CCMA&CCMB
CRM_CIC_TRIGGER_WORKSPACE	Context menu	CRM_CIC_FRAMEWORK
CL_CRM_CIC_COMPONENT_ACTIONS	Context menu	CRM_CIC_COMPONENTS
CL_CRM_CIC_COMPONENT_OBJECT	Context menu	CRM_CIC_COMPONENTS
CL_CRM_CIC_BD_DISPLAY_WS	BDD workspace	CRM_CIC_COMPONENTS
CL_CRM_CIC_BDD2	BDD	CRM_CIC_COMPONENTS

Table 3.6 Function Groups and Classes of Basic Functions

SAP Note	Description
363097	How to setup Logical Destination for Action Box RFC
128447	Trusted/Trusting systems
322517	CIC: Action Box data flow customizing with the BDD

Table 3.7 SAP Notes on Basic Functions

3.2.3 Process and Master Data Integration

IC WinClient accesses master data and processes on the CRM server. All settings defined there apply to IC WinClient and can be re-used. IC Win-

Client also provides specific features in both areas, and these are explained in the following sections.

Master Data Integration

With regard to master data, the search and display of business partners is the main function of IC WinClient, for which Slot 1 of the framework is reserved. The search can be carried out either manually or in an automated way via an *Automatic Number Identification* (ANI) within *Computer Telephony Integration* (CTI). Business partner data can be changed and created as well. Components or products installed at a business partner, for example on a particular server, can be displayed. These extended functions are available with the business-partner search workspace. This workspace is an HTML representation which stands for flexible customizing (Transaction CRMC_CIC_SEARCH_RULE). Apart from the search profiles delivered in the standard system, you can create your own by flexibly adapting the standard search profiles. Using search attributes in Customizing, you can configure, for instance, which HTML layout to use, and whether to limit the search to specific business-partner roles and/or relationship categories. You also can configure for which partner functions the identified business partners are forwarded to transaction processing or with which priority which function modules are used for searching different fields in business partner tables (see Figure 3.4).

Search and display business partners

You can define several settings for creation of business partners. For example, you can predefine in which business partner role or with what partner category business partners are created from IC WinClient. Another Customizing setting controls whether this pre-assignment may be changed by the user.

Creating business partners

Apart from industry-specific HTML templates, the standard version contains two standard layouts. CRM_CIC_SEARCH_DISPLAY is the standard proposal for a customer search in SAP CRM, while CRM_CIC_EMP_SEARCH_DISPLAY is the standard proposal for an employee search in an Employee Interaction Center. Both templates are stored in the SAP Web Repository and can be accessed via Transaction SMW0.

Besides business partner data, IC WinClient allows for the display of product-related information. This can be the presentation of product information which is displayed in a separate workspace for a specific product which is used, for example, in an order. Alternatively, installation components of a specific customer can be searched in a workspace and then presented. Further workspaces are available in the standard system for serialized products (*iObjects*).

Display of product information

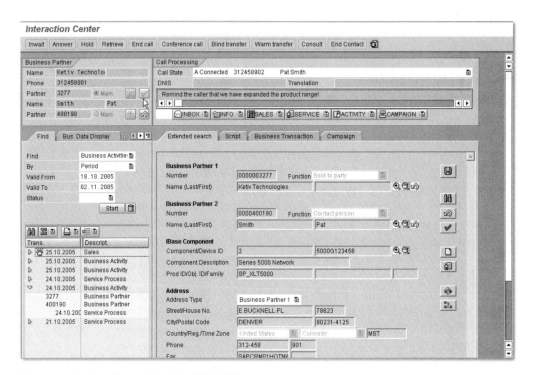

Figure 3.4 Business Partner Search in IC WinClient

Fact sheet Another option for re-using master data functions is provided by the fact sheet. The fact sheet can contain master data on the business partner from SAP CRM, processes from SAP CRM and SAP R/3 as well as data on the business partner from the SAP Business Information Warehouse. This can be configured in the **Master Data** area of the SAP Implementation Guide (SAP Reference IMG) via the Customizing activity **Customer Relationship Management · Master Data · Business Partner · Business Partner – Cockpit and Fact Sheet · Define Info Blocks and Views**. The access to this fact sheet depends on the role. The fact sheet can be called in IC WinClient in a special workspace. For this purpose, the workspace ACTIVITY_SALES_SUMM needs to be assigned to the desired workspace profile through Transaction CRMC_CIC_WSP3.

Process Integration

Interaction documentation Interactions are documented in IC WinClient via a CRM process. You can specify which CRM transaction type—and thus which business transaction category—has to be used for documenting the interaction. You can choose different transaction types for different interaction channels. Irrespective of this setting, the user can create follow-up transactions of any kind at runtime. Consequently, the Customizing definition only specifies the transaction type of the interaction record. All transaction categories are represented in the transaction workspace of IC WinClient in a slightly simplified way compared to CRM Enterprise. For the interaction record, you can define more settings in Transaction CRMC_CIC_ACT0 (see Figure 3.5).

Change View "Transaction component profile": Overview

Trn prof	Phone	E-Mail	Other	Save Bus. Activity	View	Add to BD
ACTPROF1	0002	0004	0002	Save Business Transaction Whi		☐
SALES_COMPLAINT	TSC	TSC	TSC	Save Business Transaction Whi	Standard View	☑
TELESALES	TSA	0004	TSA	Save Business Transaction Whi		☑
TELESERVICE	TSRV	TSRV	TSRV	Save Business Transaction Whi	Standard View	☑
TSRV1	SRV0	SRV0	SRV0	Save Business Transaction Whi	Standard View	☐
TSRV2	SC	SC	SC	Save Business Transaction Whi	Standard View	☑
TSRV3	SRVC	SRVC	SRVC	Save Business Transaction Whi	Standard View	☑

Figure 3.5 Customizing of Business Transactions for IC WinClient

It is possible to choose whether a detail view or a view focused on contact data is initially displayed when calling the transaction workspace. The user can switch these views at runtime. You also can configure the method of proceeding with the interaction record after ending the interaction. Several options are available:

Settings for the interaction record

▶ **Always save**

▶ **Save when user makes changes**

▶ **Save on request (when user makes changes)**

For transactions opened in the transaction workspace, it can generally be specified whether they should be transferred automatically to the business data display or whether the user should perform this task manually by clicking on a pushbutton.

Technical Information

Transaction	Description
CRMC_CIC_SEARCH_RULE	Define Profiles for Search Strategy
CRMC_CIC_SEARCH_CNTR	Define Customer-Specific Search Control
SMW0	SAP Web Repository

Table 3.8 Customizing Transactions for Process and Master Data Integration

Transaction	Description
CRMC_CIC_WSP3	Define Profiles for Automatically Created Work-spaces
CRMC_CIC_ACT0	Define Profiles for Transaction Workspaces

Table 3.8 Customizing Transactions for Process and Master Data Integration (cont.)

Function Group/Class	Description	Package
CCM1	Contact search and display	CCMA
CRM_CIC_BP_SUB	BP search subcomponent	CCMA
CL_CRM_CIC_BP_SEARCH	CIC BP search	CRM_CIC_COMPONENTS
CL_CRM_CIC_BP_EMP_SEARCH	Employee search	CRM_CIC_COMPONENTS
CL_CRM_CIC_SALES_SUMMARY	Sales Summary Workspace for CIC	CRM_CIC_COMPONENTS
CL_CRM_CIC_ONEORDER_MAINTAIN	One Order (maintain)	CRM_CIC_ORDER

Table 3.9 Function Groups and Classes of Process and Master Data Integration

SAP Note	Description
758426	HR-ALX: Enhancement of the ALE value distribution

Table 3.10 SAP Note on Master Data Integration

3.2.4 Integrating Communication Channels

Telephone, email, fax, and letter

IC WinClient provides the option to integrate several interaction channels. The SAP CTI interface SAPphone is used for the communication channel "Telephony," the SAPconnect interface for integrating asynchronous interaction media like email or fax, and SAP ArchiveLink for inbound letters. Interactions received via SAPconnect are displayed in the agent inbox of IC WinClient.

Computer Telephony Integration

The integration of Telephony in IC WinClient according to standard requires the connection of an external CTI or communication management software to SAPphone. In IC WinClient, you need only select the corresponding framework (*Telephony-enabled*) and assign one visible and two hidden components. The visible component is the call state (CALL_STATE); the hidden ones are the CTI and call-center components. If the telephony integration should be tested without IC WinClient or in IC WinClient with simulated telephone calls, you can do so via the SAP-phone test transaction SPHT.

Assigning the CTI component essentially enables the use of the telephony pushbuttons in IC WinClient (see Figure 3.6). In Transaction CICY, you can also define if and how it is possible to log on to the switch via IC Win-Client. Additionally, in Transaction CICW you can assign CTI queue names of the telephony system to individual CTI queue profiles of IC WinClient. In the administration menu, individual queues obtain descriptive texts (Transaction CICV). The logon to the queues assigned to a profile can be carried out in an automated way or manually by the agent. If logon to queues should not take place via IC WinClient, the entries in Customizing remain empty.

Softphone Controls

Figure 3.6 Call State and Telephony Pushbuttons in IC WinClient

By assigning the call center component, the processing of *call-attached data* is enabled. In this way, it is possible to identify callers via their telephone number in IC WinClient and automatically search and display the corresponding business partner data. If the telephony system includes an *Interactive Voice Response* (IVR) that already collects caller-identification data before the call is transferred to a live agent, it is possible to also use data other than the caller's telephone number during business-partner search. The configuration of the call-center component is carried out through Transaction CICG.

Call-attached data

With these components, IC WinClient also enables voice-data forwarding ('screen transfer'). To this end, all data is transferred from the business data display to telephony. Together with the call, it is then available to the receiving IC WinClient session as call-attached data on accepting the forwarding, and is visible in the business data display there.

Screen Transfer

Agent Inbox

Universal group inbox

In the agent inbox of IC WinClient, emails, faxes, and scanned letters as well as work items and planned activities can be received (see Figure 3.7). Since SAP CRM Release 5.0, there has been the additional option to place any type of CRM processes in the agent inbox of an agent group for processing, something that previously had been possible only via an enhancement on project basis. The agent inbox is designed as a group inbox: For example, all emails sent to a central email address of a company can be routed to the appropriate agent group and are then listed in the agent inbox of that particular group. This routing is done using SAP Business Workflow. Global settings for receiving messages (e.g. assigning routing rules, or determining which communication types are processed with what priority or whether CRM processes for inbound messages should be created automatically) can be defined in Transaction CRMC_CIC_MAIL_GLOBAL. You create and send messages via the email editor of IC WinClient, which provides various functions such as the maintenance of several sender addresses.

Flexible workflow support

For routing, the standard system includes the workflow template 14000004, which is assigned workflow standard tasks for email (14007925), fax (14007926), and letter (14007927). The template can be called via Transaction PFTC. The connection between an inbound message, for instance an email, and this workflow is made by assigning the BOR object CICSUPRT2 to the central email address via Transactions SO28 and CRMC_CIC_MAIL_ADDR. In its method RECEIVE, the BOR object CICSUPRT2 triggers the event MAILRECEIVED (see Transaction SWO1), which is assigned to the standard workflow as the triggering event. The agent group is assigned to the workflow in Transaction CRMC_CIC_MAIL_WF. As a prerequisite, a node for receiving emails must have been created in SAPconnect via Transaction SCOT. Additionally, the agent inbox profile maintained in Transaction CRMC_CIC_MAIL_IBXPRF needs to be assigned to a workspace in the IC WinClient profile being used, and the agent inbox use must be enabled for it (Transaction CRMC_CIC_EXT_INB_ACT).

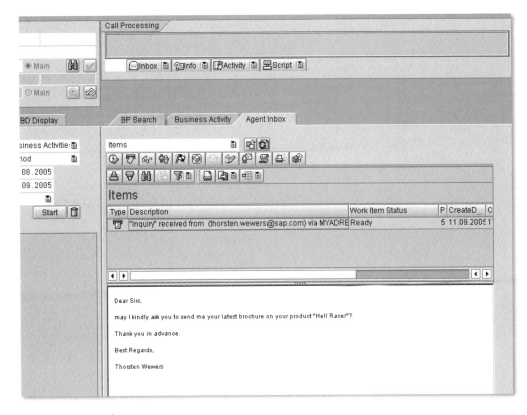

Figure 3.7 Agent Inbox

Technical Information

Transaction	Description
CICG	Define Call Center Profile
CICY	CTI administration
CICW & CICV	CTI queue
SPHA	SAPphone administration
SPHB	SAPphone system administration
SPHT	SAPphone test environment
CRMC_CIC_MAIL_GLOBAL	Global settings for agent inbox
SCOT	SAPconnect administration
PFTC	Maintain workflow tasks and templates
CRMC_CIC_MAIL_ADDR	Address Maintenance

Table 3.11 Customizing Transactions for Integrating Communication Profiles

Transaction	Description
SO28	Maintain Recipient Distribution
CRMC_CIC_MAIL_WF	Assign Agent for Email Handling
CRMC_CIC_WSP_EDITOR2	Define Editor Profiles
CRMC_CIC_MAIL_IBXPRF	Define Inbox Profiles
CRMC_CIC_EXT_INB_ACT	Activate Agent Inbox

Table 3.11 Customizing Transactions for Integrating Communication Profiles (cont.)

Function Group/Class	Description	Package
CCM5	CTI	CCMA
CCM6	Call center component	CCMA
CCMM4	Agent inbox	CCMA
CL_CCM_EMAIL*	Agent inbox classes	CCMA & CRM_CIC_COMPONENTS

Table 3.12 Function Groups and Classes for Integrating Communication Channels

SAP Note	Description
488344	Using IVR to identify Business Partner in CIC
601806	Checklist Agent Inbox Setup
697014	Support of letters in the Agent Inbox

Table 3.13 SAP Notes for Integrating Communication Channels

3.2.5 Supporting Functions

Scripting, alerts, and Knowledge Search

The main supporting functions in IC WinClient are scripting, alerts, and Knowledge Search. Additionally, broadcast messaging can be used in IC WinClient, which is discussed in more detail in the section about Interaction Center Management (see Section 3.4.2).

Interactive and Reminder Scripting

Interactive scripting

Interactive Scripts are displayed in their own workspace in IC WinClient (see Figure 3.8). They represent a sequence of questions and answering options. Interactive scripts provide possibilities beyond defining a tree structure for such a series of questions and answers.

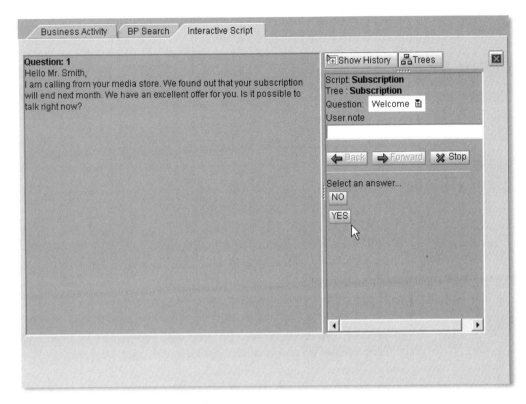

Figure 3.8 Interactive Script in IC WinClient

When selecting a certain answer, you can either simply navigate to the next question or trigger a script action. Available action types are events for stopping the script (STOP_SCRIPT) or for exiting to another script (EXIT_TO_SCRIPT <script id>). However, you can also trigger any OK code in IC WinClient or make an action-box call upon selecting an answer. This enables the integration of all workspaces configured in the action box into the interactive script. Interactive scripts can be modeled with a graphical tool in Transaction CRMM_TM_SCRIPT. Scripts created in this tool are then assigned via Transaction CICTMSCRPPROF to a script profile, which in turn needs to be assigned to the desired IC WinClient profile via its workspace or action box profile.

In addition to interactive scripts, IC WinClient also provides reminder scripting. This enables prompts of simple information texts or texts with variables during certain agent actions in IC WinClient. A list of all possible actions is available through Transaction CICA. Via Transaction CICK, these actions can then be assigned to a reminder scripting profile that in turn needs to be assigned to the desired IC WinClient profile. For these

Reminder scripting

information texts to be displayed, you also need to assign a hidden component besides the visible component in the framework (see Figure 3.9).

Figure 3.9 Reminder Script in IC WinClient

Alert Modeler

Provisioning of
Extended Notes

The alert modeler gives you the option to provide agents with extended notes in the form of text. For this purpose, either the text display of reminder scripting or the broadcast messaging display is used (see Figure 3.10). However, the alert modeler provides other functions that influence the interaction to a far greater extent than the mere display of a text message. The application can, for example, automatically trigger an action-box call when a certain situation occurs or a special event is triggered.

Figure 3.10 Alert in IC WinClient

The main purpose of the alert modeler is to grant access to the individual components of IC WinClient and also to data from the CRM server or even from an SAP BW. Within the alert modeler Customizing, you then can choose to create rules based on this data and to assign the execution of these rules to individual events. The resources available to the alert modeler (data objects, events, methods) are stored in a meta model whose XML definition can be displayed and changed via Transaction CRMC_CIC_AM_META. The modeling of the rules based on the resources stored in the meta model is carried out in Transaction CRMC_CIC_ALM_PROFILE in JavaScript. For the alerts to be executed at runtime, at least the hidden component ALRT_MODLRX must be assigned to the IC WinClient framework used, and an alert modeler profile must be assigned to this component in the IC WinClient profile.

There is a special Customizing for access to extended business-partner data. In Transaction CRMBW_CIC_ATTRIBUTES, you define which additional data for business partners is to be accessed. This can be either data from marketing attributes or from SAP BW queries. In Transaction CRMC_CIC_BP_PROFILE, the selected extended business-partner data is then assigned to a special query profile that also determines how this data will be accessed, whether, for example, by reading the data synchronously or asynchronously. Via the IC WinClient profile, this query profile must then be assigned to one of two additionally supplied hidden components (COMPANY_PROF for organization-related data or CONTACT_PROF for person-related data), which needs to be incorporated in the used framework for this purpose.

Knowledge Search

With SAP CRM Release 4.0, the CRM-proprietary search engine *Interactive Intelligent Agent* was replaced in IC WinClient and in CRM Enterprise with the Software Agent Framework and made usable for a knowledge-based search functionality. The Software Agent Framework uses the SAP NetWeaver technology TREX as a search engine, so that the IC WinClient benefits from future developments in this area. Using the Software Agent Framework, the contents of the well-known solution database are indexed by TREX. Therefore, when changing from previous releases, the customer can easily access solution database contents already created.

Software Agent Framework

With Knowledge Search, Interaction Center agents can comfortably access the solution database (see Figure 3.11). They can search for symptoms and solutions via user-defined texts or via predefined attributes. For a better structure of free-text queries, they can choose to add exclusion keywords. In this case, the Software Agent Framework subdivides large output lists whose keywords can be used for another quick restriction of the search. Output lists are displayed with probability values.

Selected solutions can be taken over into service orders or processed as response emails. It is also possible to gather feedback about the solutions provided by the solution database from the Interaction Center agents.

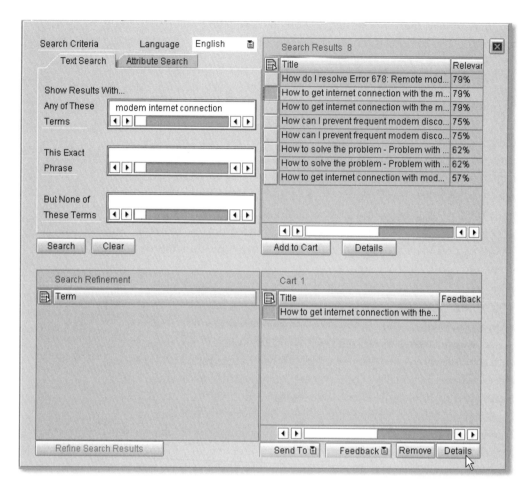

Figure 3.11 Knowledge Search in IC WinClient

Technical Information

Transaction/IMG Activity	Description
CICK	Define Reminder Scripting Profile
CICA	Define Customer-Specific Logging/Scripting Activities
CIC9	Maintain Script Texts
CIC2	Maintain Variables
CRMM_TM_SCRIPT	Maintain interactive script structure
CICTMSCRPPROF	Define Interactive Scripting Profile

Table 3.14 Customizing Transactions for Supporting Functions

Transaction/IMG Activity	Description
CRMC_CIC_AM_PROFILE	Alert modeler editor
CRMC_CIC_AM_META	Edit the alert-modeler meta model
CRMC_CIC_BP_PROFILE	Define Retrieval Profiles for Business Partner Attributes
CRMBW_CIC_ATTRIBUTES	Process BW Attributes for Business Partner
IMG · CRM · Enterprise Intelligence	Configuration of Software Agent Framework and Solution Database

Table 3.14 Customizing Transactions for Supporting Functions (cont.)

Function Group/Class	Description	Package
CCM7	Agent scripting	CCMA
CRM_TM_SCRIPTDISP	Telemarketing visible scripting	CRM_TELEMAR-KETING
CRM_TM_SCRIPTPROC	Telemarketing script processor	CRM_TELEMAR-KETING
CL_CRM_CIC_ALERT_MODELERX	CIC Alert Modeler Component	CRM_CIC_COMPONENTS
CL_CRM_CIC_BP_PROFILES	CRM CIC BP Profiles	CRM_CIC_COMPONENTS
CL_CRM_CIC_BP_PROFILES_CONTACT	CRM CIC BP Profiles	CRM_CIC_COMPONENTS
CL_CRM_CIC_CRB*	Component request broker	CRM_CIC_COMPONENTS

Table 3.15 Function Groups and Classes of Supporting Functions

SAP Note	Description
418175	CIC Reminder Scripting: List of Activities
449269	Maintaining Scripting variables
437722	Exposing data objects to the Alert Modeler
501941	Calling multiple functions in one Alert Modeler rule
656321	Replacement of Interactive Intelligent Agent
662550	Launching the Indexes Application (Software Agent Framework)

Table 3.16 SAP Notes on Supporting Functions

3.3 Interaction Center WebClient

3.3.1 Framework and Architecture

Browser-based application

The IC WebClient is built to run within a Web browser. It does not require any further local installation on the user desktop. All data displayed in the browser is provided by the SAP Web Application Server through HTTP. The communication between the browser and the SAP CRM system is carried out by Web services. For reducing the bandwidth required for communication between browser and server, special delta-handling mechanisms were implemented for the browser session (via JavaScript) and the CRM server. In order to actively display server-side events in the browser, such as signaling an inbound call in the browser, server polling is enabled by a Messaging IFrame in the browser. Therefore, the usage of IC WebClient requires a *Virtual Private Network* (VPN) in certain scenarios, where the CRM server needs to be accessed from outside (see SAP note 844929).

Multilayer architecture

On the server side, IC WebClient has a multilayer architecture shown in Figure 3.12. These architectural layers are linked to each other according to the *Model View Controller* (MVC) concept. For the presentation layer, the *Business Server Page technology* (BSP) of SAP Web Application Server is used with the *HTML Business Tag Library* (HTMLB); the business layer was additionally developed for IC WebClient in order to ensure the best separation possible of user interface and application logic. The business layer itself is divided into two layers, the *Business Object Layer* (BOL) and the *Generic Interaction Layer* (GenIL). The GenIL accesses APIs of various applications according to the model.

Business Object Layer

The BOL contains two types of objects: Entities (business objects) and query services. Using query services, you can search for specific objects within the BOL. In the standard system, the BOL contains entities for a variety of objects, e.g. business partners, transactions, or marketing campaigns. These are each represented as root nodes with attributes listed underneath based on the model. An overview is available via Transaction GENIL_MODEL_BROWSER.

Presentation layer

The presentation layer consists of views and their corresponding controllers. The purpose of a view is to visually represent elements like text fields or pushbuttons and to accept user entries. These are then forwarded to a controller, which is an ABAP class, for processing. The controller controls the entire interaction logic, e.g. whether data needs to be requested from the model based on a user entry reported by the view or whether another view should be called. In IC WebClient, every view—syntax: *myview.htm*—has exactly one controller of the same name, syntax: *myview.do*.

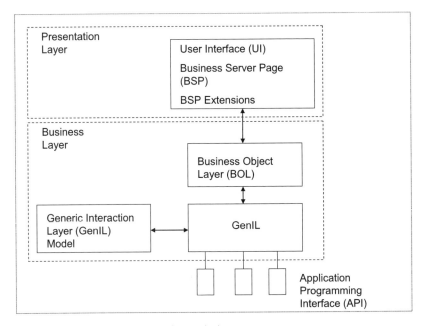

Figure 3.12 Architectural Layers of IC WebClient

The presentation layer is connected to the business layer via contexts and context nodes. This is referred to as data binding (see Figure 3.13). Every data field in a view represents one attribute of a context node. In the BSP coding of a view, this is rendered within an HTMLB input tag using the following syntax: `//context_node/attribute`. The context nodes required by a view can be found among its page attributes. They can be identified as ABAP classes with the _CN** suffix. Every context node belongs to a context. This context is in turn implemented via an ABAP class (suffix: _CTXT) which is assigned to a controller class in its attribute TYPED_CONTEXT. To display a view, its controller is called. The context of the view controller instantiates the context nodes assigned, whose attributes can then be displayed in the view. The model is accessed via methods of the controller class.

Context and context nodes

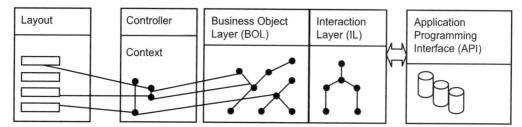

Figure 3.13 Data Binding of IC WebClient

Custom Controller Usually, a controller remains instantiated only as long as the corresponding view is displayed. As soon as the view is no longer displayed, it is deleted from the memory along with the controller data. In IC Web-Client, however, data not currently displayed should remain available. For this purpose, IC WebClient provides a special kind of controller, the custom controller. A custom controller is created and deleted by the application at points in time defined by the application. Individual view controllers thus can receive the context data they need from a (common) custom controller instead of accessing the model several times.

View set, View area and View In IC WebClient, there is another, special kind of view, the *view set*. A view set calls one or more other views and represents them in a special format. A view set contains a controller as well, however its representation is limited to providing a split screen for the called views. The screen structure of IC WebClient provides another structuring level, the view area (see Figure 3.14). A view set can consist of several view areas, each of which stores a view set or an individual view. Multiple views can be assigned to a view area. At runtime, however, one view is displayed at a certain point in time in a view area. The first view listed for a view area in the repository is the default view. This view is displayed when the view area is initially called.

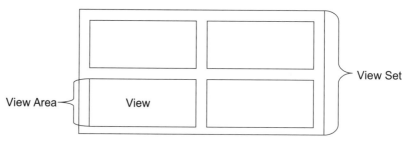

Figure 3.14 View Set, View Area, and View

The standard screen structure of IC WebClient primarily consists of four components (see Figure 3.15). Two components, the context area and the toolbar, are displayed at the top of the screen. In the context area, business- partner information, alerts, and communication channel-related data from a non-SAP system can be presented. Additionally, the context area includes the *scratch pad*—a text box available at a mouse click—in which you can enter user-defined text at any time during an interaction. All user-defined text fields of business objects provide the function of taking over text from the scratch pad in IC WebClient. A third component is the navigation area positioned at the left side of the screen. The fourth component, the work area, is assigned the largest part of the user interface. At runtime, the work area shows different view sets with different business-object data accessed either from the navigation area or from a view in the work area itself. Furthermore, broadcast messages can be displayed at the bottom of the screen, and information about the current queue status can be retrieved from a third-party system. Additionally, *breadcrumbs*, an intelligent, interaction-related navigation help, is presented above the work area. The information about screen structure and navigation links is stored in the Design Time Repository and is loaded into the Runtime Repository at runtime and thus made available to the application.

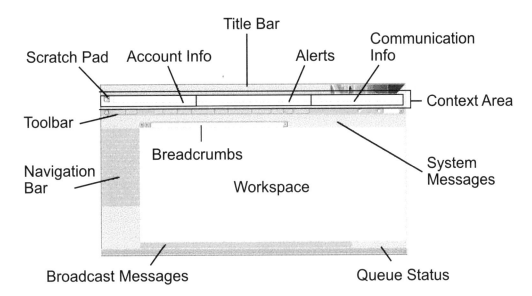

Figure 3.15 Layout of IC WebClient

Essentially, IC WebClient consists of three BSP applications, two of which are relevant at runtime: the central application (CRM_IC), the Runtime Repository of the application (CRM_IC_RT_REP), and the Design Time Repository (CRM_IC_DT_REP). The Design Time Repository contains information about standard views or view sets and navigation links.

After the central application CRM_IC has been started, the system loads all required controllers and views according to the runtime architecture presented (see Figure 3.16).

If, at runtime, you want to use your own views or view sets instead of the standard views stored in the Design Time Repository, you can do so by assigning your own framework profile (runtime framework profile) to the IC WebClient profile with so-called controller replacements in this framework profile. The replacements overrule the entries in the Runtime Repository, which are read from the Design Time Repository. The controllers and the corresponding views can be assigned to their own BSP application, which enables an extension without modification. In this case, the BSP application only receives the new or changed views and controllers; IC WebClient will continue to be started via the BSP application CRM_IC.

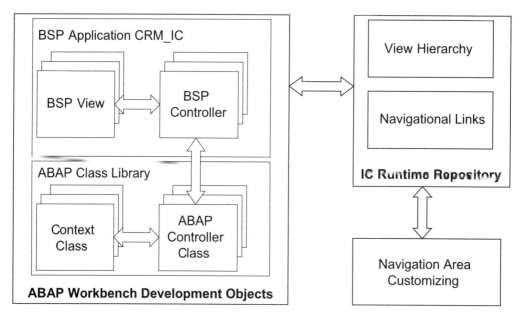

Figure 3.16 Runtime Architecture of IC WebClient

Inheritance within the ABAP classes not only allows you to implement extensions without any specific modification but lets you benefit from future developments of the standard version. Further levels of autonomy result from creating an own Runtime and Design Time Repository (see Section 4.12.2). In the case of a patch or upgrade, the copied views have to be manually reconciled in a simple way with system support.

Technical Information

The IC WebClient application is programmed in an object-oriented way. The classes used in the BSP application inherit from the superclasses listed in Table 3.17.

Part of the Framework	Superclass
View controller	CL_BSP_WD_VIEW_CONTROLLER
Custom controller	CL_BSP_WD_CUSTOM_CONTROLLER
Context	CL_BSP_WD_CONTEXT
Context node	CL_BSP_WD_CONTEXT_NODE CL_BSP_WD_CONTEXT_NODE_TV CL_BSP_WD_CONTEXT_NODE_TREE

Table 3.17 Superclasses of Framework Parts

From the inheritance hierarchy point of view, BSP classes form the top level. These BSP classes support creation of BSP applications according to the MVC concept and provide basic functions for controlling BSPs within this concept. The IC WebClient framework inherits from these classes to map framework parts like views, custom controller, contexts and context nodes. Individual parts of the application, in turn, inherit from these framework classes. At the IC WebClient application level, you need to differentiate between generated classes and the implementation classes inheriting from them (Suffix: _IMPL). The names of the classes at application level contain the name of the central application: They start with CL_CRM_IC*. There are three different classes for context nodes, where CL_BSP_WD_CONTEXT_NODE is the most basic and simple class used for binding against simple view elements such as input fields or dropdown boxes. The class CL_BSP_WD_CONTEXT_NODE_TV is the superclass for context nodes that are to be bound against a table view. The basic class for context nodes that bind against a tree structure is CL_BSP_WD_CONTEXT_NODE_TREE.

Inheritance hierarchy

Transaction/BSP Application/ IMG Activity	Description
CRM_IC	Central BSP application, application start
CRMC_IC_MAIN	Define IC WebClient Profiles
CRM_IC_RT_REP	Runtime Repository
IMG · CRM · IC WebClient · Customer-Specific System Modifications · Define IC WebClient Runtime Framework Profiles	Create and edit user-defined Runtime Repositories
CRM_IC_DT_REP	Design Time Repository

Table 3.18 BSP Applications and Customizing for the IC WebClient Framework

SAP Note	Description
759923	IC WebClient: FAQ Note
844929	Using the IC WebClient in extranet/Internet scenarios

Table 3.19 SAP Notes on the IC WebClient Framework

3.3.2 Basic Functions

Navigation bar, transaction launcher, and Activity Clipboard

The basic functions of IC WebClient are represented by the components "Navigation bar," "Transaction launcher," and the "Activity Clipboard" or the "Business data context" (BDC).

Navigation Bar

The navigation bar is displayed to the left of the screen at runtime. By selecting an entry, the corresponding view of business objects or a process is accessed in the application area of IC WebClient. The navigation bar contains a standard area for every user who has been assigned a certain navigation-bar profile via the organization model and the IC Web-Client profile. In addition, there is a personalized area. All entries are available via an index page (see Figure 3.17), where a user can select those entries from the personalized area which he or she wants to be accessible from the navigation bar at any time. In this area, the user can also define shortcuts for all entries of the navigation bar.

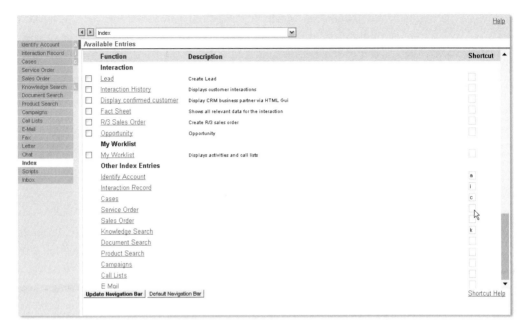

Figure 3.17 Index Page of IC WebClient

The navigation bar entries can reference standard view sets or user-defined view sets. It is also possible to define entries for any HTML pages or processes via the transaction launcher. In particular, these are processes mapped in the R/3 system or via the *People-Centric User Interface* (People-Centric UI) of CRM Enterprise. In this case, the corresponding Customizing entry for the navigation bar link is "Abox_Execution."

In versions up to and including mySAP CRM edition 2004, the navigation bar profiles are editable as XML definitions, and a wizard is available for the configuration. Since SAP CRM Release 5.0, they are edited via standard SAP Customizing tables. For customers upgrading from an earlier release to CRM 5.0, existing XML definitions are converted automatically into standard tables.

Transaction Launcher

If entries were created in the navigation bar to represent HTML pages, R/3 objects, or CRM processes via the People-Centric UI, they can be defined within the transaction launcher Customizing as different call types in a transaction launcher profile which is then assigned to the implemented IC WebClient profile. A separate session must be created for calling an HTML page and a process via the People-Centric UI. Initially, the parameter transfer is carried out only in the form of URL parameters. In the case of a People-Centric UI process, an object for the process is created in the background and is then called in change mode via the start transaction.

Calling HTML pages Calling BSPs is handled differently from calling other HTML pages. In Transaction CRMC_IC_LTX_URLS, any URLs and additional information can be maintained. Furthermore, you can define transfer parameters. This entry can then be activated via the transaction launcher wizard. For this purpose, a navigation link from a navigation bar profile is assigned to the URL, and a handler class is generated for the URL call and the parameter transfer. The name of the handler class can be defined by the user.

Calling R/3 objects Like the action box jump of IC WinClient, calling an R/3 object requires the maintenance of a logical system for the call. Additionally, you need to select the desired BOR object and the appropriate method in the transaction launcher wizard. In another step, you can configure transfer parameters via input helps. Afterwards, you determine the return parameters and specify whether the object should be listed in and be accessible from the Activity Clipboard. The name of the handler class, which is generated for this call at the completion of the wizard dialog, can again be freely selected. At runtime, the system represents R/3 objects and transactions via the *Internet Transaction Server* (ITS) (see Figure 3.18).

Calling CRM processes in the People-Centric UI When calling People-Centric UI processes, the object or transaction category, can be transferred in the transaction launcher Customizing. Additionally, the wizard supports the transfer of the transaction type. For the return data flow, the object ID is available. You can also choose whether an entry for this object should be created in the Activity Clipboard; in this case, too, the name of the handler class generated at completion of the dialog can be user-defined.

Data flow Frequently, more data needs to be transferred to the People-Centric UI process than is supported in the transaction launcher wizard. This is possible by editing the generated handler class in Transaction SE24. The data flow can be adapted manually in the method IF_CRM_IC_ACTION_HAND-LER~PREPARE_DATA_FLOW. The standard version contains examples of transferring additional data by manually enhancing this method. These examples can be found in the classes CL_CRM_IC_ABOXSAMPLE_OPPT_PRO and CL_CRM_IC_ABOXSAMPLE_LEAD_PRO. In these classes, in addition to transaction category and type, the business partners, the description of the interaction process, and its possibly associated marketing campaign are transferred from the IC WebClient context.

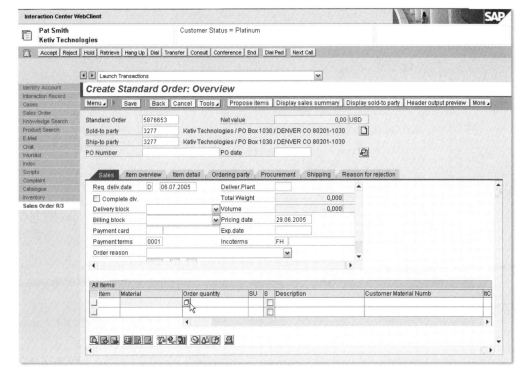

Figure 3.18 IC WebClient Jump to the R/3 System

Up to and including mySAP CRM Edition 2004, transaction launcher profiles can be called and edited as XML definitions. Since SAP CRM Release 5.0, the entries are defined in standard SAP Customizing tables. For customers upgrading from an earlier release to CRM 5.0, existing XML definitions are automatically converted into standard tables.

Activity Clipboard and Business Data Context

The Activity Clipboard (see Figure 3.19) can be regarded as the visible part of the Business Data Context. It is displayed in the view sets of transactions in IC WebClient or is part of the Business Context which additionally presents data from the document flow and the content management. The Activity Clipboard provides its own Customizing. This is where you can define the objects to be displayed for a particular activity-clipboard profile, their method of presentation, and the navigation target to be used for the detail view of the object. All objects represented can be linked via object links at the completion of an interaction. In this way, the Activity Clipboard also displays information about historical transactions. For BOR objects called or created via the transaction launcher, there is a

View of the Business Data Context

so-called *BOL wrapper*. This tool enables you to display and call BOR objects via the Activity Clipboard.

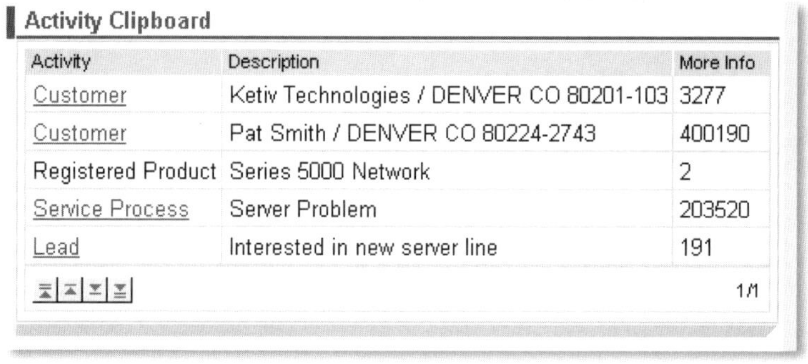
Activity Clipboard

Activity	Description	More Info
Customer	Ketiv Technologies / DENVER CO 80201-103	3277
Customer	Pat Smith / DENVER CO 80224-2743	400190
Registered Product	Series 5000 Network	2
Service Process	Server Problem	203520
Lead	Interested in new server line	191

1/1

Figure 3.19 Activity Clipboard in IC WebClient

The Business Data Context is implemented as a custom controller. As attributes, it is assigned the editable objects with the `CURRENT` prefix. Via the BOL, it is possible to access a multitude of attributes of these objects. During an interaction, the data is buffered via the context or context nodes assigned to the controller. Therefore, BOL attributes of relevant objects are available during the interaction without reading the database.

Up to and including mySAP CRM Edition 2004, Activity Clipboard profiles can be called and edited as XML definitions. Since SAP CRM Release 5.0, the entries are defined in standard SAP Customizing tables. For customers upgrading from an earlier release to CRM 5.0, existing XML definitions are automatically converted into standard tables.

Technical Information

Transaction	Description
CRMC_XMLEDITOR	Access to navigation bar profiles (component ID: LG), transaction launcher profiles (component ID: AB), Activity Clipboard profiles (component ID: AC)
CRMC_IC_LTX_URLS	Define URLs and parameters for transaction launcher
CRMC_IC_NAVBAR_PERM	Define Navigation Bar Profiles (from CRM 5.0 onwards)
CRMC_IC_ACTIONPROF	Copy/Delete Launch Transactions (from CRM 5.0 onwards)
CRMC_IC_AC_PROF	Define Activity Clipboard Profiles (from CRM 5.0 onwards)

Table 3.20 Customizing Transactions for the Basic Functions

SAP Note	Description
690500	Limitations for BOR based launch transactions
748126	Closing browser does not end launch transaction ITS session

Table 3.21 SAP Notes on Basic Functions

3.3.3 Process and Master Data Integration

Like IC WinClient, IC WebClient accesses master data and processes on the CRM server as well. All settings specified there also apply to IC Web-Client and can be re-used. IC WebClient provides some specific features in both areas, and these are explained in the following sections.

Access to master data and processes of the CRM server

Master Data Integration

All the special features of the access and display of business partner data can be configured via the account identification profile in Transaction CRMC_IC_BP_PROF and then assigned to the implemented IC Web-Client profile.

Account identification

Business-partner data is displayed in two components of the IC Web-Client screen: the context area and the work area. The display of business partner data in the context area is limited to two lines. Typically, it shows the names of customers and contact persons, but you can also display other data about the business partner from the BOL via Customizing. You also can freely determine completely different data to be displayed by assigning a special class. In the work area, besides enhanced display options for detailed information about the business partner, you also can search and create business partners (see Figure 3.20).

Business partners can be searched in an automated way, using—for example—, their telephone numbers (*Automatic Number Identification* – ANI), or manually. For an automated search via Computer Telephony Integration, search parameters other than the caller number can be supported. This is carried out flexibly by assigning an XSLT program during the maintenance of the account identification profile. An example of the business partner search based on data gathered in an Interactive Voice Response-dialog is provided by the XSLT program CRM_IC_BPIDENT_EXT_IAD_TO_ABAP, which is included in the standard system. Because IC WebClient supports the multi-channel-enabled interface ICI, the search strategy can be configured separately for every communication channel.

Automated and manual search

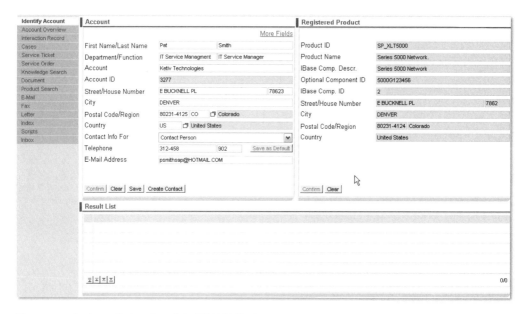

Figure 3.20 Business-Partner Search in IC WebClient

Configuration options are available for a manual search via the view set **Identify Account** in the IC WebClient work area. You can, for example, specify if the search is limited to certain business partner roles or define the maximum number of search results. Additionally, business partners can be searched using attributes of their installation components. For high-performing searches with combined search parameters in extremely large datasets, you have the option of a special search indexing. In this case, the Software Agent Framework uses the TREX search technology for indexing business partner data. TREX maintains this indexing information in main memory, enabling extremely short access times even in wildcard searches of datasets spanning several million business-partner records.

There are further configuration options for creating business partners in the work area of IC WebClient. For example, you can define which business- partner categories and roles can be created by the users of a certain IC profile.

Identification of employees in an EIC

Besides a business-to-business and a business-to-consumer identification scenario, the standard system also contains a scenario for the identification of employees to enable operation of an Employee Interaction Center using IC WebClient. To be able to access an HR system for reading the detailed data on individual employees, you need to enter a *logical system* in the identification profile. The standard system provides this option since mySAP CRM Edition 2004 (see Figure 3.21).

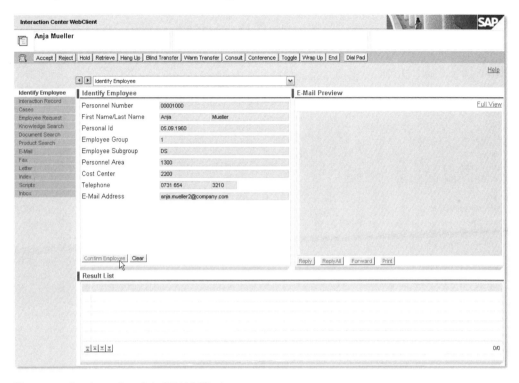

Figure 3.21 Employee Search in IC WebClient

IC WebClient provides a particular view set for searching products. This search is also used as input help in order processes, to select products for certain order items. In IC WebClient, the agent can also access serialized products (*iObjects*). In addition to search, creation, and editing functions, a special view set provides detailed information about serialized products (see Figure 3.22). Apart from that, since mySAP CRM Edition 2004, two Business Add-Ins (BAdIs) provide the option to extend the display and creation of serialized products, particularly for IC WebClient, and to flexibly specify which object links are created to the serialized product via IC WebClient.

Product search and display of product information

IC WebClient can display the fact sheet about the business partner as well. The fact sheet can contain master data on the business partner from SAP CRM, processes from SAP CRM and SAP R/3 as well as data on the business partner from the SAP Business Information Warehouse. This can be configured in the **Master Data** area of the IMG via the Customizing

Fact sheet

activity **Business partner – Cockpit and Fact Sheet · Define Info Blocks and Views**.

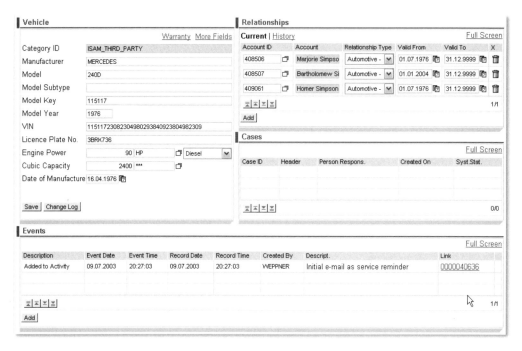

Figure 3.22 Presentation of a Serialized Product in IC WebClient

Access to this fact sheet depends on the role. IC WebClient provides a standard view set with a view (view set: *FaShAreaViewSet.htm*; view: *FaShView.htm*) for the fact sheet. There are flexible extension options for projects (see Section 4.9).

Process Integration

Interaction documentation

CRM business transactions document interactions with customers in IC WebClient. You can configure a number of things: which transaction category and which transaction type to use; in which partner functions the identified business partners are moved into the interaction process; and which value the application sets for the activity type, depending on the communication channel in the interaction process. Via the business transaction profile, you can also configure whether to use a one-document or a multi-document scenario for the processing in IC WebClient (see also SAP Note 669072).

Multi-document scenario

In a multi-document scenario, IC WebClient creates an interaction document for every interaction, e.g. an activity. The data of this document can be edited at runtime via the view set **Interaction Record**. If processes such as the creation of sales or service orders are carried out during the interaction, IC WebClient generates separate documents for these processes. These documents are linked to the interaction process via object links. For creating these documents, you can predefine one transaction type per business transaction category in the business transaction profile under **Dependent Business Transactions**. In this way, the screen is ready for input when navigating to one of these documents (see Figure 3.23).

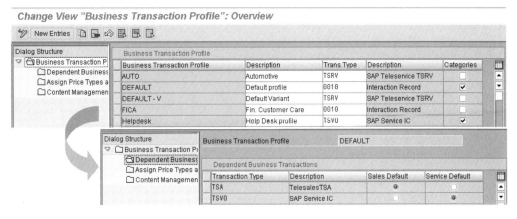

Figure 3.23 Business Transaction Customizing in IC WebClient

In a one-document scenario, interaction-related data is collected as a part of a mixed document, e.g. a service order. When navigating to the **Interaction Record** view set, that part of the service order data is then displayed which is used for documenting the interaction. When you navigate to the view set of the service order, no separate document is created but only a special format of the data related to the service order is displayed. Using a one-document scenario is worth considering if all interactions aim at executing a certain process, for example, the creation of service orders. In this case, the one-document scenario can reduce data volume.

One-document scenario

IC WebClient provides special views of a selected number of processes available in CRM Enterprise. However, all SAP CRM objects are integrated in the data model and in the BOL. Therefore, by means of the integration of start transactions, all CRM Enterprise processes are always available in IC WebClient. Special views optimized for use in an Interaction Center are available in IC WebClient for the following activity types: activity, sales order, service order (in the form of the IC WebClient service order and the service ticket), CRM case, and (since mySAP CRM 2005 or with

Special view of processes

SAP CRM Release 5.0) even lead, complaint, and sales orders from SAP ERP.

The example in Figure 3.24 shows the flexibility of the IC WebClient user interface and the benefits of the separation of UI and application logic: In one view set, several objects are accessed at the same time. The top area serves to maintain the interaction document data. In the middle, follow-up documents can be created, and all objects relevant to the interaction can be referenced. The lower area shows historical documents.

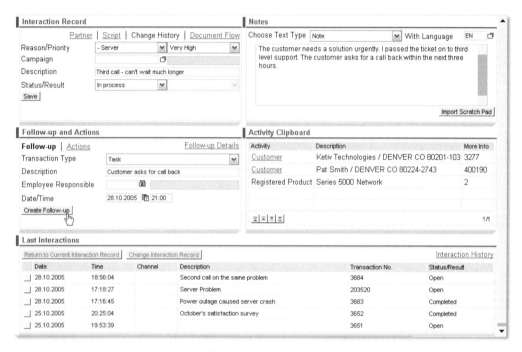

Figure 3.24 Interaction Record View Set of IC WebClient

Technical Information

Transaction/IMG Activity	Description
CRMC_IC_BP_PROF	Define Account identification Profiles
CRMC_IC_BTPFAS	Assign Partner Functions to Business Transactions
IMG · CRM · IC WebClient · Business Transaction · Define Business Transaction Profiles	Define Business Transaction Profiles

Table 3.22 Customizing Activities for Process and Master Data Integration

SAP Note	Description
707104	Account identification from attached data
669072	Customizing transactions in the IC WebClient

Table 3.23 SAP Notes on Process and Master-Data Integration

3.3.4 Integrating Communication Channels

IC WebClient provides extensive possibilities to integrate different interaction channels. There is a difference between push and pull modes in the integration of interaction channels. In push mode, the agent only declares himself ready for processing interactions via IC WebClient. Thereupon, interactions are actively prompted at his workplace according to rules stored in a communication management software. Since IC WebClient supports channels such as telephone, email, and WebChat for the push mode due to the multi-channel interface ICI, it might be possible to map concepts like universal queuing or universal routing, depending on the scope of functionality of the external communication management software. In pull mode, the inbox represents the central work list of an agent or an agent group. The entries listed therein must be actively accepted by an agent (pull mode). In the agent inbox of IC WebClient, it is possible to work with interaction channels like email, fax, and letter. The SAP interfaces SAPconnect and SAP ArchiveLink are used for this purpose. Any transaction category of an individual agent or a group is accessible via the agent inbox. In the following sections, push-mode integration is discussed under "multi-channel integration," while pull-mode integration is discussed under "agent inbox."

Integration of push and pull modes

Multi-channel Integration

In order to integrate IC WebClient with an external communication management software, at first you need to establish an HTTP connection to this external software via Transactions SM59 and CRMM_BCB_ADM. Using Transaction CRMM_IC_MCM_CCADM, you then can determine which communication channels are to be supported by this connection. With Transactions CRMC_MCM_CCPRO and CRMM_IC_MCM_CCLNK, a communication-management software profile is assigned to the connection, which in turn must be assigned to an IC WebClient profile. For every communication channel integrated via the multi-channel interface, real-time information is then displayed to the right of the context area in IC WebClient (see Figure 3.25) during the interaction processing.

Multi-channel interface for the push mode

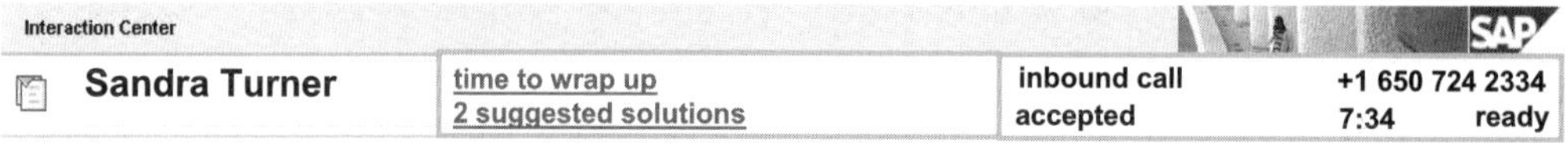

Sandra Turner	time to wrap up 2 suggested solutions	inbound call accepted	+1 650 724 2334 7:34 ready

Figure 3.25 Context Area of IC WebClient

For accepting interactions from different communication channels, IC WebClient provides several toolbars and, depending on the communication channel, automatically displays the appropriate one at the top of the screen at runtime. Special view sets are available in IC WebClient for editing emails and WebChats. For the email and WebChat communication channels, further settings can be specified.

Chat: Standard responses

Since SAP CRM Release 5.0, the WebChat communication channel lets you configure if and how the textual communication is to be stored with the interaction process. Predefined standard responses can be created for WebChat dialogs.

Email: groupware integration

For the email communication channel, you first need to configure whether emails should be received via the multi-channel interface or via the agent inbox and if the size of email attachments should be limited. Furthermore, a multitude of settings can be specified for email responses: for example if and how the reply-to address should be pre-assigned, if a general sender address should be used, or if local address books of a groupware like Microsoft Outlook or Lotus Notes should be accessed (Outlook and Notes use ActiveX Controls in the Web browser). These settings are also relevant for using the agent inbox in the email communication channel.

Up to and including mySAP CRM Edition 2004, the profiles for toolbars and for the email processing are implemented as XML definitions. Since SAP CRM Release 5.0, the entries are defined in standard SAP Customizing tables. For customers upgrading from an earlier release to SAP CRM 5.0, existing XML definitions are automatically converted into standard tables.

Agent Inbox

Universal group inbox for the pull mode

The agent inbox of IC WebClient contains interactions via email, fax, and letter. You also can search and display any kind of CRM business transaction and—since SAP CRM Release 5.0—work items, ERP sales orders, and CRM cases in the agent inbox. Within an agent inbox profile, you can configure which kinds of processes are relevant with a certain IC WebClient profile (Transaction CRMC_IC_AUI_MAINCAT).

The agent inbox of IC WebClient is designed as a group inbox. Thus, all agents of one group can use the same view of inbox entries to be processed. As soon as an agent marks an entry for processing, this is visible to the other group members. Furthermore, you can define whether these entries are displayed to the other group members in the first place.

In contrast to IC WinClient, the agent inbox of IC WebClient (see Figure 3.26) supports integrated views of output lists resulting from selections. This enables configurable, standardized quick searches such as "my open issues for this week." For these and integrated manual selections, status and priority values of the individual objects can be mapped to a standardized agent inbox status. In the user interface, a special toolbar beneath the output list provides standardized processing options for all selection results.

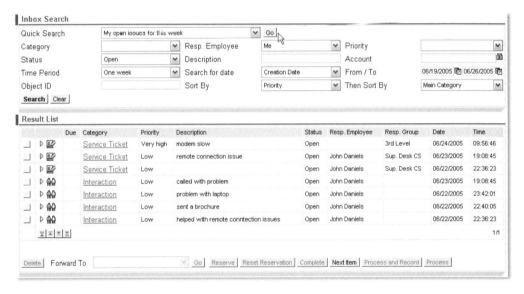

Figure 3.26 Agent Inbox in IC WebClient

IC WebClient with its agent inbox supports basically the same concept as IC WinClient (see Section 3.2.4) with regard to the inbound interaction media email, fax, and letter. For this purpose, the standard system contains a workflow template (14000164) and standard tasks for email (14008030), fax (14008031), and letter (14008032). The connection between a central email address and the workflow is established via the BOR object ICAUISUPP and its RECEIVE method, which triggers an event that in turn starts the workflow. On the other hand, the agent inbox is integrated with the SAP-proprietary ERMS (*Email Response Management*

Email, fax, and letter

System) for the email communication channel. If ERMS is to be used together with the agent inbox, in the inbound distribution (Transaction SO28), you need to assign the central address to the BOR object ERMSSUPRT2 and, in Transaction CRMC_IC_AUI_COMM, the standard task 207914 to the email (INT) communication channel.

For every communication channel, you can select either the native HTML editor of IC WebClient (see Figure 3.27) or Microsoft Word as the editor for processing the email, fax, and letter interaction media. However, this requires a local installation of Microsoft Word on the user PC. It is also possible to integrate the address book of a local groupware installation like Lotus Notes or Microsoft Outlook (see above).

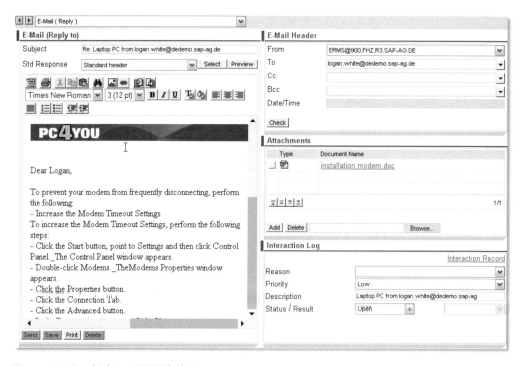

Figure 3.27 Email Editor in IC WebClient

Technical Information

Transaction	Description
CRMM_BCB_ADM	Maintain Communication Management Software Connections

Table 3.24 Customizing Transactions for Integrating Communication Channels

Transaction	Description
CRMM_IC_MCM_CCADM	Maintain System Settings for Communication management software
CRMC_MCM_CCPRO and CRMM_IC_MCM_CCLNK	Profiles for Communication management software and assignment of profiles
CRM_ICI_TRACE	Traces of the multi-channel interface ICI
CRMC_IC_AUI_PROFILE	Define Inbox Profiles
CRMC_XMLEDITOR	Access to email profile (component ID: EM), toolbar profile (component ID: WB)
CRMC_IC_TLBPROF	Define Toolbar Profiles (from CRM 5.0 onwards)
CRMC_IC_EMAIL	Define Email Profiles (from CRM 5.0 onwards)
CRMC_IC_AUI_MAINCAT	Define Element Categories for Searches
CRMC_IC_AUI_QUICKS	Define Quick Searches
CRMC_IC_AUI_MAP_STA	Map Element Status to Inbox Status
CRMC_IC_AUI_MAP_PRI	Map Element Priorities to Inbox Priorities

Table 3.24 Customizing Transactions for Integrating Communication Channels (cont.)

SAP Note	Description
707104	Account identification from attached data
669516	Using SAPphone for CTI Integration
827958	JavaScript Errors in IC WebClient, Messaging does not work
681863	IC WebClient – mail inbound – email integration
772214	Email in the PC UI: No Outlook/Notes when you enter address

Table 3.25 SAP Notes on Integrating Communication Channels

3.3.5 Supporting Functions

As in IC WinClient, the essential supporting functions in IC WebClient are scripting, alerts, and Knowledge Search. The reminder scripting is not available in IC WebClient, but the same functionality can be built via alerts.

Scripting, alerts, and Knowledge Search

Interactive Scripting

Interactive scripts   In IC WebClient, interactive scripting refers to scripts which can be displayed in their own view set (see Figure 3.28); in the WebChat view set, they can be integrated in half-screen width. In an own BSP application, the Interaction Center Manager can create a series of questions and answering options and provide them to the operative area by assigning them to a script profile or, in the case of telemarketing campaigns, by assigning them directly to a particular campaign.

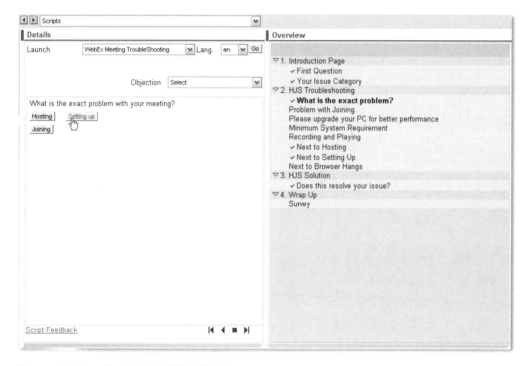

Figure 3.28 Interactive Script in IC WebClient

Manifold forms of answer recording   Besides the use of pushbuttons to represent answers and the related navigation to further questions, the interactive scripting feature of IC WebClient also supports manifold forms of answer recording which do not immediately result in a navigation. These might include recording an answer in the form of user-defined text, the selection of a dropdown box entry or of checkboxes in a list. Actions and templates can be added to an interactive script. This enables, for example, the progressive collection and storage of data about the current business partner beyond the script, or a lead qualification using a survey within the script. The standard version contains actions for updating the address data of the current business partner. It also contains templates for maintaining marketing attributes of the business partner or for integrating a CRM survey for lead qualification and, based on the collected data, creating a lead related to the business partner at the end of the script.

In interactive scripts, any attributes from the Business Data Context of IC WebClient can be used as variables. Many attributes of the identified business partners and their address data can be taken over into question-and-answer texts using *Drag & Drop*.

For executing a script, the agents can be provided with special subordinate scripts for objection handling. These can be accessed at any time during the script execution via a dropdown box. For a better structure, interactive scripts can be divided into chapters. A graphical overview over the script structure and the current position within this structure are visible throughout the execution.

Script execution

Alerts

In IC WebClient, alerts are displayed in the middle of the context area at the top of the user interface. These alerts are either simple text messages or text messages with a navigation option.

Provisioning of notes

Alerts can be configured and assigned to the currently used IC WebClient profile via an alert profile. In the standard system, the following preconfigured alerts already exist (Alert profile: DEFAULT):

▶ **Reminder** ("reminder")
This message is displayed after a certain time interval once the account was confirmed

▶ **Related documents** ("CMrelatedDocuments")
This alert is displayed if the contact data contains documents; it provides the option to navigate there via a link.

▶ **Automatically suggested solutions** ("AutoSuggest")
This alert displays the number of solutions that could previously be determined for a particular email via the solution database, and also provides a direct navigation option.

▶ **Chat notification** ("chatPosting")
This message shows the receipt of a chat request together with the sender and the first line of chat text.

For configuration of further alerts, there is a wizard to guide you through the definition process (see Chapter 4, Section 4.12).

Up to and including mySAP CRM Edition 2004, the alert profiles are stored as XML definitions. Since SAP CRM Release 5.0, the entries are defined in standard SAP Customizing tables. For customers upgrading from an earlier release to SAP CRM 5.0, existing XML definitions are automatically converted into standard tables.

Customization and enhancement

An alert is accessed via an event. A list of events available by default can be retrieved via Transaction CRMC_IC_EVENTS and also be extended using customer-specific events. Text messages can contain variables, so-called placeholders. The placeholders delivered can be retrieved via Transaction CRMC_IC_AM_PHS and also be extended by customer-specific placeholders. Input parameters and their corresponding values can be used in alerts, such as a parameter for the time unit to define how long to wait after an event occurs until a certain alert is displayed (Transaction CRMC_IC_AM_PRM). Since SAP CRM Release 5.0, all these settings are implemented via the central Transaction CRMC_IC_ALERTMODELER.

Because it is possible to use proprietary events and classes for modeling alerts, virtually any extension and adaptation can be implemented for a customer-specific use of the functionality without further modification.

Knowledge Search

Software Agent Framework

The Knowledge Search in IC WebClient is presented in its own view set and uses the Software Agent Framework for accessing various knowledge bases. The Software Agent Framework uses the TREX technology as a search engine. Via the Software Agent Framework, the contents of several knowledge bases are indexed using TREX. In the standard system, the CRM solution database, the CRM case management, and the content management are integrated as knowledge bases. Via the Software Agent Framework, a flexible extension is possible by adding more, even external, knowledge bases.

Access to various knowledge bases

With the knowledge-based search function, interaction-center agents can access the individual knowledge bases comfortably via a dropdown box. The search functionality available might be restricted by some knowledge bases. In general, it is possible to search via user-defined text or pre-defined attributes. For a better structure of free-text queries, exclusion keywords can be added. The Software Agent Framework divides large output lists into clusters whose keywords can be used for a quick restriction of the search (extended search). Output lists are displayed with probability values (see Figure 3.29).

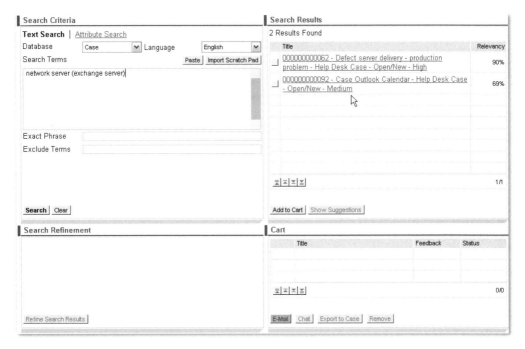

Figure 3.29 Knowledge Search in IC WebClient

Detail views are available for the entries in the output list. Additionally, the results can be easily taken over into response emails. As to case output lists, selected CRM cases can be taken over into the case processing in IC WebClient.

Technical Information

Transaction/BSP Application/ IMG Activity	Description
CRMC_IC_SCRIPT	Define Script Profiles
CRM_IC_ISE	BSP application of the script editor
CRMC_XMLEDITOR	Access to alert modeler profile (component ID: AM), event profile (component ID: EV)
CRMC_IC_EVENTS	Define Events
CRMC_IC_AM_PHS	Define Placeholders
CRMC_IC_AM_PRM	Define Input Parameters

Table 3.26 Customizing and Configuration of Supporting Functions

Transaction/BSP Application/ IMG Activity	Description
CRMC_IC_ALERTMODELER	Define Alerts and Alert Profiles (from CRM 5.0 onwards)
IMG · CRM · Enterprise Intelligence · Software Agent Framework	Settings for SAF, knowledge bases and indexing

Table 3.26 Customizing and Configuration of Supporting Functions (cont.)

SAP Note	Description
763777	Alert and Interactive Script based on CAD information
739267	Unable to Copy and Paste in the Interactive Script Editor
688307	Alert when open service order exist for account
688309	Alert when open service order exist for product
688721	Alert when there are unassigned service orders
772848	IC Scenarios requiring TREX 6.1
662550	Launching the Indexes Application (Software Agent Framework)

Table 3.27 SAP Notes on Supporting Functions

3.4 Interaction Center Management

The Interaction Center Management area of mySAP CRM Interaction Center includes an Email Response Management System (ERMS), several tools for monitoring and managing the operation of an Interaction Center, and the analytical CRM area that is relevant to Interaction Center reporting. All these contents are integrated in the CRM content of the SAP Enterprise Portal via the portal role Interaction Center Manager.

3.4.1 Email Response Management System

Rules-based email processing

With mySAP CRM Edition 2004, a complete Email Response Management System became available in mySAP CRM Interaction Center for the first time. Even earlier versions of mySAP CRM Interaction Center contain functions that can intelligently process inbound emails sent to central company addresses and forward them to the appropriate agent groups. To create complex rules requires a good knowledge of the SAP Business Workflow, however. ERMS aims at tailoring the maintenance of complex rules or sets of rules to business users. There also are extended options for automated and partially automated processing of emails and Web forms; for the latter, a Web-form handler has been integrated in the solution. Furthermore, the architecture of the solution has been designed for easy extensibility of the standard scope of functionality. Even in the standard system, ERMS already contains a multitude of functions, e.g. for the automatic answering of emails, for preparing standard responses, or for routing emails to specific agent groups based on a classification of its contents.

In ERMS, emails are received via the SAPconnect interface and then forwarded to the SAP Business Workflow. Before the workflow starts, the system can first filter out spam and other unwanted emails. The started workflow activates the ERMS Service Manager, which, in the first step, creates an XML structure for the email called "fact base." The email is analyzed using various services, and the results of this analysis are transferred to the fact base. After this process has been completed, the Service Manager starts the rule services, which are executed via the native ERMS rules engine based on the gathered facts. From the rules engine, the actions to be carried out for this email are sent back to the Service Manager, which then activates the appropriate action handlers to execute the actions.

Procedure for inbound emails

The central part of the ERMS solution from a system administrator's point of view is the Service Manager. For this component, different profiles can be created in Customizing which determine the type, number, and order of services to be used (Transaction CRMC_ERMS_SM_PROF). The services available in the standard system can be displayed via Transaction CRMC_ERMS_SM_SRV; this is also where you can add your own services. The scope of functionality of ERMS is determined by the repository it can access (Transaction CRMC_ERMS_REPOSITORY). The repository contains listings of the objects or their attributes, actions, and operators, respectively, which are known to ERMS and can be used during rule modeling and execution. All of these lists can be extended using customer-specific entries (see Figure 3.30).

Service Manager

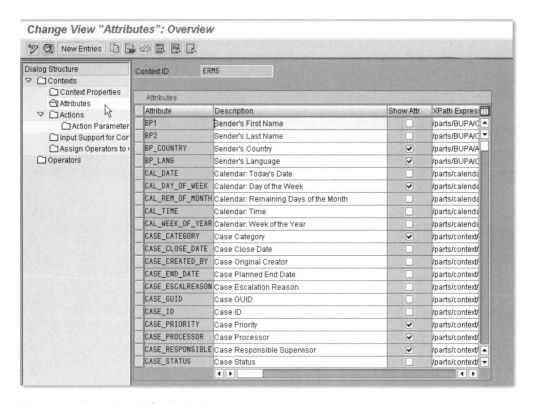

Figure 3.30 Customizing in the ERMS Repository

Rule editor The central part of the ERMS solution from an interaction center manager's point of view is the rules engine and the user-friendly Rule Modeler. It allows you to create multilevel hierarchically-structured rule sets that can be shared afterwards. The rules are edited by selecting conditions and appropriate actions from dropdown boxes. The resulting rule is also shown as text (see Figure 3.31).

Agent-related functions Interaction center agents receive ERMS emails in their agent inbox. Response emails can be edited using an HTML email editor, which provides functions such as the maintenance of standard response texts and email templates and enables the integration of a spell check. Alternatively, Microsoft Word can be integrated as the email editor in IC Web-Client.

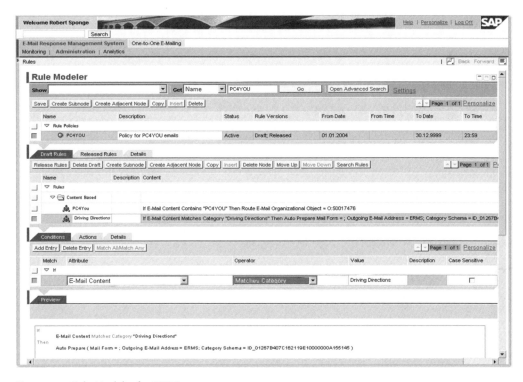

Figure 3.31 Rule Modeler for ERMS

Technical Information

For ERMS, a proprietary workflow template (WS 00200001) is delivered with a standard task for emails (207914). The workflow is started via the RECEIVE method of the BOR object ERMSSUPRT2.

Transaction/BSP Application/ IMG Activity	Description
CRMC_ERMS_SM_PROF	Define Service Manager Profiles
CRMC_ERMS_SM_SRV	Define services
CRMC_ERMS_REPOSITORY	Define Repository
CRM_ERMS_SAMPLE	BSP application containing the sample Web form
CRM_ERMS_WF_CUST	Task customizing of the ERMS workflow
SO28	Settings for Recipient Determination

Table 3.28 Customizing and Configuration of ERMS

SAP Note	Description
772848	IC Scenarios requiring TREX 6.1

Table 3.29 SAP Note on ERMS

3.4.2 Managing the Interaction Center Operation

Monitoring and messaging, knowledge management, process modeling

The management of the interaction center operation can be divided into the areas of monitoring and messaging, knowledge management, and process modeling. For these areas, mySAP CRM provides a considerable number of various functions. The following sections particularly discuss interaction center-specific functions.

Monitoring and Messaging

For monitoring and messaging, the interaction center manager can handle broadcast messaging, the manager dashboard, and a monitoring function for call lists.

Broadcast messaging

Through broadcast messaging an interaction center manager can send text messages to the agent groups in the organization for which he or she is responsible. The addressees of the messages can be specified in distribution lists freely definable within the organization and receive text messages in the form of a ticker. They can mark individual messages as read in order to stop the ticker, and display marked or archived messages in a text box. Via the administration interface, the interaction center manager can determine the maximum amount of time for which a particular message is displayed in the ticker and if it is presented in normal or bold font (high priority) (see Figure 3.32).

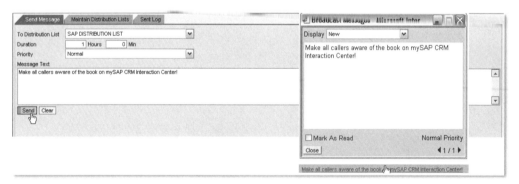

Figure 3.32 Broadcast Messaging

Since mySAP CRM Edition 2004, broadcast messaging is a BSP application that can be started via the SAP Enterprise Portal or a URL call. The use of this administration interface requires the maintenance of a broadcast messaging profile in either Transaction CRMC_CIC_BROAD or Transaction CRMC_IC_BROAD. The profile is then assigned to the IC WebClient and/or IC WinClient profile used by the agents.

The interaction center manager dashboard displays status information about the interaction center and the agent groups. This is retrieved in real time from a communication-management software (see Figure 3.33). Key performance indicators from the communication management software can be visualized. At the same time, the manager dashboard provides an extensive personalization functionality. For example, you can define threshold values based on key performance indicators. If these values are exceeded, the manager receives warning messages. Depending on the configuration, these messages are either represented as icons, texts, or pop-ups. Based on the key performance indicators from the communication-management software, user-defined key performance indicators can be configured and specified for these thresholds.

IC manager dashboard

Figure 3.33 IC Manager Dashboard

Call lists can be created either from marketing campaigns or—given periodical calls with specific customers—can be based on planned calls. Call-list monitoring is enabled via Transaction CRMD_TM_CLDIST. Alternatively, since SAP CRM Release 4.0, a BSP application can be started using the SAP Enterprise Portal or a URL call.

When monitoring call lists, varying degrees of processing detail can be retrieved. You can select individual call lists to display more detailed information. In this detail view, the processing state can also be presented with regard to the calls processed by every single agent. In the transaction, call lists can be assigned to individual agents or agent groups, who then see their call lists in IC WinClient or IC WebClient. Optionally, call lists can also be transferred to an automatic dialer for dialing and distributing the calls to the agents. When call lists are updated in the SAP system after the transfer, the dialer obtains the corresponding delta information via the SPS_MODIFY_PDCALL function module.

If a dialer processes the call list, a reference to the call list can be transferred as call-attached data along with the call to the agent's desktop. With this reference, IC WinClient and IC WebClient can call a planned activity created for the call-list entry and provide it in change mode. In IC WinClient, the reference to the call list is transferred via SAPphone. In IC WebClient, the reference is transferred via ICI and extracted from call-attached data using an XSLT program. The standard system contains several sample programs that can be adapted flexibly to the requirements of the communication management software in use (see Figure 3.34).

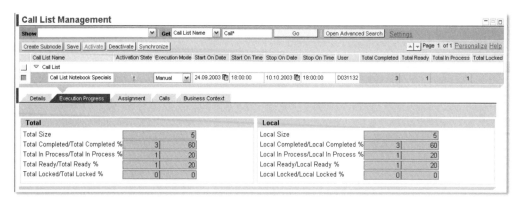

Figure 3.34 Call-List Monitoring

In some cases, the management and monitoring of outbound calls should not be carried out via call lists but rather using a direct assignment of planned calls to agents or agent groups. For this purpose, there is a special transaction for the business-transaction assignment for Interaction Centers (CRMD_BTXA) since SAP CRM Release 5.0. This transaction also provides a monitoring of the assigned planned calls. In general, the current processing status of the employees' activities can be retrieved via the *Activity monitor* (see Figure 3.35).

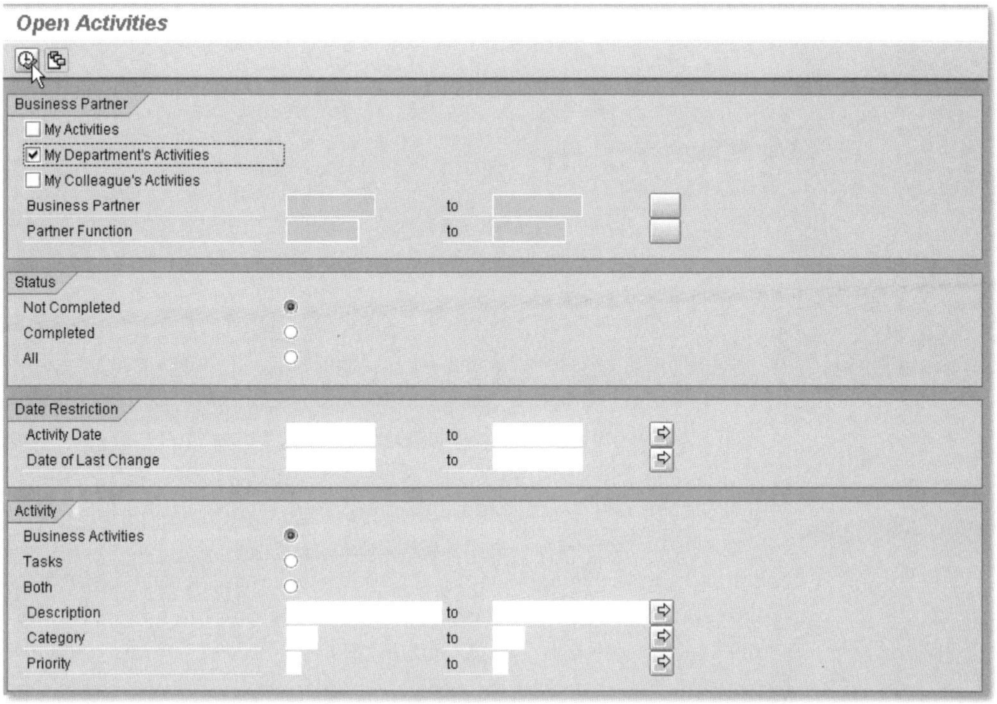

Figure 3.35 Monitoring of Business Transactions

Knowledge Management

Knowledge management includes the Software Agent Framework and the solution database, the Category Editor, and the maintenance of email templates and standard response texts. For maintaining email templates and text modules, the functionality for personalized emails from CRM Marketing has been integrated in the portal role of the Interaction Center Manager.

The solution database of SAP CRM provides the possibility to maintain problem descriptions and corresponding solutions and to provide these to the agents in the interaction center or via an e-service. The solution database can be called for administration either via Transaction IS01 or,

Solution database

since SAP CRM Release 4.0, as a BSP application via the SAP Enterprise Portal, or directly via a URL. In addition to problem and solution descriptions, further attributes, attachments, and tasks can be maintained (see Figure 3.36).

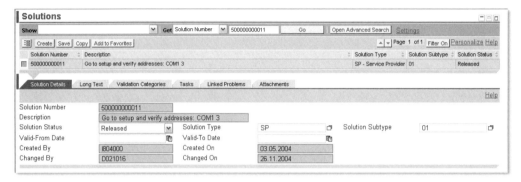

Figure 3.36 Maintenance of the Solution Database

Access to sources of knowledge The solution database is accessed via the Software Agent Framework, which is used for indexing the solution database in TREX. After indexing, several search strategies are available, including an exact, a fuzzy, or a linguistic search. Apart from the SAP CRM solution database, other sources of knowledge can be indexed and integrated for use in the interaction center via the Software Agent Framework. The standard system already contains an indexing and search option for case management, which can be integrated in IC WebClient. A BAdI enables the integration of other sources of knowledge, for example of CRM service orders, but also knowledge bases of other providers. Apart from several wizards to support the configuration, the Software Agent Framework also provides a diagnostic tool to check the selected settings for correctness and consistency (Transaction CRMC_SAF_TOOL). A BSP application provides possibilities to trigger the compilation of indexes from different sources of knowledge manually and to allow for delta compilations (CRM_EI_CMP_ADMN) (see Figure 3.37).

Category Editor Using the Category Modeler, you can build a hierarchical, multilevel classification for different applications, for example in service tickets or emails. The entries on the individual levels represent codes from a catalogue of SAP CRM. Apart from setting up the structure, the Category Modeler allows you to provide links to related objects at individual nodes of the hierarchy, for example to email standard responses, problems and solutions, or templates for service tickets. If an email is automatically categorized via ERMS, and if a standard response is assigned, this response is automatically inserted in the response email. The link to specific problems and solutions, for example, brings up the number of assigned solutions as an alert with a navigation option in the context area if you select the corresponding category in a service ticket in IC WebClient. Navigation then results in a detail view of the linked solutions. If a template in the Category Modeler is assigned to a specific classification in the service ticket, a pushbutton becomes active in IC WebClient that automatically applies all values stored in this template to the current ticket.

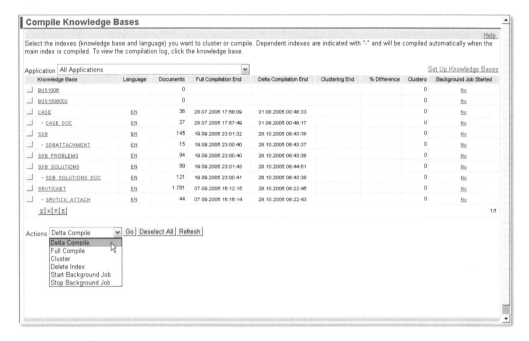

Figure 3.37 Indexing of Knowledge Bases

The Category Modeler was first provided with mySAP CRM Edition 2004. In SAP CRM Release 5.0, many additional applications were integrated. For example, the use of multilevel classification for cases, complaints or service provides has become possible with this release (see Figure 3.38).

Process Modeling

For process modeling, the interaction center manager can use the Rule Modeler and the interactive scripting editor as interaction center-specific modeling tools.

Figure 3.38 Category Modeler

Modeling of interactive scripts For interactive scripts in IC WinClient and IC WebClient, there is one graphical editor each. The editor for IC WinClient scripting (see Figure 3.39) can be opened with Transaction CRMM_TM_SCRIPT (see Section 3.2.5), the editor for IC WebClient scripting (see Figure 3.40) can be opened via the BSP application CRM_IC_ISE (see Section 3.3.5).

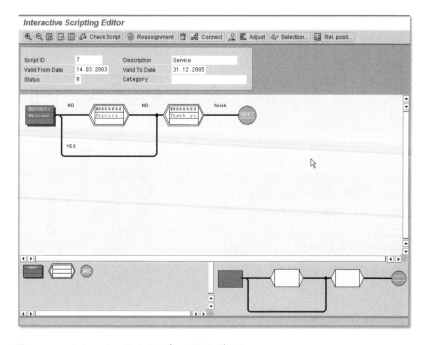

Figure 3.39 Interactive Scripting for IC WinClient

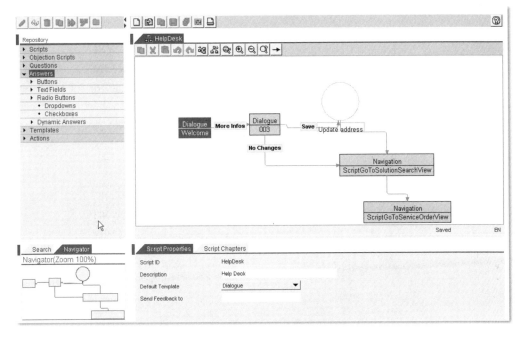

Figure 3.40 Interactive Scripting for IC WebClient

We already mentioned the Rule Modeler in connection with the Email Response Management System (see Section 3.4.1). In that context, it represents the central user interface for managing and modeling rules for email management. Further, the Rule Modeler can support other processes in the interaction center. This is possible because the Rule Modeler can separately manage several contexts for different applications. Such a context contains so-called policies (rule sets) and rules for email management. The standard system contains another context for CRM business transactions.

Rule editor

This context can be used for the forwarding of processes in IC WebClient. There is a corresponding pushbutton in the **Service Ticket** view set which calls the policies for the service ticket context stored in the rule editor. The policy delivered makes it possible to re-determine and assign the organization responsible based on information like category, status, or priority of the ticket, business partner, or product. Another context is lead management: Using the Rule Modeler, policies and rules also can be modeled for the workflow-based distribution of leads. Additionally, you can create any number of further contexts. The contexts delivered are available in Transaction CRMC_ERMS_REPOSITORY, where you can also create and configure user-defined contexts.

Rules-based forwarding of processes

Technical Information

Some of the BSP applications mentioned above, particularly the tools for managing the interaction center operation, were implemented using the People-Centric User Interface, which possesses its own framework. From this framework, you can directly start the BSP applications for the interaction center manager. For this purpose, you have to execute the page with flow logic *select.htm* in the BSP application CRM_BSP_FRAME and then select the desired BSP application on this page. In Table 3.30, People-Centric UI applications are enclosed in <...>.

Transaction/BSP Application/ IMG Activity	Description
CRM_BM	Broadcast Messaging BSP application
CRMC_IC_BROAD, CRMC_CIC_BROAD	Maintain broadcast messaging profiles
CRM_IC_MDB, CRM_IC_MDB_PERS	BSP applications for calling and personalizing the manager dashboard
CRMD_TM_CLDIST	Call List Maintenance
CRMD_CALL_LIST	Generate Business Transactions and Call Lists
CRMD_BTXA (with CRM 5.0)	Business Transaction Assignment
IS01	Maintain Problems and Solutions
<CRMM_SDB_SOL>	Maintain Solutions
<CRMM_ERM_CAT>	Category Modeler
CRMM_TM_SCRIPT	Interactive script editor for IC WinClient scripts
CRM_IC_ISE	BSP application of the interactive script editor for IC WebClient scripts
<CRMM_ERM_RULES>	Rule Modeler
CRMC_ERMS_REPOSITORY	Define Repository

Table 3.30 Customizing and Configuration of the Functions for Managing the Interaction Center Operation

SAP Note	Description
772848	IC Scenarios requiring TREX 6.1
662550	Launching the Indexes Application (Software Agent Framework)

Table 3.31 SAP Notes on Functions for Managing the Interaction Center Operation

SAP Note	Description
725408	SAF: Integration to external content management systems
739267	Interactive script editor: copy and replace

Table 3.31 SAP Notes on Functions for Managing the Interaction Center Operation (cont.)

3.4.3 Interaction Center Analytics

The interaction center-specific part of CRM Analytics consists of the interaction or contact statistics from a communication-management software, the interaction statistics from the SAP-proprietary Email Response Management System, and the evaluation options for interactive scripts. In order to integrate the interaction statistics of communication-management software in business analyses, the connection ID (or call ID) can be stored in the main CRM business transaction during the interaction.

Interaction statistics and evaluations

Since SAP CRM Release 3.0, interaction center-specific content is delivered for the SAP Business Information Warehouse. Part of this content is based on data (interaction statistics) that can be transferred via a statistics interface from a communication-management software to SAP CRM. Such data could include the connection volume, the service levels achieved, or average speed of answer. On the part of the SAP system, this is taken over by the function module SPS_STAT_DATA_GET, which is called via the CRM_CIC_CTI_LOAD report. In the CRM system, this data is then enhanced with information about business transactions, business partners, or marketing campaigns and uploaded in an SAP BW, in which the interaction statistics are stored as an InfoSource (ØCRM_CIC_CTI_1) (see Figure 3.41).

Content for SAP BW and statistics interface

SAP BW provides an ODS object (ØCRM_CTI) for the interaction statistics that lists every interaction step with its corresponding connection ID and populates two InfoCubes. The InfoCube ØCRM_CTI1 contains time-related interaction statistics which essentially provide very detailed information from the communication management software. The InfoCube ØCRM_CTI2 includes interaction statistics with references to CRM information (business partners, business transactions, marketing campaigns). This enables the creation of virtually any combination of interaction- and business-related analyses.

ODS object and InfoCubes

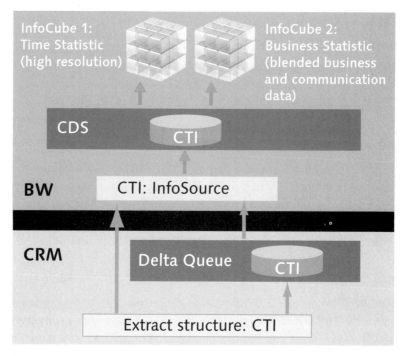

Figure 3.41 Storage of Interaction Statistics in SAP BW

ERMS interaction statistics

If you use the SAP CRM Email Response Management System, you can use it to capture interaction statistics and upload them to SAP BW in the same way. The data is found in the InfoSource 0CRM_ERMS_ITEMS_1, from which it is consistently stored via the ODS object 0CRM_ER01. The InfoCube 0CRM_ER11 provides data like volume, service level, or average speed of answer and average handling time for the Email Response Management System.

Evaluation of interactive scripts

If interactive scripts are used in the Interaction Center, data about executing individual scripts can be collected and extracted for SAP BW. This enables evaluations of the selection frequency of individual responses per script, which can be used, for example, for the analysis of a telemarketing campaign.

Technical Information

The following table lists the Web reports available for interaction statistics.

Technical Name	Description	iView
	Connection volume per	
▶ OTPL_0CRM_CTI2_CVOL_V01	▶ Customer	▶ com.sap.pct.crm.icm.intStat.CVCust
▶ OTPL_0CRM_CTI2_CVOL_V02	▶ Region	▶ com.sap.pct.crm.icm.intStat.CVRegion
▶ OTPL_0CRM_CTI2_CVOL_V03	▶ Agent	▶ com.sap.pct.crm.icm.intStat.CVAgent
▶ OTPL_0CRM_CTI2_CVOL_V04	▶ Interaction Center	▶ com.sap.pct.crm.icm.intStat.CVIC
	Service level per	
▶ OTPL_0CRM_CTI2_SL_V01	▶ Customer	▶ com.sap.pct.crm.icm.intStat.SLCust
▶ OTPL_0CRM_CTI2_SL_V02	▶ Agent	▶ com.sap.pct.crm.icm.intStat.SLRegion
▶ OTPL_0CRM_CTI2_SL_V04	▶ Interaction Center	▶ com.sap.pct.crm.icm.intStat.SLIC
	Average Speed of Answer per	
▶ OTPL_0CRM_CTI2_ASA_V01	▶ Customer	▶ com.sap.pct.crm.icm.intStat.ASACust
▶ OTPL_0CRM_CTI2_ASA_V02	▶ Region	▶ com.sap.pct.crm.icm.intStat.ASARegion
▶ OTPL_0CRM_CTI2_ASA_V04	▶ Interaction Center	▶ com.sap.pct.crm.icm.intStat.ASAIC
	Average Handling Time per	
▶ OTPL_0CRM_CTI2_AHT_V01	▶ Customer	▶ com.sap.pct.crm.icm.intStat.AHTCust
▶ OTPL_0CRM_CTI2_AHT_V02	▶ Region	▶ com.sap.pct.crm.icm.intStat.AHTRegion
▶ OTPL_0CRM_CTI2_AHT_V03	▶ Agent	▶ com.sap.pct.crm.icm.intStat.AHTAgent
▶ OTPL_0CRM_CTI2_AHT_V04	▶ Interaction Center	▶ com.sap.pct.crm.icm.intStat.AHTIC

Table 3.32 Web Reports and Corresponding iViews for Interaction Statistics

Technical Name	Description	iView
	Connection volume per	
► 0TPL_0CRM_CTI1_CVOL_V01	► Calendar day	► com.sap.pct.crm.icm.intStat.CVTime
► 0TPL_0CRM_CTI1_CVOL_V02	► Time interval and day of the week	► com.sap.pct.crm.icm.intStat.CVWeekd
► 0TPL_0CRM_CTI1_CVOL_V03	► Communication type	► com.sap.pct.crm.icm.intStat.CVChan
► 0TPL_0CRM_CTI1_CVOL_V04	► Queue ID	► com.sap.pct.crm.icm.intStat.CVQueue
	Service level per	
► 0TPL_0CRM_CTI1_SL_V01	► Calendar day	► com.sap.pct.crm.icm.intStat.SLTime
► 0TPL_0CRM_CTI1_SL_V02	► Time interval and day of the week	► com.sap.pct.crm.icm.intStat.SLWeekd
► 0TPL_0CRM_CTI1_SL_V03	► Communication type	► com.sap.pct.crm.icm.intStat.SLChan
► 0TPL_0CRM_CTI1_SL_V04	► Queue ID	► com.sap.pct.crm.icm.intStat.SLQueue
	Average Speed of Answer per	
► 0TPL_0CRM_CTI1_ASA_V01	► Calendar day	► com.sap.pct.crm.icm.intStat.ASATime
► 0TPL_0CRM_CTI1_ASA_V02	► Time interval and day of the week	► com.sap.pct.crm.icm.intStat.ASAWeekd
► 0TPL_0CRM_CTI1_ASA_V03	► Communication type	► com.sap.pct.crm.icm.intStat.ASAChan
► 0TPL_0CRM_CTI1_ASA_V04	► Queue ID	► com.sap.pct.crm.icm.intStat.ASAQueue
	Average Handling Time per	
► 0TPL_0CRM_CTI1_AHT_V01	► Calendar day	► com.sap.pct.crm.icm.intStat.AHTTime
► 0TPL_0CRM_CTI1_AHT_V02	► Time interval and day of the week	► com.sap.pct.crm.icm.intStat.AHTWeekd
► 0TPL_0CRM_CTI1_AHT_V03	► Communication type	► com.sap.pct.crm.icm.intStat.AHTChan
► 0TPL_0CRM_CTI1_AHT_V04	► Queue ID	► com.sap.pct.crm.icm.intStat.AHTQueue

Table 3.32 Web Reports and Corresponding iViews for Interaction Statistics (cont.)

Technical Name	Description	iView
	Abandonment rate per	
▶ OTPL_OCRM_ CTI1_ABR_V01	▶ Calendar day	▶ com.sap.pct.crm.icm. intStat.AbRTime
▶ OTPL_OCRM_ CTI1_ABR_V02	▶ Time interval and day of the week	▶ com.sap.pct.crm.icm. intStat.AbRWeekd
▶ OTPL_OCRM_ CTI1_ABR_V03	▶ Communication type	▶ com.sap.pct.crm.icm. intStat.AbRChan
▶ OTPL_OCRM_ CTI1_ABR_V04	▶ Queue ID	▶ com.sap.pct.crm.icm. intStat.AbRQueue

Table 3.32 Web Reports and Corresponding iViews for Interaction Statistics (cont.)

SAP Note	Description
637247	OCRM_CIC_SCRIPT does not support full update mode
536152	Performance improvement in CIC CTI extraction process

Table 3.33 SAP Notes on Interaction Statistics and Evaluations

4 Selected Customization and Extension Options

This chapter introduces some of the customization and extension options of IC WinClient and IC WebClient. This document is not intended to be complete but to provide answers to situations that frequently arise in Interaction Center projects. The examples will prepare you to meet similar customer request, using the potential of the Interaction Center framework.

4.1 Overview

The extension and customization options discussed in the following sections are adapted to the structure of Chapter 3. Extensions within the scope of the architecture are discussed in the first sections, which deal with the creation of your own workspaces or hidden components. These are followed by basic functions of the Interaction Center, such as the action box or the transaction launcher. Three sections about business partners and the fact sheet present extension examples of the integration with master data. The extensions of the business partner search in IC WebClient are just an example of general customizations in IC WebClient, which are discussed in more detail in the Interaction Center Cookbook (see Section 3.1). The process integration is described in the section about workitem execution in IC WinClient. The chapter ends with an example of the agent inbox, which illustrates the communication channels for IC WinClient and similarly for IC WebClient, and with an extension of the alerts in IC WebClient.

Numerous extension options

Experience shows that customizations of functions around the Interaction Center Manager can only be illustrated in the context of concrete customer projects. A general discussion of extensions therefore does not seem appropriate. Instead, Section 5.3 describes an extensive project example.

Interaction Center Manager

The references to the SAP Implementation Guide in this chapter are based on SAP CRM Release 4.0. To avoid too much dependency on one release, transaction codes are provided wherever possible.

4.2 Creating a Workspace with Subscreen in IC WinClient

4.2.1 Introduction

Customized workspace in application or navigation area

In Interaction Center projects, it is frequently necessary to integrate additional information and functions in the framework. One way to meet this requirement is to develop a customized workspace.

This section shows how to extend the application area of IC WinClient by a customized workspace. This new workspace then contains a subscreen with additional data about the confirmed business partner (see Figure 4.1). As with the application area, the navigation area of the Interaction Center can also be adapted.

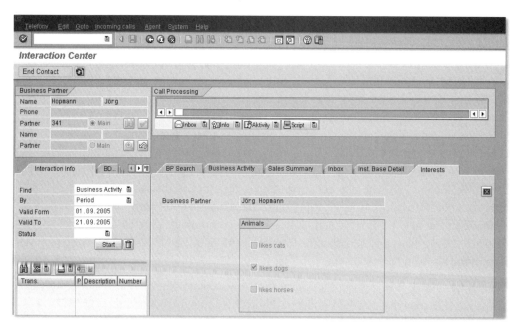

Figure 4.1 Workspace in IC WinClient After the Extension

Dynpro screens or SAP Enjoy Controls

An IC Workspace is always implemented using an ABAP Objects class. However, as it is not possible to define ABAP screens ("dynpros") within classes, we need a separate function group that contains the subscreen, including its logic. SAP Enjoy Controls (*Enjoy SAP Design*), on the other hand, can be implemented without a separate function group, as you can read in Section 4.3.

4.2.2 Implementing the Workspace Class

First, the new class ZCL_CCM_ABSTR_CMPWSP1 is created which is derived from the standard class CL_CCM_ABSTR_CMPWSP.

The CL_CCM_ABSTR_CMPWSP class is the abstract basis for IC workspaces and thus passes down the following three important interfaces.

Abstract superclass and interfaces

▶ The IF_CCM_WORKSPACE interface identifies the class as IC workspace and contains all the basic workspace methods.

▶ The IF_CCM_CMPWSP_IC_EV_HANDLER interface provides the method for the IC event handling if the workspace is supposed to respond to this handling.

▶ The IF_CRM_IC_CMPWSP_CUST interface provides methods to be called by IC Customizing transactions. It is only required if the new workspace needs to be customized.

Since this example is supposed to show a subscreen, another interface needs to be added to the new class.

Interface for Dynpro-based workspaces

▶ IF_CCM_SUBSCREEN_WORKSPACE is the subscreen interface for IC workspaces and provides appropriate methods for integration and calling.

The basic class CL_CCM_ABSTR_CMPWSP has all methods already implemented which are required for working with IC workspaces. Table 4.1 lists the most important methods of the IF_CCM_WORKSPACE interface.

Method	Description
CREATE	creates a workspace
DELETE	deletes a workspace
EXECUTE	executes a workspace
GET_ACTIONS	returns all valid actions (pushbuttons) with callback methods
GET_CONCURRENCY	characteristic: workspace supports parallel process
GET_CONTAINER	returns the workspace container
GET_DISPLAY_TEXT	returns workspace display text
GET_INTERFACE	returns the workspace interface

Table 4.1 Important Methods of IF_CCM_WORKSPACE

Method	Description
SET_LIFTIME	sets the lifetime of a workspace
SET_VISIBLE	sets the visibility of a workspace

Table 4.1 Important Methods of IF_CCM_WORKSPACE (cont.)

Initialization of the workspace and subscription to events

In this section, we first want to redefine the EXECUTE method of the IF_CCM_WORKSPACE interface, which is called once during the execution of the workspace. This is where you should place all necessary initializations of the workspace, one example being the registration for specific IC events. For this purpose, the inherited IC event gateway (attribute CIC_EVENT_GATE) provides a corresponding method that is called for every event that needs to be registered (see Listing 4.1).

```
METHOD if_ccm_workspace~execute .
* Registration of events
    CALL METHOD cic_event_gate->add_listener
        EXPORTING
            listener = me
            event    = 'SEARCH_TARGET_FOUND'.
ENDMETHOD.
```

Listing 4.1 Framework Method for Executing a Workspace

Unwanted closing of the workspace

The IF_CCM_WORKSPACE~EXECUTE method should be redefined in any case because the inherited standard version of this method checks—together with the GET_CONCURRENCY method—the permission for parallel execution. Because this is usually not permitted, a deletion of the workspace results. This can be avoided with a redefinition, even if the method is otherwise empty.

Handling events

For the handling of registered IC events, the next method to redefine is the HANDLE_EVENT method of the IF_CCM_CMPWSP_IC_EV_HANDLER interface. As an import parameter, this method receives the event name as well as the event parameters, which then can be used for controlling the workspace (see Listing 4.2). Naturally, you can only handle those events which were previously registered in the EXECUTE method, because the event handler is called only for those events.

```
METHOD if_ccm_cmpwsp_cic_ev_handler~handle_event .
    CASE event.
        WHEN 'SEARCH_TARGET_FOUND'.
```

```
*       ...
    ENDCASE.
ENDMETHOD.
```

Listing 4.2 Handler Method for Events in IC WinClient

The workspace label is initially defined in Customizing (see Section 4.2.4), but can be changed at runtime. This is done via the GET_DISPLAY_TEXT method of the IF_CCM_WORKSPACE interface which, as a result, returns the text to be displayed in the tab title (see Listing 4.3).

Labeling

```
METHOD if_ccm_workspace~get_display_text .
    text = 'Interests'(001).
ENDMETHOD.
```

Listing 4.3 Selection of the Label for the New Workspace

An IC workspace includes a toolbar on the right-hand side. This toolbar can be freely defined according to specific requirements via the GET_ ACTIONS method of the IF_CCM_WORKSPACE interface. For this purpose, there is a structure of the type CCM_WORKSPACE_CALLBACK where all the control information for the pushbutton is specified. This includes, among other things, the icon to be displayed, the OK code, and the call-back method to be called. For every pushbutton, this structure is populated with the necessary information and is then inserted in the return table. In this example, a pushbutton for closing the workspace is created (see Listing 4.4).

Pushbuttons to the right of the workspace

```
METHOD if_ccm_workspace~get_actions .
    DATA: ls_callback TYPE ccm_workspace_callback.
*   Close workspace
    CLEAR ls_callback.
    ls_callback-okcode           = 'MY_WSP_DEL'.
    ls_callback-callback_method = 'CB_DELETE_WS'.
    ls_callback-icon            = 'ICON_CLOSE'.
    ls_callback-is_active       = 'X'.
    ls_callback-quick           = 'Close
                                   workspace'(002).
    ls_callback-button_group    = '01'.
    APPEND ls_callback TO actions_and_callbacks.
ENDMETHOD.
```

Listing 4.4 Determination of Workspace Pushbuttons at Runtime

Delete workspace In this case, the callback method CB_DELETE_WS simply calls the method responsible for deleting a workspace (see Listing 4.5).

```
METHOD cb_delete_ws .
    CALL METHOD if_ccm_workspace~delete.
ENDMETHOD.
```

Listing 4.5 Callback Method for Event Handler

The DELETE method of the IF_CCM_WORKSPACE interface works in the standard version already. However, if additional cleanup tasks have to be carried out, this is the right place. For this purpose, the method is redefined and extended by the user-defined tasks. If the class was previously registered for IC events, these registrations ought to be removed here. This can be done quite easily via the REMOVE_ALL method of the IC event gateway (see Listing 4.6).

```
METHOD if_ccm_workspace~execute .
* Delete workspace
    CALL METHOD super->if_ccm_workspace~delete
        IMPORTING
            ex_not_deleted = ex_not_deleted
        EXCEPTIONS
            not_existing  = 1
            OTHERS        = 2.
    IF sy-subrc <> 0.
        MESSAGE ID sy-msgid TYPE sy-msgty NUMBER sy-msgno
        WITH sy-msgv1 sy-msgv2 sy-msgv3 sy-msgv4.
    ENDIF.
' Reset Event Gate
    CALL METHOD cic_event_gate->remove_all
        EXPORTING
            listener = me.
ENDMETHOD.
```

Listing 4.6 Framework Method for Deleting a Workspace

Determining the dynpro to be displayed The subscreen to be displayed on the new workspace still needs to be defined. As mentioned above, this is carried out via the IF_CCM_SUBSCREEN_WORKSPACE interface, which needs to be additionally included into the class because it is not inherited from the basic class.

The PBO_BEFORE method provides two return parameters used to specify the subscreen to be called. The EX_SUBSCREEN_REPID parameter trans-

fers the program name of the program or function group, and the EX_
SUBSCREEN_DYNNR parameter transfers the number of the subscreen (see
Listing 4.7).

```
METHOD if_ccm_subscreen_workspace~pbo_before .
   ex_subscreen_repid = 'SAPLZ_ADD_CIC_WSP'.
   ex_subscreen_dynnr = '0100'.
ENDMETHOD.
```

Listing 4.7 Definition of a Workspace Screen

4.2.3 Implementing the Subscreen

For implementing the subscreen, a program or a function group is
required because classes cannot contain any screens. After creating the
function group Z_ADD_CIC_WSP, a dynpro is added with the number
100 and the screen type "subscreen." In the flow logic of the dynpro, you
need to insert the PBO module INIT_0100, in which the retrieval of the
data to be displayed is implemented. In the example below, this is additional data regarding the confirmed business partner (see Listing 4.8). To
simplify things, the programming is done directly in the PBO module
instead of a separate FORM routine.

Flow logic of the
dynpro

```
MODULE init_0100 OUTPUT.
   DATA: lv_bp_guid     TYPE bu_partner_guid,
         ls_data_person TYPE bapibus1006_central_person,
         ls_data_organ  TYPE bapibus1006_central_organ,
         lv_bp_type     TYPE bu_type,
         lv_bp_name     TYPE string.

* Read partner data from GP component
   CALL FUNCTION 'CRM_CIC_BUSINESS_PARTNER_GET'
      IMPORTING
         ev_bp_guid            = lv_bp_guid

   EXCEPTIONS
      failed_to_obtain_bp = 1
      no_bp_found         = 2
      OTHERS              = 3.
   IF sy-subrc = 0.
      CALL FUNCTION 'BUPA_CENTRAL_GET_DETAIL'
         EXPORTING
            iv_partner_guid = lv_bp_guid
```

```
              IMPORTING
                  es_data_person  = ls_data_person
                  es_data_organ   = ls_data_organ
                  ev_category     = lv_bp_type.
          IF lv_bp_type = '1'.
             bp_name = ls_data_person-fullname.
          ELSEIF lv_bp_type = '2'.
             bp_name = ls_data_organ-name1.
          ENDIF.
   *    ...
          ENDIF.
      ENDMODULE.                        " init_0100  OUTPUT
```

Listing 4.8 PBO Module of the New Dynpro

By means of classical dynpro programming, the new IC workspace can now be arbitrarily enhanced or extended and thus adapted to custom requirements.

4.2.4 Customizing

Definition of the workspace in Customizing

The last step consists of customizing in order to make the new workspace known to the system. A new entry is created under **Define Customer-Specific Workspaces** in the **Customer-Specific System Modifications for IC** (Transaction CRMC_CIC_WSP0, see Figure 4.2). This is where you need to specify a name for the workspace and associate it with the implementing class (see Figure 4.3). At this point, the previously developed class ZCL_CCM_ABSTR_CMPWSP1 is to be entered. Parameters can also be maintained in this place, although they are not needed for this example.

Automatically created workspaces

Under the IMG nodes **Component Configuration** and then further **Visible Components**, a profile for automatically created workspaces is now maintained in Transaction CRMC_CIC_WSP3 (see Figure 4.4).

The easiest option is to copy one of the standard profiles. After copying, the entry is marked, and the default workspaces of this profile are opened. Now the new workspace can be inserted as a new tab in the application (or navigation) area. For this purpose, a tab ID and a tab text need to be specified (see Figure 4.5). The tab text maintained here is then displayed in the workspace in the IC if it is not dynamically changed via the redefined IF_CCM_WORKSPACE~GET_DISPLAY_TEXT method.

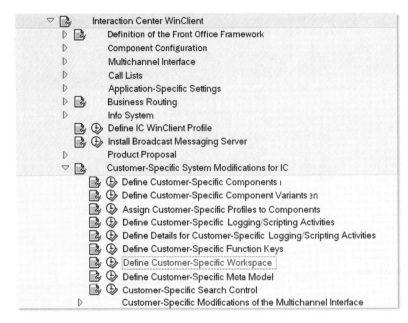

Figure 4.2 Customer-Specific System Modifications for IC

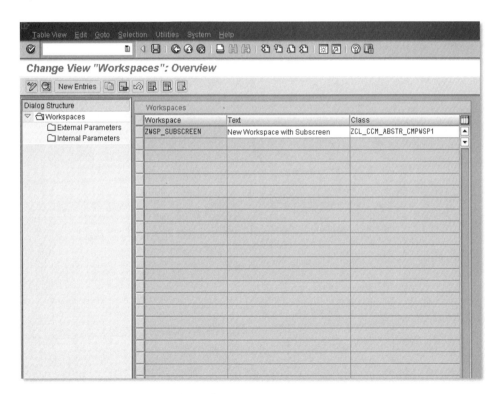

Figure 4.3 Define Customer-Specific Workspaces

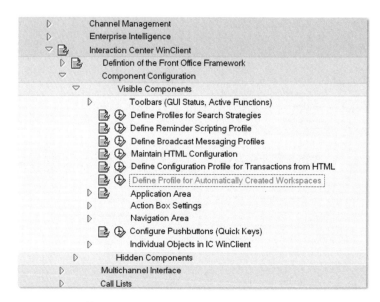

Figure 4.4 Visible Components

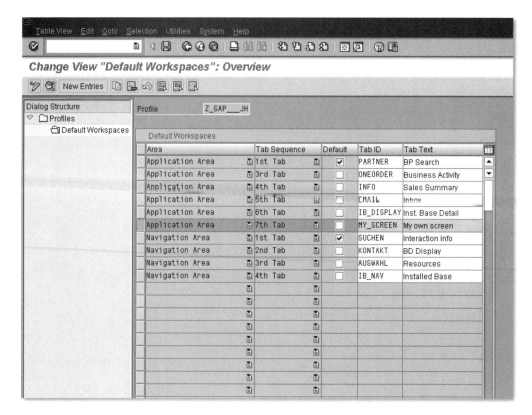

Figure 4.5 Default Workspaces

Then, the new profile for default workspaces still needs to be added to an IC WinClient profile (Transaction CICO). If no appropriate IC profile is available yet, one of the standard profiles should be copied. Afterwards, the DEFAULT_WORKSPACES attribute is set to the profile previously created for default workspaces (see Figure 4.6). Now, the Interaction Center can be started (Transaction CICO) and the new workspace can be checked.

Maintenance of the IC WinClient profile

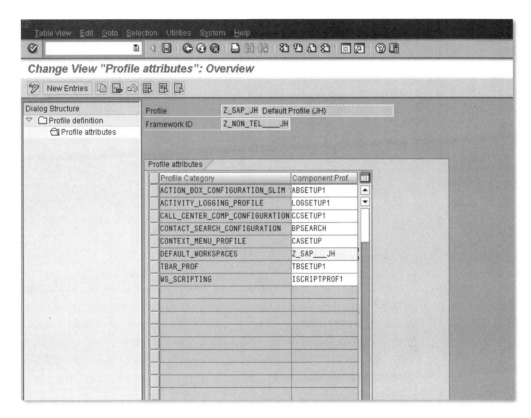

Figure 4.6 IC Profile Attributes

4.3 Creating a Workspace With Enjoy Control in IC WinClient

4.3.1 Introduction

This section describes how you can insert your own visible workspace with an SAP Enjoy Control in the application area of IC WinClient. In this case, the HTML Viewer is used as an example of an SAP Enjoy Control (see Figure 4.7).

HTML control as an example of an SAP Enjoy Control

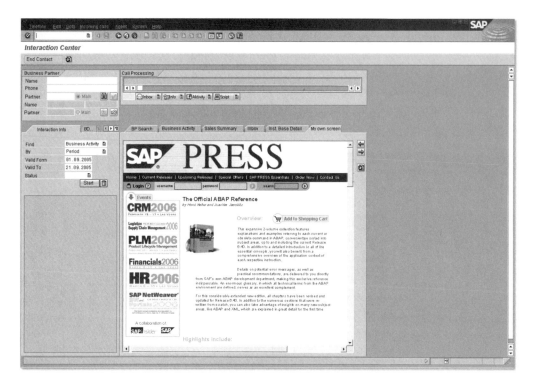

Figure 4.7 Customized Workspace With SAP Enjoy Control

Action box   Naturally, the URL itself can also be implemented using an action box configuration (see Section 3.2.2 in Chapter 3). Standard even covers the pushbuttons for Browser navigation. In this respect, it should only be regarded as an example that can easily be applied to any SAP Enjoy Controls, like the SAP Text Edit Control, the ALV grid control, or the ALV tree control. Additionally, other ActiveX controls can be integrated; the possibilities are almost infinite (see also Chapter 5, Section 5.7).

As mentioned in the previous section, an IC workspace is always implemented via an ABAP Objects class, which is used for creating and controlling the workspace.

4.3.2 Implementing the Workspace Class

First, the new class ZCL_CCM_ABSTR_CMPWSP2 is created which is derived from the standard class CL_CCM_ABSTR_CMPWSP.

Abstract   The abstract basis for IC workspaces—the CL_CCM_ABSTR_CMPWSP
superclass and   class—passes down the three interfaces IF_CCM_WORKSPACE, IF_CCM_
interfaces   CMPWSP_IC_EV_HANDLER, and IF_CRM_IC_CMPWSP_CUST. These provide

all methods necessary for working with IC workspaces. You can find more details about these interfaces in Section 4.2.2.

The HTML control itself is created in the class as a new public attribute ENJOY_CONTROL of the CL_GUI_HTML_VIEWER reference type. Via this attribute, the control can then be generated and controlled. Methods for this purpose, which make controlling rather easy, are included in the CL_GUI_HTML_VIEWER class, e.g. SHOW_URL, EXECUTE_SCRIPT, GO_BACK, GO_FORWARD, or DO_REFRESH.

HTML control

Then, the EXECUTE method of the IF_CCM_WORKSPACE interface needs to be redefined again, which calls the framework for executing the workspace. Here you can also find the necessary workspace initializations, for example the registration for IC events. Details about the IC event gateway are available in Section 4.2.2.

What is new in this context is the creation of the Enjoy Control in the workspace: Creating controls requires a GUI container in which the control is displayed. This container is provided by the workspace class with the GET_GUI_CONTAINER method of the inherited WS_DISPLAY attribute. Another very useful method of the WS_DISPLAY instance is IS_VISIBLE, with which you can check if the workspace is currently visible. The container reference returned is now used as a parameter for creating the control (see Listing 4.9).

Creation of the Enjoy Control in the workspace

```
METHOD if_ccm_workspace~execute .
   DATA: gui_container TYPE REF TO cl_gui_container.
   gui_container = ws_display->get_gui_container( ).
* Creation of Enjoy Control
   IF enjoy_control IS INITIAL.
      CREATE OBJECT enjoy_control
         EXPORTING
            parent = gui_container
         EXCEPTIONS
            OTHERS = 1.
      IF sy-subrc = 0.
* Load homepage
         CALL METHOD enjoy_control->show_url
            EXPORTING
               url = 'http://www.sap-press.com/'.
      ENDIF.
   ENDIF.
* Registration of events
```

```
       CALL METHOD cic_event_gate->add_listener
          EXPORTING
             listener = me
             event    = 'END_CONTACT'.
ENDMETHOD.
```

Listing 4.9 Creation of the HTML Control

If the control has been successfully created, it can be used immediately. In the example, the SAP PRESS website (*http://www.sap-press.com*) is loaded into the HTML control via the SHOW_URL method mentioned previously.

Reinitialization at "End Contact" This is what should also happen when Interaction Center is reset via the **End Contact** pushbutton. In order to achieve this behavior, the class needs to register for the IC event END_CONTACT—via the EXECUTE method—and to implement event handling. To this end, the HANDLE_EVENT method of the IF_CCM_CMPWSP_CIC_EV_HANDLER interface is available (see Listing 4.10).

```
METHOD if_ccm_cmpwsp_cic_ev_handler~handle_event .
   CASE event.
      WHEN 'END_CONTACT'.
*      Reload start page
      IF enjoy_control IS NOT INITIAL.
         CALL METHOD enjoy_control->show_url
            EXPORTING
                url = 'http://www.sap-press.de/'.
      ENDIF.
   ENDCASE.
ENDMETHOD.
```

Listing 4.10 Handler Method for Events of IC WinClient

Pushbuttons to the right of the workspace In this example, the toolbar to the right of the workspace, which was mentioned in the previous section, is used to provide the typical Web-browser navigation functions. For this purpose, the GET_ACTIONS method of the IF_CCM_WORKSPACE interface is redefined, and the callback structure of the type CCM_WORKSPACE_CALLBACK is populated for every pushbutton and inserted in the return table (see Listing 4.11).

```
METHOD if_ccm_workspace~get_actions .
   DATA: ls_callback TYPE ccm_workspace_callback.
*  Backward Navigation
```

```
      CLEAR ls_callback.
      ls_callback-okcode          = 'MY_WSP_BACK'.
      ls_callback-callback_method = 'CB_GOBACK'.
      ls_callback-icon            = 'ICON_ARROW_LEFT'.
      ls_callback-is_active       = 'X'.
      ls_callback-quick           = 'Back'(001).
      ls_callback-button_group    = '01'.
      APPEND ls_callback TO actions_and_callbacks.
*     Forward navigation
      CLEAR ls_callback.
      ls_callback-okcode          = 'MY_WSP_FORW'.
      ls_callback-callback_method = 'CB_GOFORWARD'.
      ls_callback-icon            = 'ICON_ARROW_RIGHT'.
      ls_callback-is_active       = 'X'.
      ls_callback-quick           = 'Forward'(002).
      ls_callback-button_group    = '01'.
      APPEND ls_callback TO actions_and_callbacks.
*     Update
      CLEAR ls_callback.
      ls_callback-okcode          = 'MY_WSP_RFRSH'.
      ls_callback-callback_method = 'CB_REFRESH'.
      ls_callback-icon            = 'ICON_REFRESH'.
      ls_callback-is_active       = 'X'.
      ls_callback-quick           = 'Update'(003).
      ls_callback-button_group    = '02'.
      APPEND ls_callback TO actions_and_callbacks.
ENDMETHOD.
```

Listing 4.11 Specification of Workspace Pushbuttons

Via the BUTTON_GROUP field, the pushbuttons can be grouped; that is, a small gap is inserted between the pushbuttons.

Grouping of the Pushbuttons

Finally, the callback methods for the pushbuttons need to be implemented. Each of these methods calls another method of the Enjoy Control which corresponds to the pushbutton function (see Listing 4.12).

Callback methods

```
METHOD cb_goback .
* Backward navigation
   IF enjoy_control IS NOT INITIAL.
      CALL METHOD enjoy_control->go_back.
   ENDIF.
ENDMETHOD.
```

```
METHOD cb_goforward .
* Forward navigation
   IF enjoy_control IS NOT INITIAL.
      CALL METHOD enjoy_control->go_forward.
   ENDIF.
ENDMETHOD.
METHOD cb_refresh .
* Update
   IF enjoy_control IS NOT INITIAL.
      CALL METHOD enjoy_control->do_refresh.
   ENDIF.
ENDMETHOD.
```

Listing 4.12 Callback Methods for Controlling the HTML Control

This completes the implementation phase. The only thing you still have to do is customize in order to make the new workspace known to the system.

4.3.3 Customizing

Definition of the workspace in Customizing

The customizing necessary for displaying the new workspace in the Interaction Center corresponds exactly to that described in Section 4.2. In the **Customer-Specific System Modifications for IC**, the new workspace needs to be created under **Define Customer-Specific Workspaces** (Transaction CRMC_CIC_WSP0). Here, a name for the workspace (ZWSP_ENJOY) is defined and associated with the class ZCL_CCM_ABSTR_CMPWSP2 which has just been developed (see Figure 4.8).

Automatically created workspaces

Now, a profile for automatically created workspaces is maintained in the Component Configuration under Visible Components. Under the **Default Workspaces** of this profile, the new workspace can be inserted as a new tab in the application or in the navigation area (Transaction CRMC_CIC_WSP3); for this purpose, you need to implement a tab ID and a tab text (see Figure 4.9).

Maintenance of the IC WinClient profile

The new profile for default workspaces now needs to be entered in an IC WinClient profile as DEFAULT_WORKSPACES attribute. A more detailed description and illustrations of these customizing activities can be found in Section 4.2.4.

The Interaction Center is ready to be started. The new workspace is displayed in the application area.

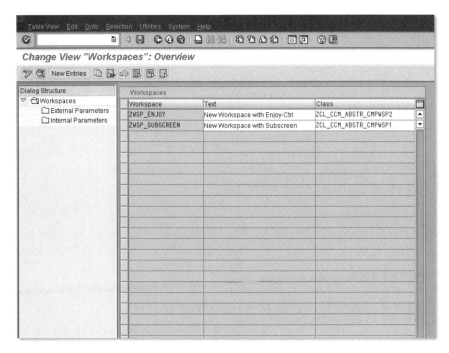

Figure 4.8 Define Customer-Specific Workspaces

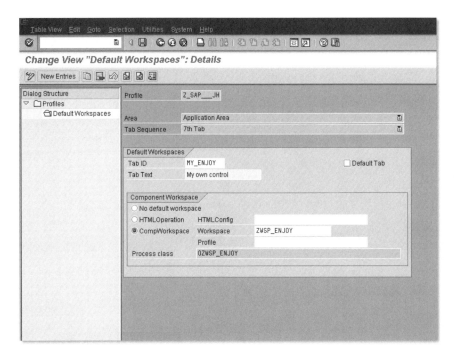

Figure 4.9 Detail View of the Default Workspaces

4.4 Using Hidden Components in IC WinClient

4.4.1 Introduction

Modification-free enhancement of the IC WinClient behavior

In projects, it is frequently necessary to respond to specific events with customer-specific programming. This can involve a change of the focused workspace after confirming the business partner, or the calculation of further relevant values. An experienced project developer will always try to provide this functionality without modifications, that is without changing the SAP standard programs. For this purpose, hidden components can be used.

In many situations, IC WinClient triggers its own events (*IC events*) for which function modules register themselves in order to perform the desired tasks. The registration for the events takes place in the hidden component.

4.4.2 Implementing the Workspace Class

Like a workspace

The hidden component is essentially a workspace that is not displayed. For this reason, it is derived from the abstract class CL_CCM_ABSTR_CMPWSP.

In this class, the CREATE method must be redefined from the IF_CCM_WORKSPACE interface. This method is called once during the creation of the hidden component and is therefore suited best for the registration of function modules for events in IC WinClient (see Figure 4.10).

Subscription to events

The following code represents the response to the event SEARCH_TARGET_FOUND—a business partner was found and confirmed. The function module Z_CRM_CIC_HIDDEN_CALLBACK is to be called (see Listing 4.13).

```
METHOD if_ccm_workspace~create .
  DATA: ls_subscriber TYPE cic0_subscriber,
        ls_event TYPE cic0_event,
        ls_cb_fct TYPE cic0_funcname.
  CALL METHOD super->if_ccm_workspace~create
    EXPORTING
      proc_instance     = proc_instance
      proc_cl_id        = proc_cl_id
      workspace_manager = workspace_manager
      abox_admin        = abox_admin
      workspace_display = workspace_display
```

```
    RECEIVING
        workspace          = workspace.
        ls_subscriber      = 'ZWSP_HIDDEN'.
        ls_cb_fct          = 'Z_CRM_CIC_HIDDEN_CALLBACK'.
        ls_event           = 'SEARCH_TARGET_FOUND'.
    CALL FUNCTION 'CIC_EVENT_SUBSCRIBE'
        EXPORTING
            event                         = ls_event
            subscriber                    = ls_subscriber
            callback_function             = ls_cb_fct
            handle                        = '1'
        EXCEPTIONS
            already_subscribed_to_event = 1
            OTHERS                        = 2.
ENDMETHOD.
```

Listing 4.13 Registration of the Hidden Component for the Event SEARCH_TARGET_FOUND

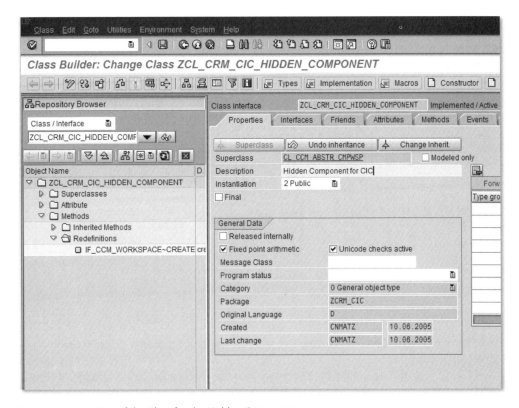

Figure 4.10 Creation of the Class for the Hidden Component

The implementation of the method and the corresponding function module are designed in a way to enable the same function module to handle different events.

Definition as a component
This class now needs to be entered as an Interaction Center component in Customizing under **CRM · Interaction Center WinClient · Customer-Specific System Modifications for IC · Define Customer-Specific Components** (Transaction CICD; see Figure 4.11).

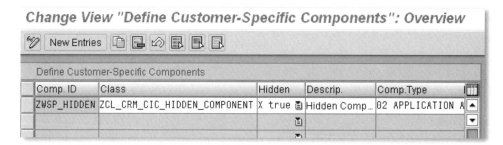

Figure 4.11 Define Class as Customer-Specific Component

Maintenance of hidden components in the framework
For the component to be called in IC WinClient, it must be integrated in the framework as a hidden component (see Figure 4.12). This can be done, for example, in a copy of the NON-TELEPHONY framework.

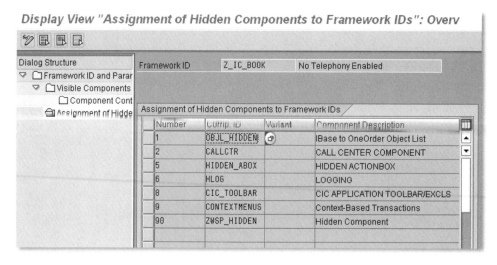

Figure 4.12 Integrate the Component as a Hidden Component in the Framework

After assigning this framework to the Interaction Center profile, the new functionality can be used.

Eventually, the function module itself must be implemented. As an example, a function module will be called that shows the name of the confirmed business partner in a popup. The function module called needs to provide a specific interface (see Listing 4.14).

Callback function module

```
FUNCTION z_crm_cic_hidden_callback.
*"----------------------------------------------------
*"*"Local interface:
*"  IMPORTING
*"     REFERENCE(EVENT)  TYPE  CIC0_EVENT
*"     REFERENCE(HANDLE) TYPE  CIC0_HANDLE
*"     REFERENCE(P1) OPTIONAL
*"     REFERENCE(P2) OPTIONAL
*"     REFERENCE(P3) OPTIONAL
*"     REFERENCE(P4) OPTIONAL
*"     REFERENCE(P5) OPTIONAL
*"  TABLES
*"      EVENT_ERRORS TYPE  CIC1_EERRORTAB
*"      T1
*"      T2
*"      T3
*"      T4
*"      T5
*"----------------------------------------------------
  DATA:
    ls_bps_confirmed TYPE crmt_cic_bpident,
    ls_partner_guid  TYPE bu_partner_guid,
    ls_partner_descr TYPE bus000flds-descrip_long.
  CASE event.
    WHEN 'SEARCH_TARGET_FOUND'.
      ls_bps_confirmed = p1.
      IF ls_bps_confirmed-partner1_guid IS NOT INITIAL.
        ls_partner_guid =
          ls_bps_confirmed-partner1_guid.
      ELSEIF ls_bps_confirmed-partner2_guid
        IS NOT INITIAL.
        ls_partner_guid =
          ls_bps_confirmed-partner2_guid.
      ENDIF.
      IF ls_partner_guid IS NOT INITIAL.
        CALL FUNCTION 'BUP_PARTNER_DESCRIPTION_GET'
```

```
           EXPORTING
             i_partnerguid      = ls_partner_guid
           IMPORTING
             e_description_long = ls_partner_descr
           EXCEPTIONS
             OTHERS             = 4.
        MESSAGE i001(00) WITH
          ' The following business partner has been
            confirmed:'(001)
          space ls_partner_descr.
      ENDIF.
    ENDCASE.
ENDFUNCTION.
```

Listing 4.14 Callback Function Module for an IC WinClient Event

If a business partner is found and confirmed in IC WinClient, a popup is displayed as shown in Figure 4.13.

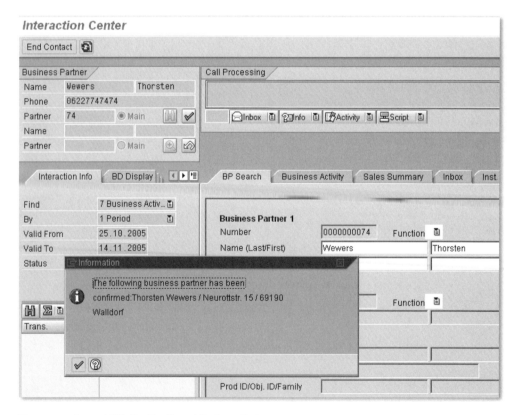

Figure 4.13 Popup With the Confirmed Business Partner

4.5 Using the Action Box in IC WinClient

4.5.1 Introduction

The following short example shows how to use the action box in IC Win-Client. For this purpose, the current document is shown in the transaction workspace along with the change documents.

Example change documents

In IC WinClient, functionalities can be integrated that are already available in other places. The desired function can exist in the most diverse forms, for instance as a report, a function module, or a class method. In order to call the functionality, it must be integrated in an object from the Business Object Repository (BOR), because the action box uses calls from BOR-object methods for starting these functions.

BOR methods

In the following example, the action box calls a function module that displays the change documents of the CRM business transaction currently displayed in the transaction workspace in a window.

4.5.2 Implementation Steps

For displaying the change documents, we use a function module from the SAP standard that needs to be called with the transaction number and the transaction category. The name of the function module is CRM_CDORDER_DISPLAY. It should be possible to call the display irrespective of the current transaction category, but only within IC WinClient.

> **Note**
>
> To simplify things, an existing BOR object (TSTC, Transaction) is used. In the real project, you most likely would create a new BOR object for this purpose, in which, for example, a number of additional functions for IC WinClient would be combined. However, the creation and maintenance of BOR objects is not subject of this book. Therefore, the extension of the BOR object is described.

BOR object type TSTC

To integrate the functionality, you need to perform the following steps:

▶ Extension of the BOR object
▶ Extension of Customizing for the action box

4.5.3 Extending the BOR Object

Reusability

First, the BOR object is extended by a method and three attributes. The actual functionality is stored in the method; this is where the function module is called. In the attributes, the various parameters required for calling the function module are determined. The use of attributes is not necessary, but should be considered because it is desirable to re-use the BOR object for other additional functions.

Business Object Builder

The BOR object is extended in Business Object Builder which can be called directly, for example using Transaction SWO1. There, the ZTSTC subtype of the existing TSTC object is created first (see Figure 4.14).

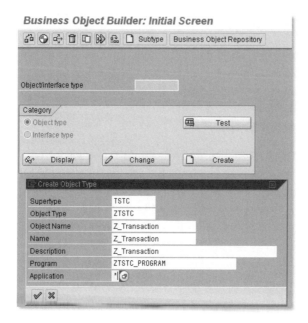

Figure 4.14 Create Subtype of the TSTC Object

Virtual attributes

The subtype then obtains three new (virtual) attributes:

▶ currentOneOrder
  (virtual, reference: CRMD_ORDERADM_H-GUID)

▶ currentObjectID
  (virtual, reference: CRMD_ORDERADM_H-OBJECT_ID)

▶ currentBusType
  (virtual, reference: CRMD_ORDERADM_H-OBJECT_TYPE)

These three attributes must be provided with the appropriate source code so that they will be populated at runtime (see Listing 4.15).

```
get_property currentoneorder changing container.
DATA: lv_guid TYPE crmt_object_guid.
CALL FUNCTION 'CRM_INTLAY_GET_HEADER_GUID'
  IMPORTING
    ev_header_guid = lv_guid.
    object-currentoneorder = lv_guid.
    swc_set_element container 'currentOneOrder'
                    object-currentoneorder.
end_property.
*------------------------------------------------------------
get_property currentobjectid changing container.
DATA: lv_guid      TYPE crmt_object_guid,
      lv_object_id TYPE crmt_object_id.
swc_get_property self 'currentOneOrder' lv_guid.
CALL FUNCTION 'CRM_ORDERADM_H_READ_OW'
  EXPORTING
    iv_orderadm_h_guid    = lv_guid
  IMPORTING
    ev_object_id          = lv_object_id
  EXCEPTIONS
    admin_header_not_found = 1
    OTHERS                = 2.
IF sy-subrc <> 0.
ENDIF.
object-currentobjectid = lv_object_id.
swc_set_element container 'currentObjectID'
              object-currentobjectid.
end_property.
*------------------------------------------------------------
get_property currentbustype changing container.
DATA: lv_guid TYPE crmt_object_guid,
      lv_bus  TYPE crmd_orderadm_h-object_type.
      swc_get_property self 'currentOneOrder' lv_guid.
CALL FUNCTION 'CRM_ORDERADM_H_READ_OW'
  EXPORTING
    iv_orderadm_h_guid    = lv_guid
  IMPORTING
    ev_object_type        = lv_bus
  EXCEPTIONS
    admin_header_not_found = 1
    OTHERS                = 2.
```

```
IF sy-subrc <> 0.
ENDIF.
object-currentbustype = lv_bus.
swc_set_element container 'currentBusType'
                  object-currentbustype.
end_property.
```

Listing 4.15 BOR Object Attributes for Determining the Parameters

Object method

Furthermore, the getChangeDocsPopup method needs to be created as a synchronous dialog method with the source code in Listing 4.16.

```
begin_method getchangedocspopup changing container.
DATA: lv_object_id TYPE crmt_object_id,
      lv_bus       LIKE crmd_orderadm_h-object_type.
IF object-key-code <> 'CIC0'.
  MESSAGE e001(00) WITH text-001.
  "Displayed only for Transaction CICO!
  EXIT.
ENDIF.
swc_get_property self 'currentObjectID' lv_object_id.
swc_get_property self 'currentBusType'  lv_bus.
IF lv_object_id IS NOT INITIAL AND
   lv_bus IS NOT INITIAL.
  CALL FUNCTION 'CRM_CDORDER_DISPLAY'
    EXPORTING
      iv_object             = lv_object_id
      iv_bus                = lv_bus
      i_screen_start_column = 5
      i_screen_start_line   = 5
      i_screen_end_column   = 140
      i_screen_end_line     = 25.
ELSE.
  MESSAGE i001(00) WITH text-002.
  "Document not saved yet,
  "no change documents
ENDIF.
end_method.
```

Listing 4.16 BOR Object Method for Calling the Action Box

After the attributes and the method have been assigned the release status **implemented**, and the new BOR object has also been marked as **implemented**, the object type can now be generated. The object should then appear as shown in Figure 4.15.

Sharing the method and the object type

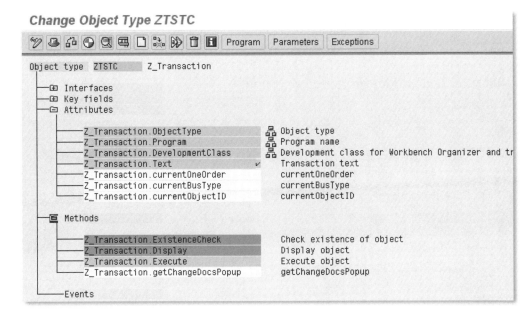

Figure 4.15 New BOR Object ZTSTC

Afterwards, the standard SAP object TSTC needs to be delegated to the new BOR object ZTSTC. This is done in the initial screen of Business Object Builder via the menu option **Settings · Delegate** (see Figure 4.16).

Delegation

Change View "Customizing Object Types": Details

| 🖉 New Entries 📋 📇 ⟋ 📇 📇 🔁 | | | |

| Object Type | TSTC | Transaction |
| Person responsible | WEWERS| | |

Delegate

| Delegation type | ZTSTC | Z_Transaction |
| ☐ GUI-specific | | |

Figure 4.16 Delegation of the BOR Object TSTC to the ZTSTC Subtype

4.5.4 Customizing

Configuration of the action box

After the BOR object has been extended successfully, the new method only needs to be integrated in the Customizing of the action box. This can be done in Customizing under **CRM · Interaction Center WinClient · Component Configuration · Visible Components · Action Box Settings · Define Configuration Profile for Action Box** or directly via Transaction EWFC0 (see Figure 4.17).

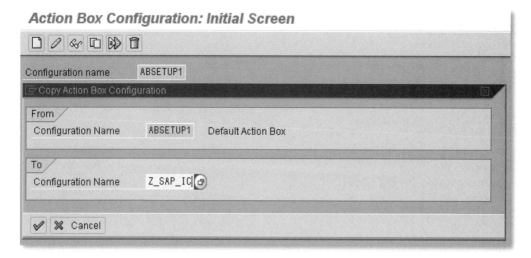

Figure 4.17 Copy Action Box Profile

First, the standard profile ABSETUP1 is copied as Z_SAP_IC in order to then make the changes to the copy.

Afterwards, you create a new entry "Display Change Documents" in the **Info** group, for example. In doing so, the entry must be assigned a transaction code—for a direct entry in the OK code field of the action box—and the desired method of the BOR object must be selected (see Figure 4.18).

Note

Calls in other systems specifying the logical system

When selecting the method, you can also specify a logical system; that is, you can also call methods of another SAP system, for example of a sales order from the R/3 back-end system (see Chapter 3, Section 3.2.2).

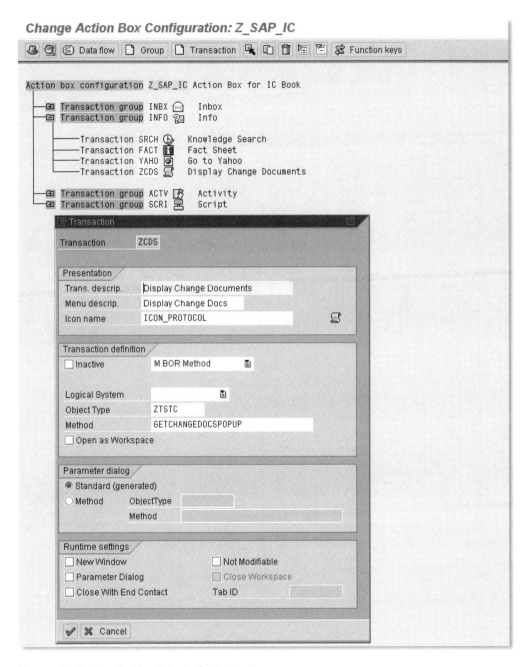

_Change Action Box Configuration: Z_SAP_IC_

Data flow | Group | Transaction | Function keys

Action box configuration Z_SAP_IC Action Box for IC Book

Transaction group INBX Inbox
Transaction group INFO Info

Transaction SRCH Knowledge Search
Transaction FACT Fact Sheet
Transaction YAHO Go to Yahoo
Transaction ZCDS Display Change Documents

Transaction group ACTV Activity
Transaction group SCRI Script

Transaction

Transaction ZCDS

Presentation
Trans. descrip. Display Change Documents
Menu descrip. Display Change Docs
Icon name ICON_PROTOCOL

Transaction definition
☐ Inactive M BOR Method

Logical System
Object Type ZTSTC
Method GETCHANGEDOCSPOPUP
☐ Open as Workspace

Parameter dialog
◉ Standard (generated)
○ Method ObjectType
Method

Runtime settings
☐ New Window ☐ Not Modifiable
☐ Parameter Dialog ☐ Close Workspace
☐ Close With End Contact Tab ID

✓ ✗ Cancel

Figure 4.18 Creating the New Entry in the Action Box

In our example, the data flow also needs to be created for the method (see Figure 4.19). This makes it possible to exchange data between the current application and the method of the BOR object.

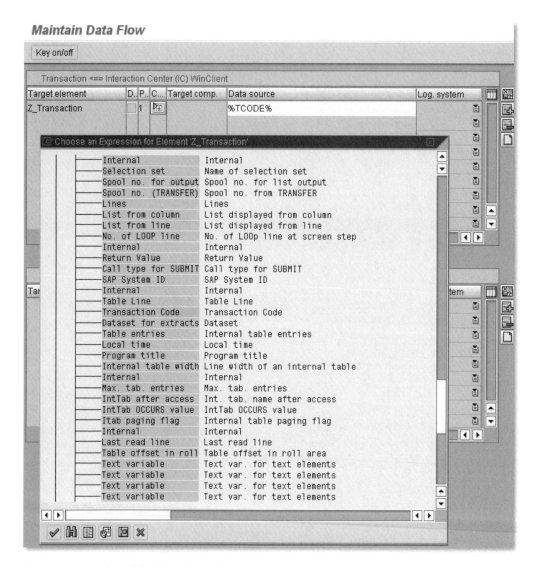

Figure 4.19 Data Flow of the Entry for the Action Box

Data flow   Because the standard SAP Object is the transaction, a transaction code is expected as entry value. This value is a required entry field, which means that if you forget to enter it IC WinClient asks the user to enter a value in a dialog during the execution of the function from the action box. However, this is not recommended in most cases.

For this reason, the current transaction code is transferred from the system fields and is then checked through the query if the call is made from IC WinClient (Transaction CIC0).

After the new action box profile has been assigned to IC WinClient, the new function can be executed at the next startup of the Interaction Center.

4.6 Using the Transaction Launcher in IC WebClient

4.6.1 Introduction

External services can be called in IC WebClient, much in the same way as with the action box in IC WinClient. The only prerequisite is that the desired service is available via a URL.

Calling any URL

The function enabling the integration of external services is the transaction launcher. The external services can be called from the same SAP CRM system, from other SAP systems, from an intranet, or from the Internet.

Via a wizard, the system generates a transaction launcher class that controls the call and the parameter transfer. It is always advisable to first have the system generate the class and then make the necessary extensions to the generated class; you should not copy classes because of the manual rework that needs to be done in Customizing.

Support from wizard

In the following example, we want to integrate the news page of Google (*http://news.google.com*) in such a way that news in the user's logon language is searched for automatically.

The integration is carried out in three steps:

▶ Create the URL and, if necessary, URL parameters
▶ Integrate the URL via the transaction launcher wizard
▶ Customize the generated transaction launcher class

4.6.2 Creating the URL

First, a URL needs to be created with the appropriate URL parameters (see Figure 4.20). At runtime, the parameters can be populated with values from the application (see Figure 4.21 and Figure 4.22).

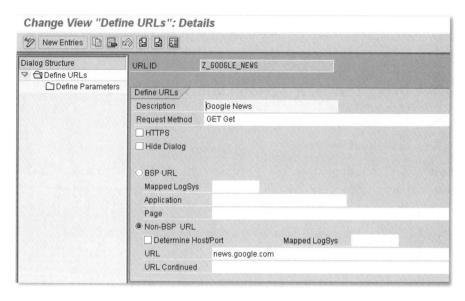

Figure 4.20 Transaction Launcher: Creating the URL ...

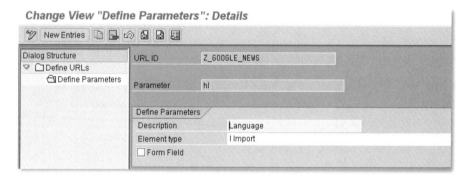

Figure 4.21 ... and the First Parameter ...

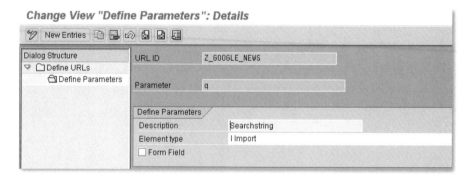

Figure 4.22 ... and the Second Parameter

You can create the URL in Customizing under **CRM · Interaction Center WebClient · Transaction Launcher · Define URLs and Parameters** (Transaction CRMC_IC_LTX_URLS).

Definition of the URL

> **Note**
>
> It is always possible to manipulate the URL directly in the generated class without having specified parameters in Customizing.

4.6.3 Integrating the URL

Using a wizard, the desired URL can be integrated in the transaction launcher profile. In doing this, however, you have to be aware that the wizard changes both a profile from the transaction launcher and a profile from the navigation bar.

Working on the profile of the transaction launcher and the navigation bar

For this reason, a new entry needs to be maintained in the navigation bar to which the URL to be started is bound. Afterwards, the wizard can be run, and this creates the entry in the transaction launcher profile and generates the corresponding class (see Figure 4.23).

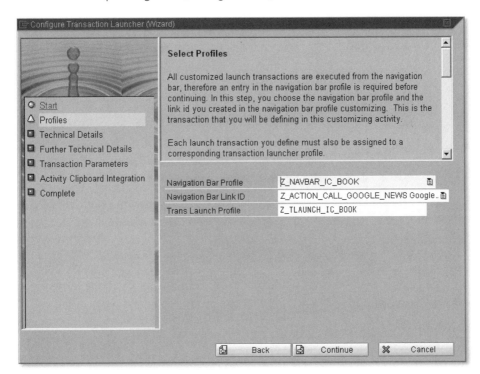

Figure 4.23 Start the Transaction-Launcher Wizard

In the following, the class name (see Figure 4.24) of the generated transaction launcher class needs to be specified, and the URL from Customizing needs to be assigned (see Figure 4.25).

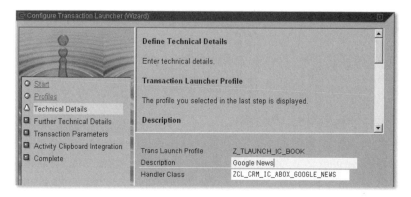

Figure 4.24 Specify Class Name for the Generator

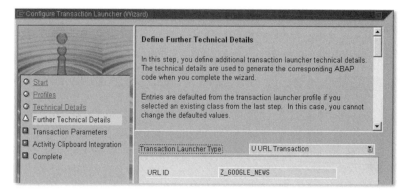

Figure 4.25 Select URL

4.6.4 Customizing the Generated Class

The generated source code now can be customized to populate the URL
parameters with the desired values. The values are determined and transferred to the URL via the PREPARE_DATA_FLOW method from the IF_
CRM_IC_ACTION_HANDER interface (see Figure 4.26).

In the example, the parameter hl is to be populated with the user's logon
language and "SAP" is to be transferred to the q parameter as the search
term (see Figure 4.27). After the new profiles for the navigation bar and
the transaction launcher have been integrated in the IC WebClient profile, it is possible to read the latest SAP news in IC WebClient as well (see
Figure 4.28).

```
METHOD if_crm_ic_action_handler~prepare_data_flow .

  DATA: __bdc     TYPE REF TO cl_crm_ic_cucobdc_impl,
        __source TYPE        string,
        __line   TYPE        string,
        __value  TYPE        string,
        lang_iso TYPE        laiso.

  super->if_crm_ic_action_handler~prepare_data_flow( ).

  __bdc ?= gv_view_controller->get_custom_controller( 'CuCoBDC' )."#EC NOTEXT

  add_parameter( iv_name  = 'hl'
                 iv_value = __value ).

| add_parameter( iv_name  = 'q'
                 iv_value = __value ).

* Data flow is complete - set to false if data is missing
  gv_data_flow_complete = abap_true.
```

Figure 4.26 Generated Source Code for the Transaction Launcher

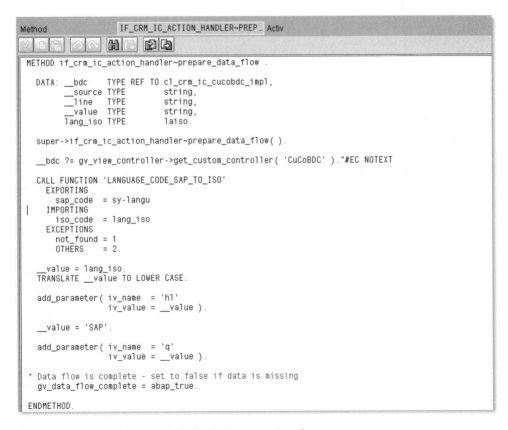

```
METHOD if_crm_ic_action_handler~prepare_data_flow .

  DATA: __bdc     TYPE REF TO cl_crm_ic_cucobdc_impl,
        __source TYPE        string,
        __line   TYPE        string,
        __value  TYPE        string,
        lang_iso TYPE        laiso.

  super->if_crm_ic_action_handler~prepare_data_flow( ).

  __bdc ?= gv_view_controller->get_custom_controller( 'CuCoBDC' )."#EC NOTEXT

  CALL FUNCTION 'LANGUAGE_CODE_SAP_TO_ISO'
    EXPORTING
      sap_code = sy-langu
|   IMPORTING
      iso_code = lang_iso
    EXCEPTIONS
      not_found = 1
      OTHERS    = 2.

  __value = lang_iso.
  TRANSLATE __value TO LOWER CASE.

  add_parameter( iv_name  = 'hl'
                 iv_value = __value ).

  __value = 'SAP'.

  add_parameter( iv_name  = 'q'
                 iv_value = __value ).

* Data flow is complete - set to false if data is missing
  gv_data_flow_complete = abap_true.

ENDMETHOD.
```

Figure 4.27 Customized Source Code for the Parameter Transfer

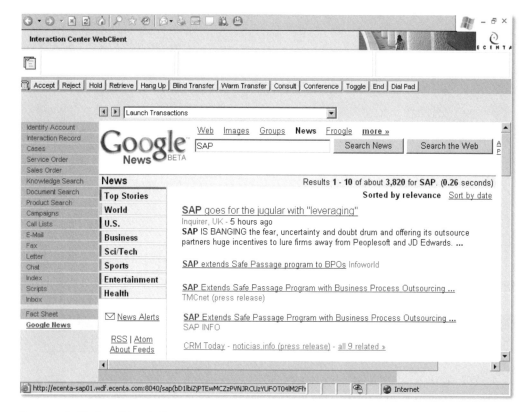

Figure 4.28 Display of Google News

Note

The generated class is created as a local object (Package $TMP). The object directory entry must be changed to a transportable package if you want to transport the settings to another system.

4.7 Extending the Business Partner Search in IC WinClient by New Search Fields

4.7.1 Introduction

Frequent requirement in customer projects

We will next explain how to extend the business partner search in Interaction Center by individual fields. The procedures vary depending on the selected scenario (IC WinClient or IC WebClient). In this first example, the business partner search of IC WinClient (see Figure 4.29) is to be extended by the fields **Search Term 1** and **Search Term 2**. These fields exist in the business partner master record and are used for searching additional terms to describe the business partner. The search for these terms is a very common requirement in customer projects.

In Section 4.8, the business partner search in IC WebClient is extended by the same fields.

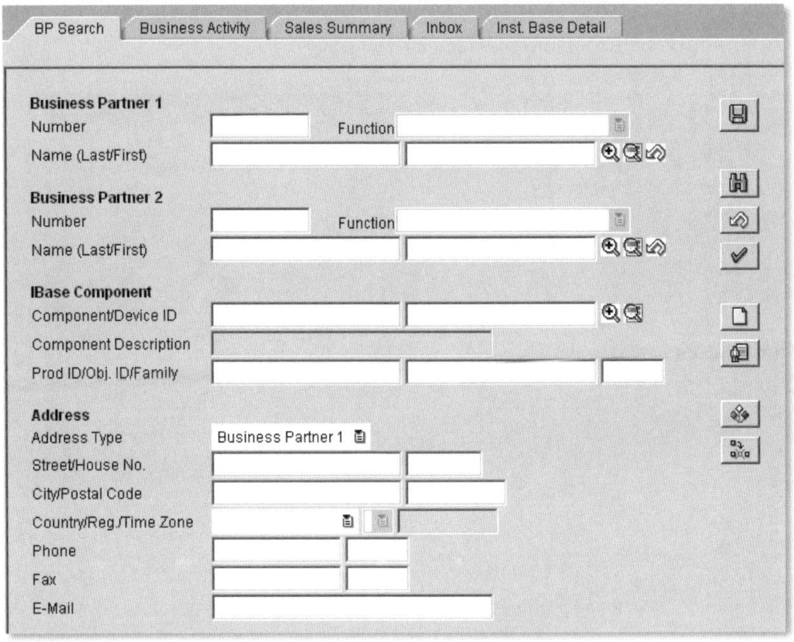

Figure 4.29 Standard Business Partner Search in IC WinClient

4.7.2 Implementing Searchable Fields

As with all other customizations and extensions, work on the extended business partner search should be done in a separate IC WinClient profile that must be copied from a standard profile, for example 00000001. This can be done in the IMG via **CRM · Interaction Center WinClient · Define IC WebClient Profile** or directly via Transaction CICO. [margin: Separate IC WinClient profile]

A search profile is stored in the IC WinClient profile **CRM · Interaction Center WinClient · Component Configuration · Visible Components · Define Profiles for Search Strategies** (Transaction CRMC_CIC_SEARCH_RULE) which you can either use directly or copy into the customer namespace. For the example, we copy the standard profile BPSEARCH and store it in the IC WinClient profile. When copying the profile, you need to ensure that all dependent entries are copied as well. [margin: Separate search profile]

Search types in the search profile The search profile contains different search types that specify which information is used for searching a business partner, for example ANI for Automatic Number Identification. The relevant search type for searching the business partner workspace is NORM. The search type also defines which form is used for entering the search parameters (see Figure 4.30). In this case, it is the HTML template CRM_CIC_SEARCH_DISPLAY. This template corresponds to the user interface of the agent.

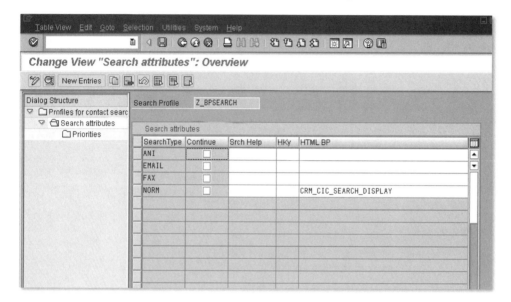

Figure 4.30 Customizing the Search Profile

In order to insert the new search fields in the template and include them in the search, two steps are required: The fields need to be activated in Customizing, and the template needs to be extended. The second step in particular requires some source code, but on the other hand, you are free to choose the layout of the new fields.

Searchable fields The first step is carried out in Customizing under **CRM Customizing · Interaction Center WinClient · Customer-Specific System Modifications for IC · Define Customer-Specific Search Control** (Transaction CRMC_CIC_SEARCH_CNTR). All kinds of fields for an HTML page are listed there. An "X" in the last column indicates if this field will be used during the search or not. For this example, the fields BP1_SRCHTREM1 and BP1_SRCHTERM2 should be enabled (see Figure 4.31). It is always possible to copy the entries to the customer namespace and change them there or to modify the default settings. For a minimal change like the one described here, it makes more sense to choose the modification option.

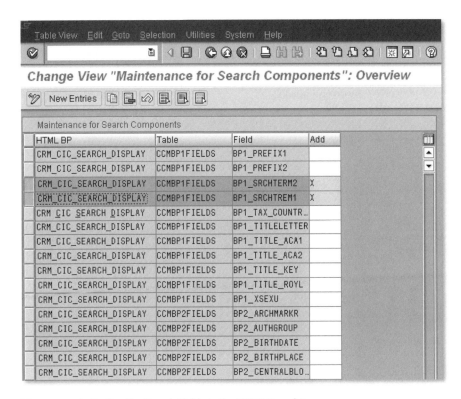

Figure 4.31 Activating the Search Fields in the HTML Template

The second step is to change the layout of the HTML page. Although you could perform this task in the customer namespace as well, it is not done in this example for the reasons previously described. The HTML templates can be found via Transaction SMW0 in the SAP Web Repository in the CRM_CIC_COMPONENTS package. For editing, the HTML page can be exported, changed on the local computer and then be re-imported.

Layout changes

> **Note**
>
> When naming the local template file, please make sure that it is saved with the ".htm" file extension. A file with the ".html" extension is not correctly identified during the import process. At the same time, the name of the exported page should correspond to the name chosen on the CRM system.

Naming the HTML file

The HTML page can be edited with any HTML or text editor. This example simply inserts the appropriate new fields (see Listing 4.17).

```
<TR>
<TH align=left width=28%>
<TD width=72%>
<NOBR><INPUT name=BP1_SRCHTREM1 size=25 type=TEXT/PLAIN>
<INPUT name=BP1_SRCHTERM2 size=25 maxLength=35
type=TEXT/PLAIN>
</NOBR>
</TD>
</TR>
```

Listing 4.17 Extension of the HTML Page

Labeling the new fields The labeling of entry fields in the user interface can be carried out in different ways. The easiest way to do it is through hard-coding the text in the HTML page. The downside to this method is the lack of language dependency. Alternatively, you have the option to use a specific notation which contains the field name. Listing 4.18 shows the HTML source code which needs to be inserted in the table layout.

```
<TH align=left width=28%><NOBR><!--%%BP1_SRCHTREM1%-->/>
<!--%%BP1_SRCHTERM2%--></NOBR> </TH>
```

Listing 4.18 Labeling the New Entry Fields

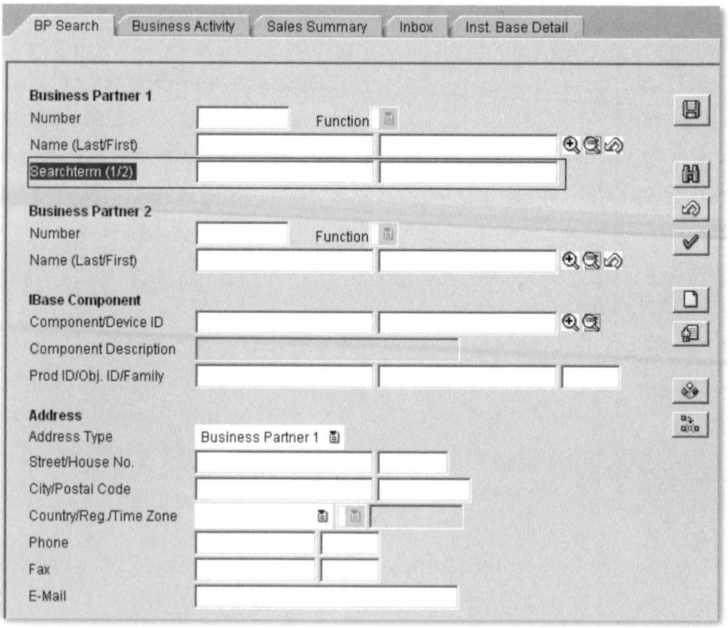

Figure 4.32 IC WinClient With New Fields in the Business Partner Search

When IC WinClient is started, the agent now sees a business search screen extended by the corresponding fields (see Figure 4.32).

4.7.3 Implementing Complex Searches

The extension described so far is applicable in all those cases dealing with searchable business partner fields. Occasionally in a customer project you might find that, in spite of the multitude of searchable fields, the desired field was not planned for ahead of time by SAP. Even in this situation, it is possible to extend the search.

Searching non-standard fields

As an example, we use the search for the credit-card number. This is not included in the search structures CCMBP1FIELDS and CCMBP2FIELDS of the Data Dictionary and therefore must be added to the search structures using APPEND structures. In the concrete example, the fields ZZ_CCNUM and ZZ_CCINS with the data element CCNUM or CCINS, respectively, are added to the structures (see Figure 4.33).

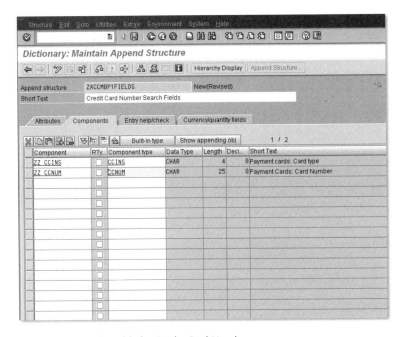

Figure 4.33 Search Fields for Credit-Card Number

After the Data Dictionary has been prepared, all steps described above need to be carried out. Provided that a separate IC WinClient profile has been created, the fields have to be entered and activated for the HTML template CRM_CIC_SEARCH_DISPLAY in Customizing under **CRM · Interaction Center WinClient · Customer-Specific System Modifica-**

Definition of fields and extension of the HTML layout

tions for IC · **Define Customer-Specific Search Control** (Transaction CRMC_CIC_SEARCH_CNTR). Afterwards, the template needs to be extended like the HTML layout shown in Listing 4.17 and Listing 4.18.

Extension of the search function

In the last step, the search function itself needs to be extended, because it does not know a field named ZZ_CCINS or ZZ_CCNUM and therefore would not include it during the search process. The search takes place in the CCMCS_BP_SEARCH2 function module of the CRM_CIC_BP_SUB function group and can be easily amended there. Listing 4.19 shows some example source code.

```
. . .
* Check whether searching for the credit card
      number is possible
  IF NOT bpl_data-zz_ccnum IS INITIAL AND
      NOT bpl_data-zz_ccins IS INITIAL.
* Credit card number filled => Search possible
      CALL FUNCTION 'BUP_PARTNER_GET_BY_CARD_DETAIL'
        EXPORTING
          I_CCINS                   = bpl_data-zz_ccins
          I_CCNUM                   = bpl_data-zz_ccnum
        TABLES
          T_PARTNER                 = lt_bpartner
        EXCEPTIONS
          NO_PARTNER_FOUND          = 1
          WRONG_PARAMETERS          = 2
          OTHERS                    = 3.
      IF SY-SUBRC = 0.
        READ TABLE lt_bpartner ASSIGNING <ls_bpartner>
          INDEX 1.
* Transfer BP to search
        CALL FUNCTION 'CONVERSION_EXIT_ALPHA_INPUT'
          EXPORTING
            input = <ls_bpartner>-partner
          IMPORTING
            output = ccmsearch_struct-bpl_partner.
      ENDIF.
  ENDIF.
. . .
```

Listing 4.19 Function Module for the Business Partner Search for a Credit Card Number

4.8 Extending the Business Partner Search in IC WebClient by New Search Fields

4.8.1 Introduction

Similar to Section 4.7, this example deals with extending the IC Web-Client search functionality for business partners by the two fields **Search Term 1** and **Search Term 2**. This principle of extending the UI does not depend on the view being changed and is therefore generally applicable.

Applicable also to general view extensions

4.8.2 Settings in Customizing and Defining a Customized View and Repository

The IC WebClient Workbench (Transaction BSP_WD_WORBENCH), which has been available since mySAP CRM Edition 2004, is suitable for supporting the implementation of the request. However, this section of the book aims at discussing the basic principle of view extensions, with the goal of enabling you to "have a look behind the scenes." The use of the workbench is always advisable in a customer project for carrying out general tasks such as replacing controller, context, and context node classes, or creating new views or view sets. The IC WebClient Cookbook describes in great detail how to work with the IC WebClient Workbench and its wizards.

Another possibility: Implementation of the Workbench

When proceeding manually, the first step for extending views or changing the layout is always to copy the corresponding view and the associated controller to the customer namespace. For this purpose, a new package (for example, Z_TEST) and a new BSP application (for example, ZCRM_IC) are created. View and controller are in this case *BuPaSearchB2B.htm* and *BuPaSearchB2B.do*. Afterwards, you have to replace the standard controller with the customer-specific controller in Customizing (IMG path in IC WebClient: **Customer-Specific System Modifications · Define IC WebClient Runtime Framework Profiles**). Up to and including mySAP CRM Edition 2004, simple XML tags are required in the framework profile for this task (see Listing 4.20 and Figure 4.34). From SAP CRM Release 5.0 onwards, a familiar table-maintenance option is available.

Creating the customer-specific view, controller, and controller replacement

```
<ControllerReplacements>
  <ControllerReplacement>
    <ReplacedController>
      BuPaSearchB2B
    </ReplacedController>
    <ReplacingControler>
```

```
        ZCRM_IC/BuPaSearchB2B
      </ReplacingController>
    </ControllerReplacement>
  </ControllerReplacements>
```

Listing 4.20 Controller Replacements in XML Notation (prior to SAP CRM Release 5.0)

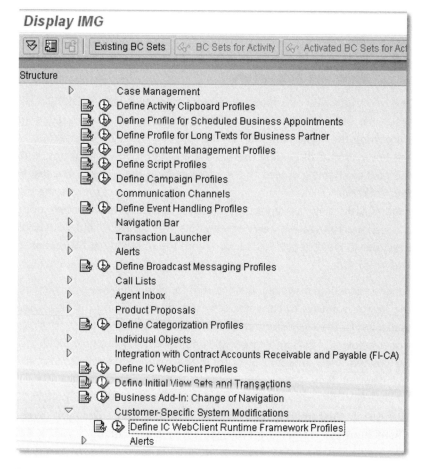

Figure 4.34 Customer-Specific System Modification in the Customizing of IC Web-Client

4.8.3 Extending View, Controller, and Context

Derivation of controller, context, and context node classes
According to the description in Section 3.3.1, the controller, the context, and the class of the context node to be extended need to be replaced with customized classes. For this purpose, in the package mentioned above, three classes have to be created and derived from the correspond-

ing classes of the original view. In this example, the following classes need to be replaced:

► **Controller class**

  ▻ Original: CL_CRM_IC_BUPASEARCHB2B_IMPL

  ▻ New: ZCL_CRM_IC_BUPASEARCHB2B_IMPL

► **Context class**

  ▻ Original: CL_CRM_IC_BUPASEARCHB2B_CTXT

  ▻ New: ZCL_CRM_IC_BUPASEARCHB2B_CTXT

► **Context node class**

  ▻ Original: CL_CRM_IC_BUPASEARCHB2B_CN02

  ▻ New: ZCL_CRM_IC_BUPASEARCHB2B_CN02

The name of the controller class has to be stored in the copied view and in the controller in the corresponding objects of the BSP application ZCRM_IC.

In the next step you need to ensure that the new context is used. The context of every view is instantiated in the WD_CREATE_CONTEXT method of the corresponding controller class. Therefore, you need to redefine this method and insert the source code as shown in Listing 4.21.

Connecting classes

```
CALL METHOD super->wd_create_context.
* Create customized context
context = cl_bsp_wd_context=>get_instance(
          iv_controller = me
          iv_type = 'ZCL_CRM_IC_BUPASEARCHB2B_CTXT' ).
typed_context ?= context.
```

Listing 4.21 Creating the New Context in the Controller

The same needs to be done in the context class. The context node to contain the new search fields is **CONTACTPERSONSASBP.** For exchanging this context node, the CREATE_CONTEXT_NODES method of the context class has to be redefined; in SAP CRM 4.0, it is the constructor of the context class that must be redefined. The smartest way to do this is through inheritance: The inherited method first creates the context as usual. Then, you delete the entry of the context node to be exchanged and create it again, this time using the type of the enhanced class. In the last step, a reference to the data of the current business partner is written to the context node, i.e., the node is bound against the data model. Listing 4.22 shows the full source code.

```
DATA: model TYPE REF TO if_bsp_model,
      coll_wrapper          TYPE REF TO
        cl_bsp_wd_collection_wrapper,
      bupacontroller        TYPE REF TO
        cl_crm_ic_bupacontroller,
      searchcontactasbp_    TYPE REF TO
        cl_crm_ic_bupacontroller_cn16.
CALL METHOD super->create_context_nodes
  EXPORTING
    controller = controller.
* Delete standard context node: model_id as lower case!
  owner->delete_model( model_id = 'searchcontactasbp' ).
* Create context node
model = owner->create_model(
  class_name       = 'ZCL_CRM_IC_BUPASEARCHB2B_CN02'
  model_id         = 'SearchContactAsBP' ).
searchcontactasbp ?= model.
CLEAR model.
* Bind to custom controller
bupacontroller ?=
  controller->get_custom_controller( 'BuPaController' ).
searchcontactasbp_ =
  bupacontroller->typed_context->searchcontactasbp.
coll_wrapper =
  searchcontactasbp_->get_collection_wrapper( ).
searchcontactasbp->set_collection_wrapper(
  coll_wrapper ).
```

Listing 4.22 Creating a New Context Node

Browser for the GenIL model

The basic steps described above are essentially carried out by the IC Web-Client Workbench. The next step definitely requires working in the Data Dictionary: The two search fields, **Search Term 1** and **Search Term 2**, are not part of the search structure in IC WebClient, as you can easily tell from Transaction GENIL_MODEL_BROWSER (see Figure 4.35). Therefore, you first need to extend the corresponding structure of the data model, CRMST_HEADER_SEARCH_BUIL, by the required fields. This is done without modification in an APPEND structure (see Figure 4.36).

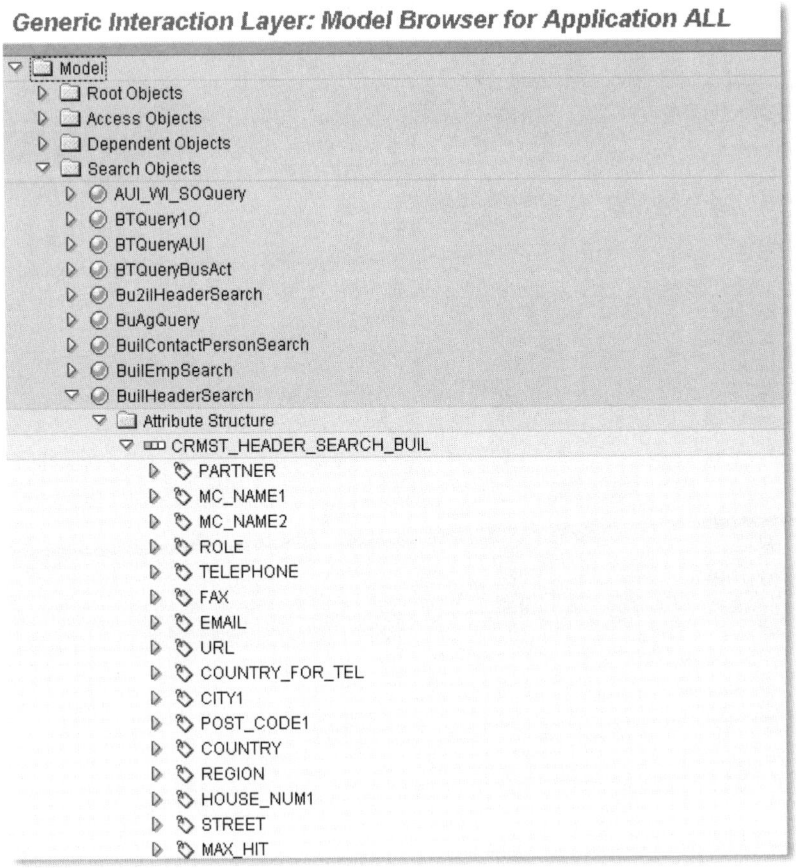

```
▽ 🗀 Model
   ▷ 🗀 Root Objects
   ▷ 🗀 Access Objects
   ▷ 🗀 Dependent Objects
   ▽ 🗀 Search Objects
      ▷ ◎ AUI_WI_SOQuery
      ▷ ◎ BTQuery1O
      ▷ ◎ BTQueryAUI
      ▷ ◎ BTQueryBusAct
      ▷ ◎ Bu2ilHeaderSearch
      ▷ ◎ BuAgQuery
      ▷ ◎ BuilContactPersonSearch
      ▷ ◎ BuilEmpSearch
      ▽ ◎ BuilHeaderSearch
         ▽ 🗀 Attribute Structure
            ▽ 🖭 CRMST_HEADER_SEARCH_BUIL
               ▷ ◈ PARTNER
               ▷ ◈ MC_NAME1
               ▷ ◈ MC_NAME2
               ▷ ◈ ROLE
               ▷ ◈ TELEPHONE
               ▷ ◈ FAX
               ▷ ◈ EMAIL
               ▷ ◈ URL
               ▷ ◈ COUNTRY_FOR_TEL
               ▷ ◈ CITY1
               ▷ ◈ POST_CODE1
               ▷ ◈ COUNTRY
               ▷ ◈ REGION
               ▷ ◈ HOUSE_NUM1
               ▷ ◈ STREET
               ▷ ◈ MAX_HIT
```

Figure 4.35 Business Partner Search Structure in the GenIL of IC WebClient

Data binding

The next step is supported by the IC WebClient Workbench again, in other words, extending the new context node by the new search fields. To enable data binding between model and view, the class requires a GET method for data retrieval, a GET_M method for determining the data type and a SET method for writing the data entered to the model. In most cases, the source code of these methods is the same between two different fields (except for the field name). This is only an example of the source code of a GET method to illustrate the data binding between Business Object Layer and UI level (see Listing 4.23).

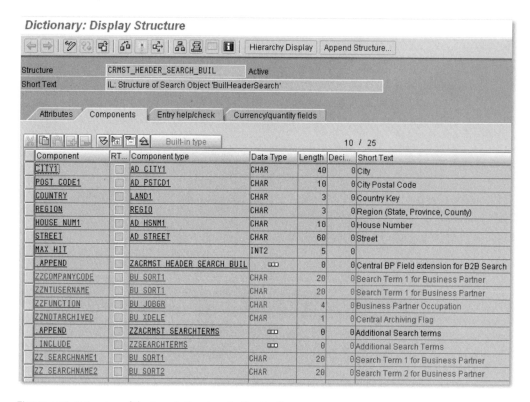

Dictionary: Display Structure

⬅️ ➡️ | 🖉 📝 🕹️ | 🔠 ⓘ 🔄 | 🖳 🖥️ ⬜ ⓘ | Hierarchy Display | Append Structure...

| Structure | CRMST_HEADER_SEARCH_BUIL | Active |
| Short Text | IL: Structure of Search Object 'BuilHeaderSearch' | |

| Attributes | Components | Entry help/check | Currency/quantity fields |

✂️ 📋 📄 📑 | ✅ 🔲 📋 🔼 Built-in type | 10 / 25

Component	RT...	Component type	Data Type	Length	Deci...	Short Text
CITY1	☐	AD_CITY1	CHAR	40	0	City
POST_CODE1	☐	AD_PSTCD1	CHAR	10	0	City Postal Code
COUNTRY	☐	LAND1	CHAR	3	0	Country Key
REGION	☐	REGIO	CHAR	3	0	Region (State, Province, County)
HOUSE_NUM1	☐	AD_HSNM1	CHAR	10	0	House Number
STREET	☐	AD_STREET	CHAR	60	0	Street
MAX_HIT	☐		INT2	5	0	
.APPEND	☐	ZACRMST_HEADER_SEARCH_BUIL	⬛	0	0	Central BP Field extension for B2B Search
ZZCOMPANYCODE	☐	BU_SORT1	CHAR	20	0	Search Term 1 for Business Partner
ZZNTUSERNAME	☐	BU_SORT1	CHAR	20	0	Search Term 1 for Business Partner
ZZFUNCTION	☐	BU_JOBGR	CHAR	4	0	Business Partner Occupation
ZZNOTARCHIVED	☐	BU_XDELE	CHAR	1	0	Central Archiving Flag
.APPEND	☐	ZZACRMST_SEARCHTERMS	⬛	0	0	Additional Search terms
.INCLUDE	☐	ZZSEARCHTERMS	⬛	0	0	Additional Search Terms
ZZ_SEARCHNAME1	☐	BU_SORT1	CHAR	20	0	Search Term 1 for Business Partner
ZZ_SEARCHNAME2	☐	BU_SORT2	CHAR	20	0	Search Term 2 for Business Partner

Figure 4.36 Extension of the Search Structure in the GenIL

```
METHOD get_m_searchname1 .
  DATA: current TYPE REF TO
          if_bol_bo_property_access.
  DATA: dref    TYPE REF TO data.

  value = ''.                        "#EC NOTEXT
  IF iterator IS BOUND.
    current = iterator->get_current( ).
  ELSE.
    current = collection_wrapper->get_current( ).
  ENDIF.
  IF current IS NOT BOUND.
    RETURN.
  ENDIF.

  dref = current->get_property( 'ZZ_SEARCHNAME1' ).
```

```
IF dref IS NOT BOUND.
  value = ''.                              "#EC NOTEXT
  RETURN.
ENDIF.
TRY.
value = if_bsp_model_util~convert_to_string(
data_ref      = dref
attribute_path = attribute_path ).
  CATCH cx_bsp_conv_illegal_ref.
    FIELD-SYMBOLS: <l_data> type DATA.
    assign dref->* to <l_data>.
    value = ''.                          "#EC NOTEXT

  CATCH cx_root.
    value = ''.                          "#EC NOTEXT
ENDTRY.
ENDMETHOD.
```

Listing 4.23 GET Method of the Context Node

If the methods exist in the context node, they can also be used in the Layout extensions view. In the layout, for example, this appears as shown in Listing 4.24.

```
<crmic:gridLayoutCell columnIndex="1"
  rowIndex="<%=lv_r3  %>"
  colSpan="3">
    <crmic:label design = "label"
      id     = "ContactName2"
      for    = "//SearchContactAsBP/SearchName1"
      text   = "<%= otr(z_test/searchterm1) %>"/>
</crmic:gridLayoutCell>
<crmic:gridLayoutCell columnIndex="<%=lv_c4  %>"
  rowIndex="<%=lv_r3  %>"
  colSpan="<%=lv_colspan2  %>">
    <crmic:inputField id = "SearchName1"
      width     = "100%"
      maxlength = "35"
      focus     = "TRUE"
      value     = "//SearchContactAsBP/SearchName1" />
</crmic:gridLayoutCell>
```

Listing 4.24 Extension of the View Layout by New Fields

At this point, the IC WebClient already displays the search fields. Even so, the fields do not affect the search process because their values are not yet included as search parameters. To accomplish this, the EH_ONSEARCH method of the controller class is redefined. Calling the original method takes care of the standard search, of setting the results in the corresponding custom controller, and of the navigation to a new view. Accordingly, the search results must be read from the custom controller and filtered by parameters, and a new navigation may need to be carried out. This can be done, for example, as outlined in Listing 4.25.

> **Note**
>
> If the number of hits specified in Customizing is too low, this can result in an empty set of hits.

```
* Definitions
  DATA:
     . . .
* Call inherited method
  CALL METHOD super->eh_onsearch.
     . . .
* Get additional search criteria from context
  lr_wrapper ?=
       lv_bupacontroller->
       typed_context->
       searchcontactasbp->
       get_collection_wrapper( ).
  lr entity ?= lr_wrapper->get_current( ).
  CALL METHOD lr_entity->get_property_as_value
    EXPORTING
      iv_attr_name = 'ZZ_SEARCHTERM1'
    IMPORTING
      ev_result    = lv_searchterm1.
     . . .
* Filter by additional search criteria
  lr_current ?= bo_col->get_first( ).
  WHILE lr_current IS BOUND.
    IF lv_searchterm1 IS NOT INITIAL.
     CALL METHOD lr_current->get_property_as_value
       EXPORTING
         iv_attr_name = 'ZZ_SEARCHTERM1'
```

```
   IMPORTING
      ev_result  = lv_value.
   FIND lv_searchterm1 IN lv_value IGNORING CASE.
   IF sy-subrc <> 0.
     bo_col->remove( iv_bo = lr_current ).
   ENDIF.
   lr_current ?= bo_col->get_next( ).
  ENDWHILE.
* "Overwrite" navigation of the inherited method,
* if necessary
   IF bo_col->size( ) = 0.
*     Nothing found!
     lv_msgsrv =
       cl_bsp_wd_message_service=>get_instance( ).
     lv_msgsrv->add_message( iv_msg_type   = 'I'
                             iv_msg_id     =
                             'CRM_IC_APPL_UI_BPID'
                             iv_msg_number = '011' ).
     view_manager->navigate(
                source_rep_view = rep_view
                outbound_plug   = 'showEmpty' ).
     EXIT.
   ENDIF.
  ENDIF.
```

Listing 4.25 Redefined Search Method of the View Controller (Extract)

If you now restart IC WebClient, you receive an extended business partner search as illustrated in Figure 4.37.

View Extensions

The effort necessary to extend views is determined by the properties of the data model. In the easiest situation, the relevant data already exists in the data model. In this case, the context node class only needs to be extended by the appropriate GET, GET_M and SET methods for reading and writing the data to the relevant field. This can be carried out easily using the IC WebClient Workbench.

IC WebClient Workbench

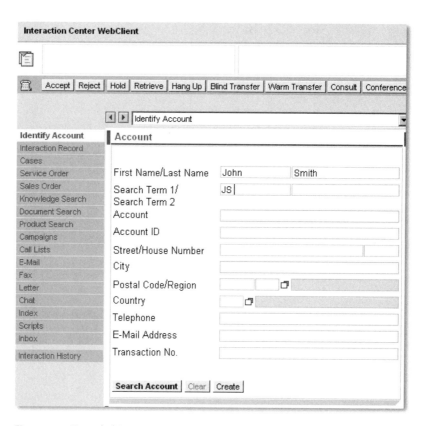

Figure 4.37 Extended Business Partner Search

GenIL extensions In the second situation, the relevant fields are not yet contained in the structures of the data model. In this case, the structures of the data model must be extended. You also must extend the methods in the data model classes in the GenIL that are responsible for transferring data between model and database. The framework of IC WebClient provides various possibilities for doing this. One sample implementation for a model extension is given with the CL_CRM_GENIL_SAMPLE_COMP class.

As a variant of the situation described in the previous paragraph, a search object is extended as described in this section. In this case, you do not necessarily need to extend the GenIL because the data is only used as a search parameter and is not transferred to a real object layer for further processing and final storage in the database.

4.9 Fact Sheet Enhancement

4.9.1 Introduction

The fact sheet is often used to present a variety of customer data in an overview. The following sections describe how to integrate customized information in the fact sheet. The extensions apply to both IC WinClient and IC WebClient.

A fact sheet consists of independent info blocks that can be combined as necessary. The info blocks themselves show information about the current business partner, and you can access both master and transaction data. Thus, it is possible to display the recent orders of a customer or similar information. Since the data retrieval can be programmed, it is even possible to obtain data from any system (for example SAP R/3, SAP BW, or non-SAP systems), provided that it is retrievable by the SAP CRM system.

Info blocks from any system

4.9.2 Creating and Customizing Info Blocks

Although the fact sheet is displayed as a Web page, you do not need any HTML expertise in order to create an info block. Via auxiliary classes, the data is prepared as XML so that it can automatically be displayed on the Web page.

No HTML knowledge required

An info block can be created in two ways: as the modification of a copy of an existing info block or as a new info block. The second case requires the creation of a class as a derivation of the CL_CRM_CCKPT_IOS class. This class then obtains all methods necessary for presenting the data (see Figure 4.38).

Programming in ABAP classes

The data to be displayed in the fact sheet later on is determined via the GET_REPORT method (see Figure 4.39). The return parameter ET_XML_OUT then contains the data for the presentation.

> **Note**
>
> Although the return parameter starts with ET_, it is not a table but just a string.

This is an example of the required source code for displaying all telephone numbers of the current business partner that were saved with the standard address.

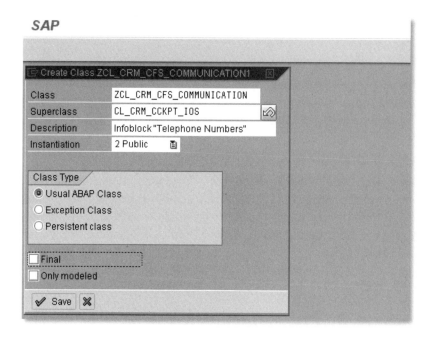

Figure 4.38 Creating the Class for the Info Block

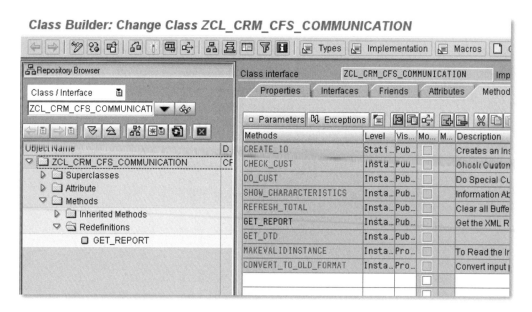

Figure 4.39 Redefinition of the GET_REPORT Method

Implementation of the method The data is to be presented in a one-column table. This is why the template CRMTE_CCKPT_XML_IB_HEADER_1S is used for the subheading and the template CRMTE_CCKPT_XML_IB_ITEM_1S is used for the telephone numbers (see Listing 4.26).

```
METHOD get_report .
  CONSTANTS:
    lc_newline TYPE string
               VALUE cl_abap_char_utilities=>newline.
  DATA:
    lr_xml_container    TYPE REF TO
                          cl_crm_cckpt_xmlcontainer,
    lt_xml_obj_ranges   TYPE crmt_cckpt_xml_ta,
    ls_template         TYPE crmt_cckpt_template,
    lv_line             TYPE crmt_cckpt_xmlline,
    lt_xml              TYPE crmt_cckpt_xml_ta,
    ls_xml              LIKE LINE OF lt_xml.
  DATA:
    lt_rangetab         TYPE crmt_cckpt_objranges_ta,
    ls_rangetab         LIKE LINE OF lt_rangetab,
    ls_range            TYPE crmt_cckpt_range,
    lv_partner          TYPE bu_partner.
  DATA:
    lt_adtel            TYPE bapiadtel_t,
    ls_adtel            TYPE bapiadtel,
    lt_adfax            TYPE bapiadfax_t,
    ls_adfax            TYPE bapiadfax,
    lt_adsmtp           TYPE bapiadsmtp_t,
    ls_adsmtp           TYPE bapiadsmtp.

  CALL METHOD me->convert_to_old_format
    EXPORTING
      iv_new_container = it_xml_obj_ranges
    IMPORTING
      ev_old_container = lt_xml_obj_ranges.
  CREATE OBJECT lr_xml_container
    EXPORTING
      it_xmlcontainer = lt_xml_obj_ranges.
  CALL METHOD lr_xml_container->getrangetabs
    IMPORTING
      et_rangetabs = lt_rangetab.
```

```
* Get BP range
  READ TABLE lt_rangetab INTO ls_rangetab
    WITH KEY objtype = 'BUS1006'.
  CHECK sy-subrc = 0.

* Only 1 BP should be found
  DESCRIBE TABLE ls_rangetab-rangetab[] LINES sy-tfill.
  CHECK sy-tfill = 1.

* Get BP number
  READ TABLE ls_rangetab-rangetab[] INTO ls_range
    INDEX 1.
  CHECK ls_range-sign    = 'I'            AND
        ls_range-option  = 'EQ'           AND
        ls_range-low     IS NOT INITIAL AND
        ls_range-high    IS     INITIAL.
  lv_partner = ls_range-low.

* Read phone and fax data
  CALL FUNCTION 'BUPA_ADDRESS_READ_DETAIL'
    EXPORTING
      iv_partner            = lv_partner
      iv_xaddress           = space
      iv_xadtel             = 'X'
    TABLES
      et_adtel              = lt_adtel
    EXCEPTIONS
      no_partner_specified  = 1
      no_valid_record_found = 2
      OTHERS                = 3.
  CHECK sy-subrc = 0.

* Build XML data -----------------------------
* Build 1st heading (optional)
  CALL METHOD
      crmcl_cckpt_templatesplitter=>get_template
    EXPORTING
      iv_name    = 'CRMTE_CCKPT_XML_IB_HEADER_1S'
    IMPORTING
      ev_template = ls_template.
```

```
lv_line = 'Telephone Number'(001).
CALL METHOD
    crmcl_cckpt_templatesplitter=>fill_template
  EXPORTING
    iv_tagname  = 'S1'
    iv_string   = lv_line
  CHANGING
    cv_template = ls_template.
APPEND LINES OF ls_template-template[] TO lt_xml[].

* 2. Compose data
  LOOP AT lt_adtel INTO ls_adtel.
    CALL METHOD
        crmcl_cckpt_templatesplitter=>get_template
      EXPORTING
        iv_name     = 'CRMTE_CCKPT_XML_IB_ITEM_1S'
      IMPORTING
        ev_template = ls_template.
    lv_line = ls_adtel-tel_no.
    CALL METHOD
        crmcl_cckpt_templatesplitter=>fill_template
      EXPORTING
        iv_tagname  = 'S1'
        iv_string   = lv_line
      CHANGING
        cv_template = ls_template.
    APPEND LINES OF ls_template-template[] TO lt_xml[].
  ENDLOOP.

  CALL METHOD
      crmcl_cckpt_templatesplitter=>get_template
    EXPORTING
      iv_name     = 'CRMTE_CCKPT_XML_IB_BORDER'
    IMPORTING
      ev_template = ls_template.
  CALL METHOD crmcl_cckpt_templatesplitter=>inserttable
    EXPORTING
      iv_table    = lt_xml[]
      iv_tag      = 'ROW'
    CHANGING
```

```
        cv_template = ls_template.
        lt_xml[]    = ls_template-template[].

* 3. Prepare data for output
  CALL METHOD
      crmcl_cckpt_templatesplitter=>get_template
    EXPORTING
      iv_name     = 'CRMTE_CCKPT_XML_IB'
    IMPORTING
      ev_template = ls_template.
      lv_line     = gv_myname.
  CALL METHOD
      crmcl_cckpt_templatesplitter=>fill_template
    EXPORTING
      iv_tagname  = 'HEADER'
      iv_string   = lv_line
    CHANGING
      cv_template = ls_template.
  CALL METHOD
      crmcl_cckpt_templatesplitter=>fill_template
    EXPORTING
      iv_tagname  = 'SHORTHEADER'
      iv_string   = lv_line
    CHANGING
      cv_template = ls_template.
  CALL METHOD crmcl_cckpt_templatesplitter=>inserttable
    EXPORTING
      iv_table    = lt_xml[]
      iv_tag      = 'INFOBLOCK'
    CHANGING
      cv_template = ls_template.
      lt_xml[]    = ls_template-template[].

* Return XML data -----------------------------
  LOOP AT lt_xml INTO ls_xml.
    CONCATENATE et_xml_out lc_newline ls_xml
      INTO et_xml_out.
  ENDLOOP.
ENDMETHOD.
```

Listing 4.26 Method for Obtaining Data and Preparing It as XML String

If several columns are used for the presentation, you can use the corresponding templates with the `HEADER_xS` or `ITEM_xS` suffix, where "x" specifies the number of columns. When the `CRMCL_CCKPT_TEMPLATE-SPLITTER=>FILL_TEMPLATE` method is called, the columns are then populated with the values `S1` to `Sx` for the `IV_TAGNAME` parameter.

Multi-column presentations

After the info block is created, it must be made known to the system. For this purpose, the class needs to be entered in the Customizing view `CRMV_CCKPT_CLASS`. This Customizing view must be maintained directly in Transaction SM30, it is not available in the IMG (see Figure 4.40 and Figure 4.41).

Storing the info block in Customizing

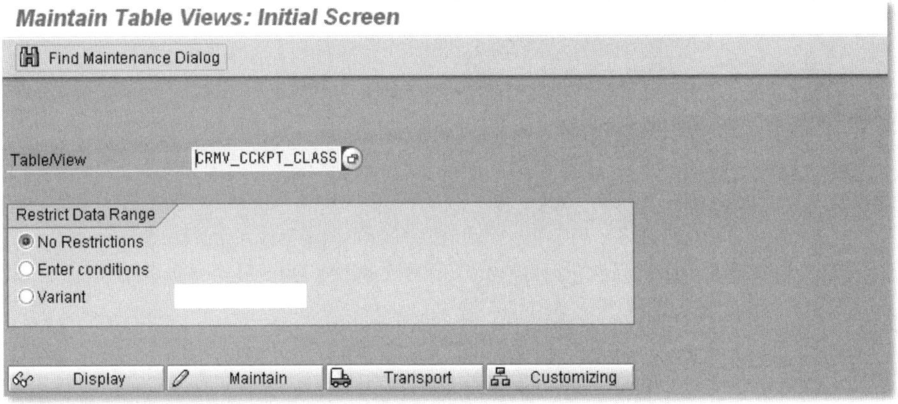

Maintain Table Views: Initial Screen

Find Maintenance Dialog		

Table/View   `CRMV_CCKPT_CLASS`

Restrict Data Range
- No Restrictions
- Enter conditions
- Variant

Display   Maintain   Transport   Customizing

Figure 4.40 Calling the View for the Info Block Classes

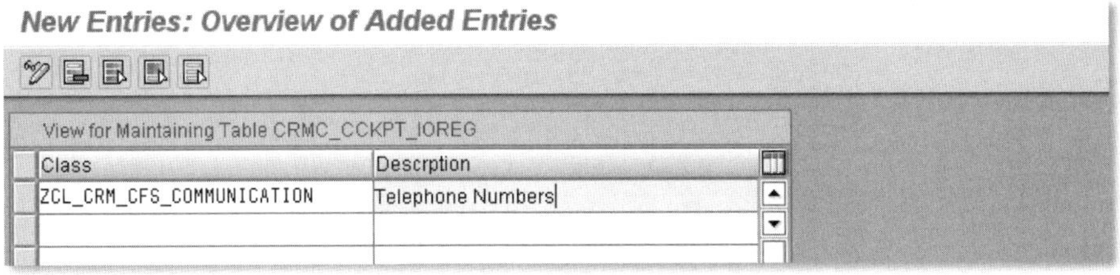

New Entries: Overview of Added Entries

View for Maintaining Table CRMC_CCKPT_IOREG

Class	Descrption	
ZCL_CRM_CFS_COMMUNICATION	Telephone Numbers	

Figure 4.41 Entering the New Class as an Info Block Class

4.9.3 Customizing the Fact Sheet

After the class has been declared as an info-block class, it can now be used in a fact sheet in Customizing. This is carried out in three steps:

Link to the fact sheet

1. Assign the info block class to an info block

2. Create or change a fact sheet

3. Assign the info blocks to the fact sheet

At first, the info block class is assigned to an info block (IMG path: **CRM · Master Data · Business Partner · Business Partner – Cockpit and Fact Sheet · Define Info Blocks and Views**). Extended settings may need to be maintained where necessary (see Figure 4.42).

Figure 4.42 Assigning the Info Block Class to an Info Block

Afterwards, a new fact sheet is created or an existing sheet is changed (see Figure 4.43). Finally, the info blocks are assigned to the fact sheet, and the order of the presentation is defined (see Figure 4.44).

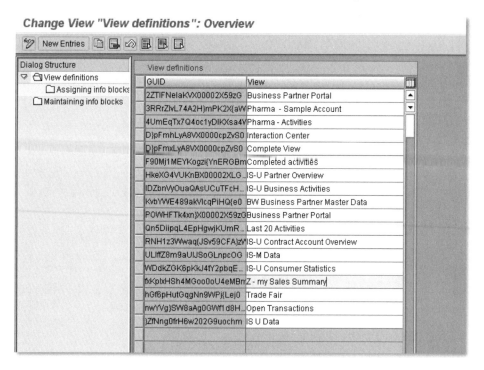

Figure 4.43 Creating a New Fact Sheet

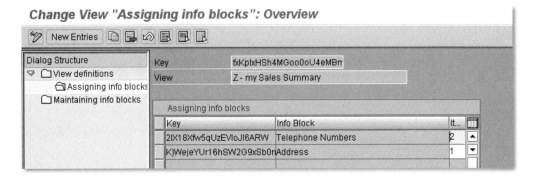

Change View "Assigning info blocks": Overview

Figure 4.44 Assigning the Info Blocks to a Fact Sheet

When the fact sheet is called in the Interaction Center, all telephone numbers of the confirmed business partner are now displayed as requested (see Figure 4.45 and Figure 4.46).

Interaction Center

End Contact

Business Partner		
Name	Wewers	Thorsten
Phone	06227747474	
Partner	74	⦿ Main
Name		
Partner		⚪ Main

Call Processing

| 🗐Inbox | ❓Info | 📋Activity | 🖵Script |

| Interaction Info | BD Display | ◀ ▶ | | BP Search | Business Activity | Sales Summary | Inbox | Inst. Base Detail |

Find	7 Business Activ...
By	1 Period
Valid From	27.08.2005
Valid To	16.09.2005
Status	
	Start 🗑

Trans.	P	Descripti...	Number

View: Z - my Sales Summary **Personalize**

Address
Address
Dear
Thorsten Wewers
Neurottstr. 15
69190 Walldorf

Telephone Numbers
Telephone Number
+496227747474
+496227700000

Figure 4.45 New Fact Sheet in IC WinClient ...

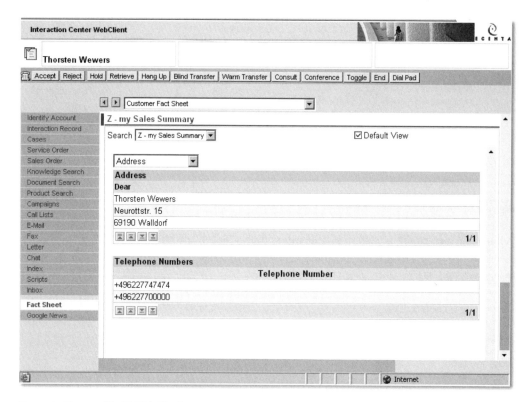

Figure 4.46 ... and in IC WebClient

4.10 Executing Workitems in IC WinClient

4.10.1 Introduction

Workflow scenarios on the standard system

The Workflow Inbox—found in the application area of the Interaction Center—displays the most different types of workitems. From Service Release 1 of SAP CRM Release 4.0, several workflow scenarios have been delivered, for example:

▶ Escalations

▶ Forwarding

▶ Consultations

▶ Notifications

▶ Approvals

These scenarios are available for all CRM business transactions and can be seamlessly executed in the People-Centric UI of CRM. When workitems are executed in IC WinClient on the standard system, the Interaction

Center is left, and the associated business transaction is displayed in another transaction.

One of the basic concepts of the Interaction Center, however, is to present all information that an agent needs to process interactions and transactions in one single transaction and distributed among several tabs. Thus prepared, the agent can quickly and easily access all necessary information.

Information integration as the basic concept of the IC

Accordingly, it would be a significant advantage if the business transactions transferred to the agent via workitems were also displayed in the transaction workspace of the Interaction Center (see Figure 4.47).

Transaction workspace

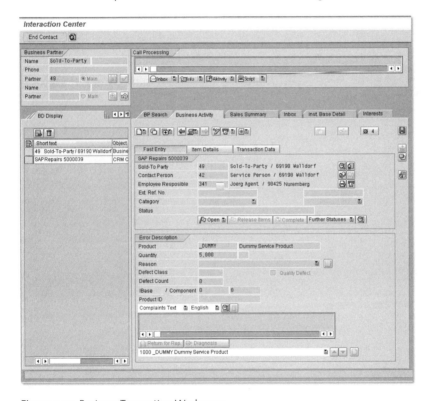

Figure 4.47 Business Transaction Workspace

4.10.2 Implementing the Object Method

In order to call a CRM business transaction in the transaction workspace, a new BOR method is required that determines the workspace for the relevant business transaction and places it into display or process mode in the foreground. In this context, some standard function modules can be used advantageously.

BOR method for workitem execution

The function module CRM_CIC_TRIGGER_OBJ_PROCESSING, to which the object key and the object type of the transaction are transferred, triggers the processing of the relevant business transaction in the Interaction Center. In this case, the object key corresponds to the GUID of the business transaction (see Figure 4.48).

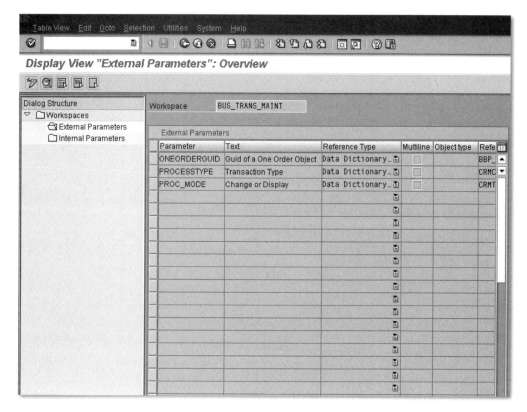

Figure 4.48 Parameters of the Business Transaction Workspace

The standard system deals with the object types listed in Table 4.2.

CRM Business Transaction	Object Type (Activity Type)
Business transaction	BUS20001
Task	BUS2000125
Opportunity	BUS2000111
Service contract	BUS2000112

Table 4.2 Supported Object Types of the CRM_CIC_TRIGGER_OBJ_PROCESSING Function Module

CRM Business Transaction	Object Type (Activity Type)
Purchase contract	BUS2000113
Sales contract	BUS2000121
Financial contract	BUS2000114
Service confirmation	BUS2000117
Purchase scheduling agreement	BUS2000118
Complaint	BUS2000120
Lead	BUS2000108
Service process	BUS2000116
Sales transaction	BUS2000115
Activity	BUS2000110
Contact	BUS2000126
Product	BUS1178

Table 4.2 Supported Object Types of the CRM_CIC_TRIGGER_OBJ_PROCESSING Function Module (cont.)

All other BOR objects are called via the standard function SWO_INVOKE in display (DISPLAY) or edit (EDIT) mode.

Using the Workspace Manager (reference of the type IF_CCM_ WORKSPACE_MANAGER), the CRM_CIC_TRIGGER_WS_ONEORDER function searches the business transaction workspace in the application area of the Interaction Center. The standard name of this workspace is BUS_TRANS_ MAINT. If it does not exist yet, it is created by the Workspace Manager; if it does exist, it is placed in the foreground. The decision whether the workspace is visible at the start of the Interaction Center already is taken in Customizing for default workspaces (see Figure 4.49). In both cases, the business object to be displayed is provided and is thus presented in the workspace.

Calling the transaction workspace

The complete method for displaying business transactions in the Interaction Center is thus structured as shown in Listing 4.27. In this case, the import parameter corresponds to the GUID of the transaction to be opened. With this GUID, the object type is determined first. Using this information, the object processing described above is then triggered and the workspace is opened.

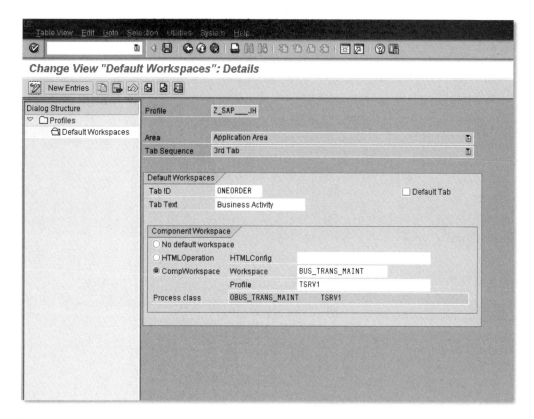

Figure 4.49 Default Workspace BUS_TRANS_MAINT

```
METHOD show_item .
  DATA: ls_guid       TYPE crmt_object_guid,
        ls_orderadm_h TYPE crmt_orderadm_h_wrk,
        li_wsp        TYPE REF TO if_ccm_workspace,
        ls_objkey     TYPE swo_typeid,
        ls_objtype    TYPE swo_objtyp,
        ls_abox_admin TYPE cic00_impdata_event,
        ls_call_cont  TYPE swcont,
        ls_cmpconf    TYPE ccmcmpconf.

  IF sy-tcode = 'CIC0'.
    CALL METHOD
      cl_crm_cic_workspace_util=>find_by_name
      EXPORTING
        im_name    = 'BUS_TRANS_MAINT'
      RECEIVING
```

```
       re_workspace = lr_wsp.
  ENDIF.

  IF lr_wsp IS NOT INITIAL.
* Interaction Center scenario
    ls_guid = iv_bor_guid.
    CALL FUNCTION 'CRM_ORDERADM_H_READ_OB'
      EXPORTING
        iv_guid                    = ls_guid
      IMPORTING
        es_orderadm_h_wrk          = ls_orderadm_h
      EXCEPTIONS
        parameter_error            = 1
        record_not_found           = 2
        at_least_one_record_not found = 3
        OTHERS                     = 4.
    IF sy-subrc <> 0.
      MESSAGE ID sy-msgid TYPE sy-msgty NUMBER sy-msgno
              WITH sy-msgv1 sy-msgv2 sy-msgv3 sy-msgv4.
    ENDIF.

*    Trigger workspace
    ls_objtype = ls_orderadm_h-object_type.
    ls_objkey  = iv_bor_guid.
    CALL FUNCTION 'CRM_CIC_TRIGGER_OBJ_PROCESSING'
      EXPORTING
        iv_objkey  = ls_objkey
        iv_objtype = ls_objtype.
    ls_call_cont-element = 'PINFOGUID'.
    ls_call_cont-value = iv_bor_guid.
    APPEND ls_call_cont TO ls_abox_admin-call_cont.
    ls_call_cont-element = 'PINFOTYPE'.
    ls_call_cont-value = ls_orderadm_h-object_type.
    APPEND ls_call_cont TO ls_abox_admin-call_cont.

    CALL FUNCTION 'CRM_CIC_TRIGGER_WS_ONEORDER'
      EXPORTING
        iv_cmpwsp    = 'BUS_TRANS_MAINT'
        iv_cmpconf   = ls_cmpconf
        is_abox_admin = ls_abox_admin.
```

```
    ELSE.
*     Call in full-screen mode
      SUBMIT crm_wf_modeler_submit_lo
         WITH guid    EQ iv_bor_guid
         WITH mode    EQ 'C'
         AND RETURN.
    ENDIF.
ENDMETHOD.
```

Listing 4.27 Method for Calling a CRM Business Transaction in IC WinClient

Implementing the BOR method in the workflow This method then can be used in the corresponding standard task of the workflow step to be executed in IC WinClient, either by integrating it in a method of the Business Object Repository or directly in an ABAP Objects method.

4.11 Extending the Agent Inbox

4.11.1 Introduction

ERMS With mySAP CRM Edition 2004, SAP provides its customers with the Email Response Management System, which offers extensive functions for IC WebClient, that were designed for complex requirements. With SAP CRM Release 5.0, these functions are also available for IC WinClient.

Extensions of the simple Inbox Workflow as "ERMS light" If you do not need the complete Email Response Management System (ERMS) functionality, you can easily integrate individual functions in IC WinClient. This example shows how to provide a separate automatic acknowledgment of receipt and a separate priority for every inbound email address by extending the inbox workflow. In the standard agent inbox, these settings can only be specified globally, that is, per channel.

The description is fairly detailed because we cannot expect every reader to be familiar with workflows. If you are an experienced user of workflows however, you will realize very quickly that the extensions require only a few steps and can be carried out completely without modifications.

4.11.2 Extending the Inbox Customizing

Standard process for the agent inbox With regard to its basic structure, the agent inbox (in both IC WinClient and IC WebClient) is a smart combination of the SAPconnect inbound distribution (Transaction SO28), a business object (CICSUPRT2 for IC WinClient, ICAUISUPP for IC WebClient), and a workflow controlling the actual processing of the inbound correspondence, by email or fax (see also Sections 3.2.4 and 3.3.4). The workflow also transports letters, but is in this case not started via the inbound distribution but via an ArchiveLink scenario for inbound documents.

This example of email and fax covers all parts of the standard solution previously mentioned except for the inbound distribution. The descriptions refer to IC WinClient, but also apply to IC WebClient. First, a new Customizing table ZCCMMAILADDRCON2 is created with the fields shown in Figure 4.50, the delivery class C, and the table view maintenance setting **Display/Maintenance allowed**.

Separate Customizing table

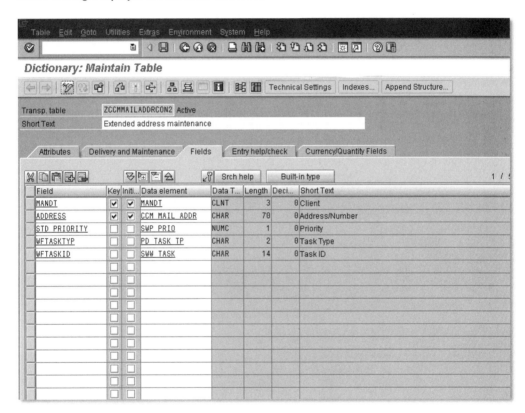

Figure 4.50 Definition of the Address-Dependent Customizing Table

Using the table maintenance generator (to be found in the **Utilities** menu of the table maintenance dialog; see Figure 4.51), you generate the maintenance interface for this table, which is then attached to the IMG structure under **Customer Relationship Management · Interaction Center WinClient · Component Configuration · Visible Components · Application Area · Agent Inbox Settings** (see Figure 4.52). For this purpose,

Generating the table maintenance

Transaction S_IMG_EXTENSION can be used: A new node is added here, with a new extension ID under the path mentioned above, in which a new maintenance object `ZMAILADDR_EXT` of the type **Customizing Object** is created. This maintenance object is then assigned to the ZCCMMAILADDRCON2 table and Transaction SM30 (table view/maintenance).

The new Customizing can now be used and is shown in Figure 4.53.

With the new table, all inbound emails can be assigned their own priorities. If the highest priority (1) is maintained, the system additionally sends an express notification. For the automatic acknowledgments of receipt, several standard tasks (type TS) are deployed, which are created in the next step.

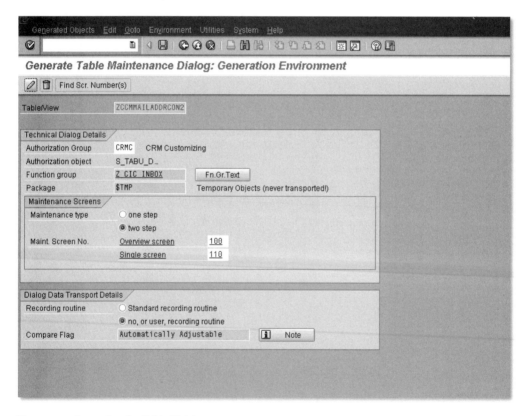

Figure 4.51 Generating the Table Maintenance

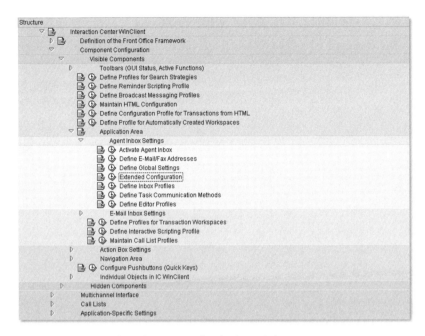

Figure 4.52 New Node in Customizing for the Agent Inbox

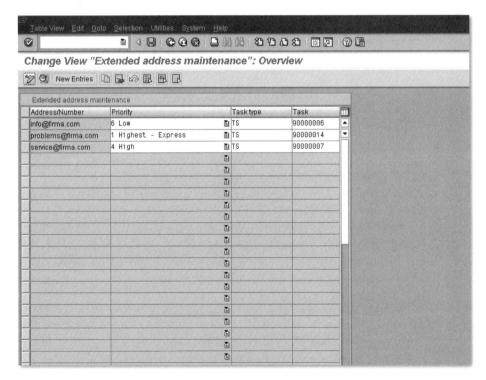

Figure 4.53 Customizing "Extended Address Maintenance"

4.11.3 Extending the Inbox Workflow

Standard task as a carrier of the acknowledgment of receipt In the standard inbox workflow, the standard task TS14007921 is used for the automatic acknowledgment of email receipt. This now needs to be copied for every text needed as an acknowledgment of receipt. In doing this, the text is integrated in the task description (see Figure 4.54).

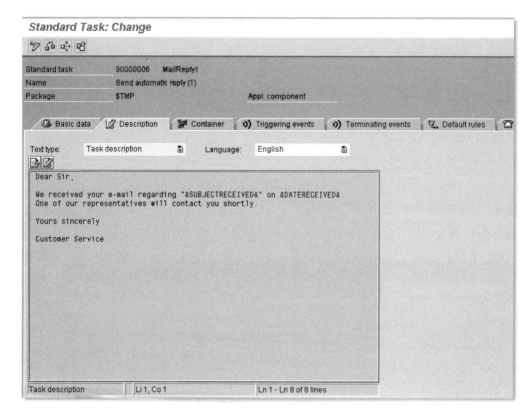

Figure 4.54 Standard Task "Send Automatic Reply"

These new standard tasks can now be entered in the Customizing table created in the first step. For changing the inbox workflow, a copy of the standard workflow template WS14000004 is created using Transaction PFTC. In order to switch to this new workflow, the triggering event for the standard workflow must be disabled and the one for the new workflow must be enabled.

Extensions of the workflow container Then, the container of the workflow copy needs to be extended by a new element **AcknTask** of the type SWWWIHEAD-WI_RH_TASK (see Figure 4.55). This is where the task for the automatic acknowledgment of receipt will be stored temporarily later.

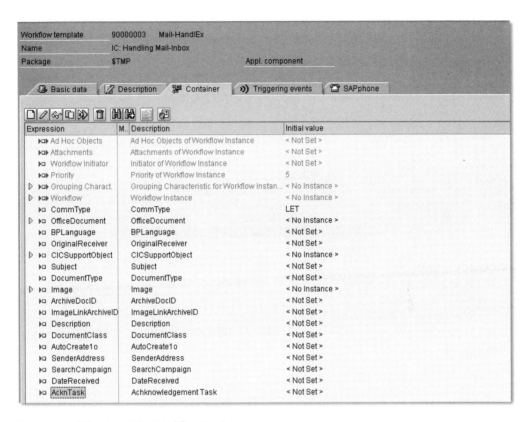

Expression	M..	Description	Initial value
▶□▶ Ad Hoc Objects		Ad Hoc Objects of Workflow Instance	< Not Set >
▶□▶ Attachments		Attachments of Workflow Instance	< Not Set >
▶□ Workflow Initiator		Initiator of Workflow Instance	< Not Set >
▶□▶ Priority		Priority of Workflow Instance	5
▷ ▶□▶ Grouping Charact.		Grouping Characteristic for Workflow Instan...	< No Instance >
▷ ▶□▶ Workflow		Workflow Instance	< No Instance >
▶□ CommType		CommType	LET
▷ ▶□ OfficeDocument		OfficeDocument	< No Instance >
▶□ BPLanguage		BPLanguage	< Not Set >
▶□ OriginalReceiver		OriginalReceiver	< Not Set >
▷ ▶□ CICSupportObject		CICSupportObject	< No Instance >
▶□ Subject		Subject	< Not Set >
▶□ DocumentType		DocumentType	< Not Set >
▷ ▶□ Image		Image	< No Instance >
▶□ ArchiveDocID		ArchiveDocID	< Not Set >
▶□ ImageLinkArchiveID		ImageLinkArchiveID	< Not Set >
▶□ Description		Description	< Not Set >
▶□ DocumentClass		DocumentClass	< Not Set >
▶□ AutoCreate1o		AutoCreate1o	< Not Set >
▶□ SenderAddress		SenderAddress	< Not Set >
▶□ SearchCampaign		SearchCampaign	< Not Set >
▶□ DateReceived		DateReceived	< Not Set >
▶□ AcknTask		Achknowledgement Task	< Not Set >

Figure 4.55 Extension of the Workflow Container

In the next step, the condition 000210 is extended by the `AcknTask <>` `' '` expression in Workflow Builder. As a result, the system does not send an acknowledgment at runtime if no standard task for the specific address is maintained in Customizing.

Finally, the property **Task Determined by Expression** must be enabled by the &ACKNTASK& expression in the Activity 000152. This ensures that the task used in this step is the task stored in the workflow container (element **AcknTask**) (see Figure 4.56).

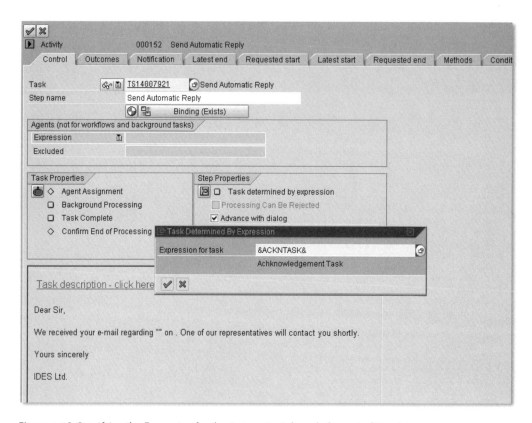

Figure 4.56 Specifying the Expression for the Automatic Acknowledgment of Receipt

4.11.4 Extending the Business Object

In order to extend the object type CICSUPRT2, a subtype ZCICSUPRT2 is created in Transaction SWO1.

Virtual attribute in the BOR object type

An additional virtual attribute **AcknowledgementTask** of the type SWW-WIHEAD-WI_RH_TASK has to be created in this object, which reads the corresponding Customizing from the ZCCMMAILADDRCON2 table (see Listing 4.28).

```
GET_PROPERTY ACKNOWLEDGEMENTTASK CHANGING CONTAINER.
  DATA: ls_original_receiver TYPE soxna-fullname.
  ls_original_receiver = object-key.
  SELECT SINGLE WFTASKID FROM zccmmailaddrcon2
    INTO OBJECT-ACKNOWLEDGEMENTTASK
      WHERE address = ls_original_receiver.
```

```
SWC_SET_ELEMENT CONTAINER 'AcknowledgementTask'
     OBJECT-ACKNOWLEDGEMENTTASK.
END_PROPERTY.
```

Listing 4.28 Determining the Standard Task from Customizing

The RECEIVE method only consists of one call of the function module **RECEIVE method**
CCM_MAIL_RECEIVE_DOCUMENT, which processes the receipt of an
email (or a fax) and—among other things—populates the workflow container. To extend this function module, the copy ZCCM_MAIL_RECEIVE_
DOCUMENT is created. Now the new workflow container element **Ackn-
Task** can be filled here using the virtual attribute (see Listing 4.29). The
function module can be integrated by redefining the RECEIVE method.

```
FUNCTION zccm_mail_receive_document.
*"----------------------------------------------------------
*"*"Local interface:
*"  IMPORTING
*"     REFERENCE(I_OFFICEOBJECT) TYPE  OBJ_RECORD
*"     REFERENCE(I_RECEIVER) TYPE  OBJ_RECORD
*"----------------------------------------------------------
  INCLUDE <cntn01>.
  INCLUDE rswtgdso.
  ...
  DATA: comm_type TYPE ad_comm,
        ...
        lv_offset TYPE I,
        ls_task type swwwihead-wi_rh_task.
  ...
** Populate container for event
  swc_container l_container.
  swc_create_container l_container.
  ...
  swc_get_property i_receiver
                   'AcknowledgementTask' ls_task.
  swc_set_element l_container 'AcknTask' ls_task.

** Start workflow
  ...
ENDFUNCTION.
```

Listing 4.29 Function Module for the Workflow Start

As a last step, the new priority needs to be set: For this purpose, the Com-
puteDeadline method is redefined and, after copying the original code,
extended by reading the corresponding Customizing entry from the
ZCCMMAILADDRCON2 table (see Listing 4.30).

```
begin_method computedeadline changing container.
DATA: date LIKE sy-datum,
 ...
      ls_sender_addr TYPE soxna-fullname,
      ls_addcust TYPE zccmmailaddrcon2.
 ...
* Read standard values from Customizing
 ...
* Read additional Customizing
TRANSLATE ls_original_receiver TO LOWER CASE.
SELECT SINGLE * FROM zccmmailaddrcon2
  INTO ls_addcust
    WHERE address = ls_original_receiver.
IF sy-subrc = 0.
  ls_global_set-std_priority = ls_addcust-std_priority.
ENDIF.

* Call BADI
 ...
* Return result
 ...
swc_set_element container 'NewWfPriority'
  ls_global_set-std_priority.

end_method.
```

Listing 4.30 Redefined Method for Calculating the Address-Dependent Workflow Priority

The agent-inbox extensions described here are just examples, and the
objects mentioned are also accessible for additional extensions. Beyond a
certain volume, the implementation of the ERMS should naturally be
considered, although the general mechanism discussed in this section
applies to both the agent inbox and the ERMS.

4.12 Alerts in IC WebClient

4.12.1 Introduction

The following example is intended to further illustrate the functionality of alerts in IC WebClient. In general, alerts can be used to provide text notes to the agents whenever a certain situation occurs. This section deals with an alert that is triggered as soon as the agent confirms a business partner and this business partner is listed in a call list of a marketing campaign.

Marketing campaigns as examples

As with most of the examples discussed here, the individual steps are settings in Customizing and user-defined extensions in the ABAP classes.

4.12.2 Settings in Framework Customizing and Defining a Customized View and Link Repository

This example aims at triggering an alert when the agent confirms a business partner, in other words when he or she presses the **Confirm** pushbutton after searching for a business partner. The alert should be triggered as soon as the business partner shows up in a call list assigned to the agent. At the same time, the alert is to be connected to a navigational link, which allows for the navigation to the marketing campaign associated with the call list.

Alert with navigation

As in the other examples, you first need to copy the desired objects to the customer namespace. The example is based on a B2B scenario so that the controller *BuPaDetailB2B.do* and the corresponding view *BuPaDetailB2B.htm* have to be copied. Since the source code should be completed so as to be dependent on an event, a new separate controller class must also be created as a subordinate class of the original controller class CL_CRM_IC_BUPADETAILB2B_IMPL. After that has been done and the corresponding controller replacement has been carried out in Customizing, the *BuPaDetailB2B.htm* view is replaced with the corresponding view from the customer namespace when starting IC WebClient. The wizards in the IC WebClient Workbench perform all these for you automatically (see also Section 4.8).

Controller replacement

You should also prepare here for the new navigational link. First, you have to create a separate Runtime (for example ZCRM_IC_RT_REP) and Design Time Repository (for example ZCRM_IC_DT_REP). Then, the XML file *CRM_IC.xml* needs to be copied from the standard SAP Runtime Repository into the separate one, where the path pointing to the XML file *CRM_IC_ALL_NavLinks.xml* must be changed to refer to the newly created

Navigational link in the runtime repository

Design Time Repository. The corresponding original file *CRM_IC_ALL_ NavLinks.xml* then must be copied from the standard location to the customer namespace. After these steps are complete, you need to insert one line in the XML file *CRM_IC_ALL_NavLinks.xml* that points to a new XML file, for example:

```
<%@ include file="Add_AlertNavigationalLinks.xml" %>
```

Accordingly, a page fragment named *Add_AlertNavigationalLinks.xml* must be created in a separate Design Time Repository. It contains the definition of the new navigational link. It could look as shown in Listing 4.31.

```
<NavigationalLink name="AlertToCallDetailsLarge">
<Source viewRef="contextAreaView"
        outboundPlugRef="default"/>
<Targets>
<Target viewRef="ClmCallListDetailsLarge"
        inboundPlugRef="inboundplugid"/>
</Targets></NavigationalLink>
```

Listing 4.31 Definition of the New Navigational Link

Changing the Runtime Repository in the IC WebClient profile The last step consists in adapting the BSP application in Customizing using the XML file which is dealing with the controller replacement as well. This is carried out via the IC WebClient Customizing setting **Customer-Specific System Modifications · Define IC WebClient Runtime Framework Profiles** under the **RuntimeRepositorySource** tag (see Listing 4.32).

```
<RuntimeRepositorySource type="BSP">
  <BspApplication>ZCRM_IC_RT_REP</BspApplication>
  <PageName>CRM_IC.xml</PageName>
</RuntimeRepositorySource>
```

Listing 4.32 Exchanging the Runtime Repository in Customizing

After the IC WebClient is restarted, not only the *BuPaDetailB2B.htm* view but also the Runtime and Design Time Repositories have been exchanged and thus a newly defined navigational link has been integrated.

4.12.3 Customizing the Alert Definition

Triggering via events Alerts are defined depending on start and end events of IC WebClient. Thus, triggering an event in the ABAP source code triggers an alert if it was defined accordingly.

The alert definition takes place in Customizing and consists of two steps (see Figure 4.57). The description is based on the ABAP configuration of IC WebClient in mySAP CRM Edition 2004.

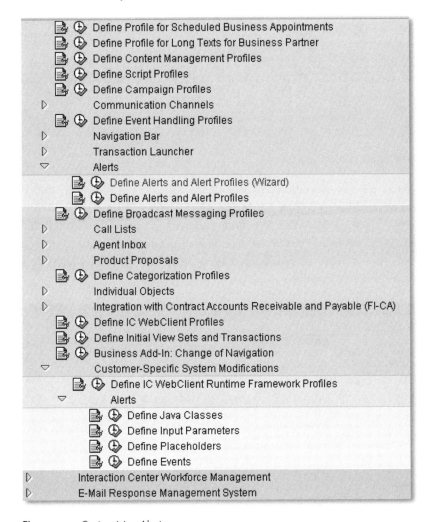

Figure 4.57 Customizing Alerts

In the first step, the event must be published in Customizing (see Figure 4.58). The corresponding IMG path is **Customer-Specific System Modifications · Alerts · Define Events** (Transaction CRMC_IC_EVENTS). You only need to specify the technical name of the event along with a short description and the event type (ABAP event, triggered in ABAP). All events entered here are later available for the alert definition.

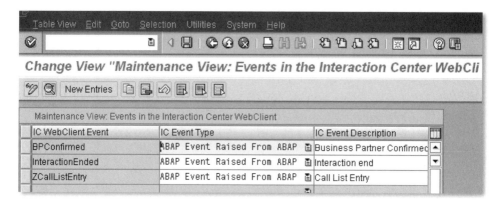

Figure 4.58 Customizing Events

The actual alert definition also takes place in the IC WebClient Customizing under **Alerts · Define Alerts and Alert Profiles (Wizard)** or via Transaction CRMC_IC_AMWZ. The wizard consists of seven steps. In the first step, you are asked for the name of an alert profile (see Figure 4.59). You can either choose an existing profile or create a new one by entering a name and a description.

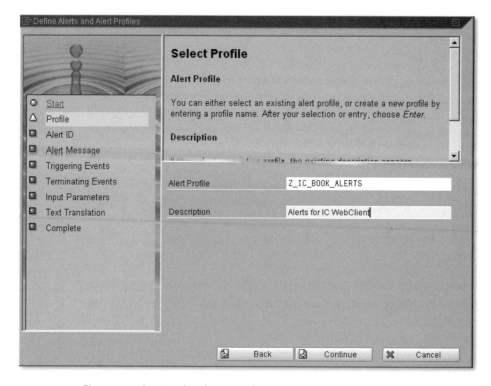

Figure 4.59 Starting the Alert Wizard

In the second step, you need to enter an alert ID, a description, and a **Basic alert data** class (see Figure 4.60). The ID and the description can be freely selected. In this example, from the selection you enter "CL_CRM_IC_ALERT_ GENERIC" in the **Class** field. The **Java Class** field remains blank.

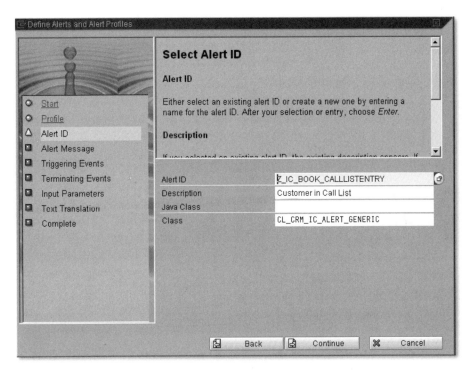

Figure 4.60 Selection of the Alert ID and the Alert Class

In the next step of the wizard, you can specify the alert text and, option- **Alert text, tooltip** ally, a tooltip or a navigational link (see Figure 4.61). Here you need to **and navigational** enter the alert text and the ID of the navigational link created above **link** ("AlertToCallDetailsLarge").

In the fourth and fifth steps, the triggering and the terminating events are **Triggering and** specified. In this example, the triggering event is the event triggered in **terminating event** the source code when the alert condition is met ("ZCallListEntry," see Figure 4.62). As the terminating event we choose "InteractionEnded," because in this example the information refers to the current business partner (see Figure 4.63). As soon as the transaction concerning this business partner is closed, the alert must be closed as well.

In the sixth step, parameters for the alert can be defined (see Figure **Alert parameters** 4.64). However, this only makes sense together with a selected Java class. Therefore, this step is not relevant for this example.

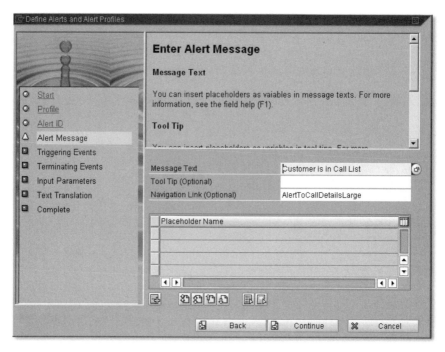

Figure 4.61 Definition of the Alert Text and the Navigational Link

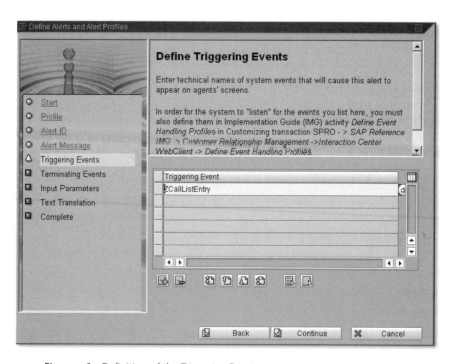

Figure 4.62 Definition of the Triggering Event

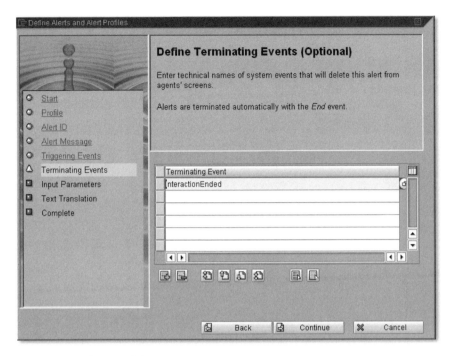

Figure 4.63 Definition of the Terminating Event

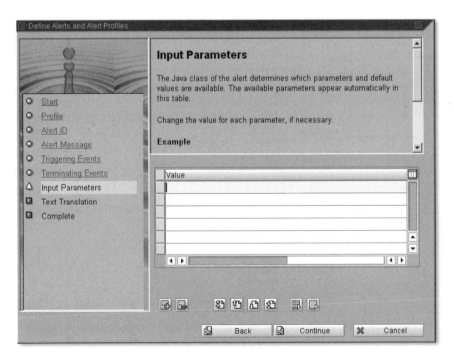

Figure 4.64 Definition of Parameters (Java Configuration Only)

As the final step of the wizard, the alert text can be translated into different application languages (see Figure 4.65).

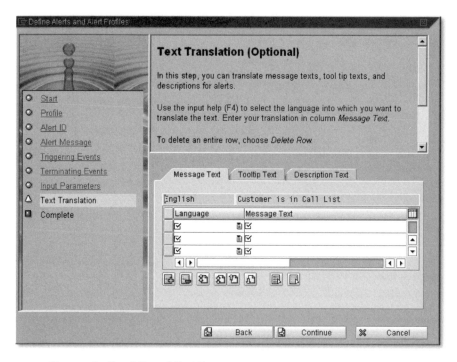

Figure 4.65 Translation of Alert Text

4.12.4 Triggering the Alert

Up to now, the functionality of IC WebClient has not been significantly modified. The corresponding controller, the views and the controller class are stored in the customer namespace, and a new navigational link and an alert have been defined and integrated in IC WebClient. In order to trigger the alert, a crucial task still needs to be performed: extending the source code.

In this example, extension is carried out as follows: First, a new class ZCL_IC_BOOK_SERVICE_TOOLS is defined. By defining such a service class, methods or functionalities needed in several places of the customer extensions can be created centrally. This is easiest when methods and attributes are static.

In this service class, we define three methods: One method reads the current customer, the second checks whether the customer is included in a call list, and the third method places the call list found into the marketing custom controller as the current call list. Then, the EH_CONFIRM method is redefined in the controller class to call the methods of the service class in the correct order. This eventually triggers the alert if the proper conditions are met. The source code in Listing 4.33 triggers this process.

```
METHOD eh_onconfirm .
  DATA:
    lr_customer TYPE REF TO if_bol_bo_property_access,
    lv_bp_guid  TYPE        bu_partner_guid.
* Call super method
  CALL METHOD super->eh_onconfirm.
* Read current customer
  lr_customer =
    zcl_ic_book_service_tools=>get_current_customer( ).
* Read BP GUID
  IF lr_customer IS BOUND.
    CALL METHOD lr_customer->get_property_as_value
      EXPORTING
        iv_attr_name = 'BP_GUID'
      IMPORTING
        ev_result    = lv_bp_guid.
  ENDIF.
  CHECK lv_bp_guid IS NOT INITIAL.
* Check for campaign
  CALL METHOD zcl_ic_book_service_tools=>check_campaign
    EXPORTING
      iv_bp_guid = lv_bp_guid.
  IF zcl_ic_book_service_tools=>
    gs_mktpl_tggrp-project_guid IS NOT INITIAL.
* Set first call list found as the current call list
    CALL METHOD
      zcl_ic_book_service_tools=>set_current_campaign
      EXPORTING
        iv_cl_pid = zcl_ic_book_service_tools=>
                      gs_mktpl_tggrp-project_guid.
  ENDIF.
ENDMETHOD.
```

Listing 4.33 Redefined Controller Method at Business Partner Confirmation

For reading the current customer/business partner in the service class, a method is defined which includes the return parameter rr_customer of the type IF_BOL_BO_PROPERTY_ACCESS (see Listing 4.34).

```
METHOD get_current_customer .
  DATA:
    lr_bdc      TYPE REF TO cl_crm_ic_cucobdc_impl,
    lr_coll_wr TYPE REF TO cl_bsp_wd_collection_wrapper.
* Get business data context
  lr_bdc ?=
    cl_crm_ic_services=>contextarea_contr
    ->get_custom_controller( 'CuCoBDC' ).
* Get collection
  lr_coll_wr ?= lr_bdc->typed_context
    ->currentcustomer->get_collection_wrapper( ).
* Get current customer
  rr_customer ?= lr_coll_wr->get_current( ).
ENDMETHOD.
```

Listing 4.34 Method for Reading the Business Partner Found

The method for checking the call lists includes the import parameter iv_
bp_guid of the type BU_PARTNER_GUID (see Listing 4.35).

```
METHOD check_campaign .
  DATA:
    lr_event       TYPE REF TO   cl_crm_ic_event,
    lr_event_srv   TYPE REF TO   if_crm_ic_event_srv,
    lt_tm_index    TYPE TABLE OF crmd_tm_iact_bp,
    ls_tm_index    TYPE          crmd_tm_iact_bp,
    lt_tm_calls    TYPE TABLE OF crmd_tm_iact,
    ls_tm_calls    TYPE          crmd_tm_iact,
    lt_mktg_tg_i   TYPE TABLE OF crmd_mkttg_tg_i,
    ls_mktg_tg_i   TYPE          crmd_mkttg_tg_i,
    lt_mktpl_tggrp TYPE TABLE OF crmd_mktpl_tggrp,
    ls_mktpl_tggrp TYPE          crmd_mktpl_tggrp.

  CLEAR gs_mktpl_tggrp.
* Read target group
  Select * FROM crmd_mkttg_tg_i INTO TABLE lt_mktg_tg_i
                        WHERE bp_guid = iv_bp_guid.
  CHECK sy-subrc = 0.

  READ TABLE lt_mktg_tg_i INTO ls_mktg_tg_i INDEX 1.
* Read campaign details
  SELECT * FROM crmd_mktpl_tggrp INTO TABLE
```

```
   lt_mktpl_tggrp WHERE targetgrp_guid =
   ls_mktg_tg_i-tg_guid.
CHECK sy-subrc = Ø.

READ TABLE lt_mktpl_tggrp INTO ls_mktpl_tggrp
                           INDEX 1.

IF sy-subrc = Ø.
  CREATE OBJECT lr_event.
  lr_event->set_name ('ZCallListEntry').
  lr_event_srv = cl_crm_ic_services
  =>get_event_srv_instance ().
  lr_event_srv->raise (lr_event).
  zcl_ic_book_service_tools=>gs_mktpl_tggrp =
  ls_mktpl_tggrp.
ENDIF.

ENDMETHOD.
```

Listing 4.35 Method for Searching for Call Lists

The SET_CURRENT_CAMPAIGN method includes the import parameter iv_
cl_pid of the type CRMT_GENIL_OBJECT_GUID and places the transferred call list as the current call list in the marketing custom controller
(see Listing 4.36).

```
METHOD set_current_campaign.
  DATA:
    lr_bol             TYPE REF TO cl_crm_bol_core,
    lr_mkt_controller  TYPE REF TO
                           cl_crm_ic_mktcontroller,
    lr_campaign        TYPE REF TO cl_crm_bol_entity.

  CLASS cl_crm_appl_intlay_campaign DEFINITION LOAD.

  CHECK iv_mkt_guid IS NOT INITIAL.

  TRY.
    lr_mkt_controller ?=
      cl_crm_ic_services=>
        contextarea_contr->get_custom_controller
                           ( 'MKTController').
```

```
CHECK lr_mkt_controller IS BOUND.
  lr_bol = cl_crm_bol_core=>get_instance ().
  lr_campaign = lr_bol->get_root_entity
    (iv_object_name =
        cl_crm_appl_intlay_campaign=>co_tn_campaign
      iv_object_guid = iv_mkt_guid).
  CHECK lr_campaign is bound.
    lr_mkt_controller->set_current_campaign
                          (campaign=lr_campaign).
  CATCH cx_crm_genil_model_error.
ENDTRY.

ENDMETHOD.
```

Listing 4.36 Method for Setting the Campaign in Custom Controller

The results are the following: The agent confirms a business partner (see Figure 4.66). If the business partner is included in a call list, IC WebClient displays an alert to notify the agent accordingly (see Figure 4.67). If the agent clicks the alert—which functions as a navigational link—the call list containing the customer and details about the campaign are automatically displayed (see Figure 4.68).

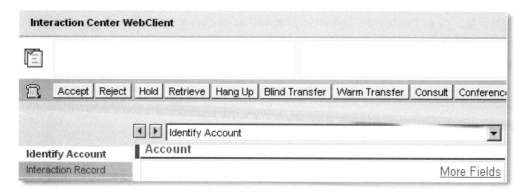

Figure 4.66 IC WebClient View Before Clicking the Confirm Pushbutton

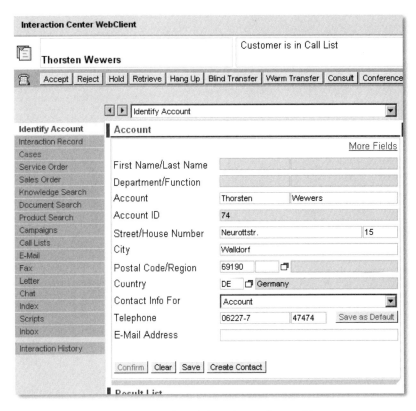

Figure 4.67 IC WebClient View After Clicking the Confirm Pushbutton

Figure 4.68 IC WebClient View After Navigating to the Call List

5 Selected Examples From Customer Projects

This chapter illustrates the versatility of implementing mySAP CRM Interaction Center in customer projects using six examples from different industries and companies of different sizes. These examples can generate ideas for other, similar projects. Technical details are given, which can be of direct help in comparable situations.

5.1 Overview

The customer projects in this chapter were selected because they clearly demonstrate the value of Interaction Center in a variety of industries and company sizes. The consulting firm ecenta AG was involved in all the projects and responsible for a part of each solution. We describe the projects in as much detail as possible, while at the same time meeting legal requirements and protecting customers' anonymity.

We tried to present an attractive selection in spite of the requirement for anonymity. Sections 5.2 and 5.3 introduce a complete scenario of a CRM Service process, including the analytical parts, in a Business Information Warehouse. We follow that up with an example from the consumer goods industry (Section 5.4), which shows a sophisticated email and letter integration as well as numerous extensions for capturing marketing-relevant customer data. Section 5.5 presents an employee interaction center that was introduced by a midsized HR outsourcing company with a short project timeframe. Section 5.6 proves that the Interaction Center is suited for supporting the internal sales-support processes of an IT company. The chapter ends with an illustration of a customized solution integrating the Interaction Center with third-party computer-telephony integration (CTI) software in a logistics company (Section 5.7).

Different industries and company sizes

5.2 Support Help Desk Based on IC WinClient

5.2.1 Customer and Problem

For companies with worldwide operations, the ability to provide first-class 24x7 service for their products is of crucial importance. This applies in this case to a leading technology company whose products are deployed all over the world. The company gains a significant amount of

Product support around the clock

its revenues with services related to its own products. Many of these services are maintenance and troubleshooting tasks where certain contractual response and solution times must be met. In order to track adherence to these agreements and thus continuously improve the performance of the overall service, this customer built up a comprehensive reporting system in SAP BW in parallel to the CRM project. This section first describes the CRM solution, Section 5.3 discusses the BW solution.

Flexible enhancement with further processes For supporting its own service processes in the software area, the customer was looking for a solution that had to meet several important requirements. One of those requirements was that all employees needed to access this data at any time, which could be implemented most easily with standard software. Apart from that, the software must be robust and flexible at the same time in order to map future requirements. The solution had to take into account the company's intention to also include the hardware-support process in mySAP CRM in the future. This placed special demands on the functions of the *installed base* (installation components). In an extreme case, the customer needed to provide comprehensive information on the configuration, construction-change status, etc. of all delivered products in order to provide the service employee with the necessary information for a support case before he visited the respective site.

5.2.2 Project Description

The implementation was initially based on SAP CRM Release 3.0. The extensions provided by SAP with the subsequent mySAP CRM 3.1 and 4.0, were integrated in the company solution in the course of the continuous development and enhancement of the application.

Business Process

Three-step support process with 5,000 employees The more than 5,000 employees of the service area work in three so-called lines. The point of contact for the customer is the *front office*, which receives requests and checks the knowledge database for existing solutions. If no solution can be found, the front office forwards the request to the *back office*. Product and solution specialists work in this area. If the back office cannot help either, the request is submitted to *product development*.

Remedy, permanent solution The solution process is run through twice. In the first pass, for example, a way might be found for the customer to restart the system. Then, a solution is worked out which permanently solves the problem (see Figure 5.1).

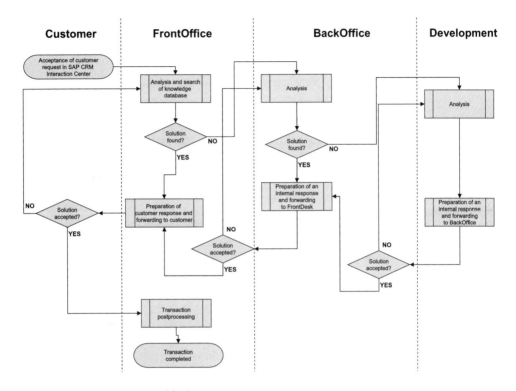

Figure 5.1 Solution Process (Simplified)

Highly simplified, the procedure is similar in both phases:

▶ **Step 1: Data entry**
The front office enters the transaction as a service request. It contains the customer data, the internal departments in charge, the product information, the problem description and the maintenance contract information. Using the maintenance contract, the system calculates when the first-aid or the complete solution needs to be provided to the customer.

▶ **Step 2: Front-office analysis**
The front office searches the knowledge database of the company for a solution. If sufficient information can be found, a response for the customer is prepared. However, if further analysis from product specialists is found to be necessary, the transaction is escalated to the back office (see below for an explanation of the term "escalation").

▶ **Step 3a: Response to the customer**

The customer can either accept or decline the response from the front office. If the customer accepts it, the transaction is postprocessed—for example, entered in the knowledge database—and closed. If the customer does not accept the response, the transaction is transferred back to the analysis phase (Step 2).

▶ **Step 3b: Escalation to the back office**

In the back office, product experts are at work. If they can solve the problem, they create an internal response for the front office. Otherwise, they escalate it to product development.

▶ **Step 4a: Internal response to the front office**

The front office has the same option as the customer; that is, it can either accept or decline the response. When declined, the transaction goes back to the back office; otherwise the front office prepares a response for the customer (Step 2).

▶ **Step 4b: Escalation to development**

The development department has no further escalation option. It must solve the problem and prepare the internal response for the back office. The latter can decline the response again and demand an improved solution.

CRM service order with follow-up documents

Technically, the processing of a customer request as a service order has been solved via follow-up documents. The employees in front office, back office, and development work with the follow-up documents, enter information and change the document status. They can forward the entire transaction to other colleagues or escalate it to the next service line if they think that more in-depth knowledge is required.

User Interface

Solution executable in IC WinClient and in IC WebClient

The decision about the user interface was made in favor of IC WinClient. Thus, a single interface can provide all the functions needed by the service employee for his daily work. Only for some administrative tasks must a user quit IC WinClient. With the availability of mySAP CRM 4.0 and thus of IC WebClient, an upgrade project was successfully completed for migrating to this user interface based on mySAP CRM Edition 2004. Both user interfaces support the same business-process logic in the solution and use the respective parts of the interface. These descriptions are based on IC WinClient but also apply to IC WebClient.

5.2.3 Solution Outline

The complexity of the service processes placed different demands on the software. One of these demands was the storage of the installation (*Installed Base*), which triggered the service process, in the service order. Owing to the product structure, a multilevel selection of the installation was necessary, and this functionality was not available in the standard version at the time of the implementation. The installation provides information on the products installed by the customer, in cases where the product can be entered in the service request. Using a structured presentation of the installations, it is easier for the service employees to correctly enter the service orders and find orders already entered for further processing. In a search, the number of hits can be restricted by the installation.

Installation components of the end customer

There were other challenges: To make the service available 24 hours a day, the service process is mapped across a worldwide organization divided into many steps, as described above. The resulting organizational structure is very complex. In order to support the individual service employees in finding the correct contact person for their questions despite these complex organizational structures, only the "approved" recipients are determined and offered for selection for forwarding, based on the CRM organization model.

Organizational structure

There are two types of forwarding. "Dispatching" refers to the forwarding within the same organizational level, while "escalation" means transferring the service request to the next service level. Both of these types of forwarding are implemented via the action box. Dispatching enables the processing of service requests around the clock, for example if a service employee from Europe transfers the service request to a colleague in the United States. If the front office cannot solve the problem, though, it is escalated to the back office.

Dispatching and escalation

An essential idea of forwarding is the division into the responsible agent and the responsible group. This ensures that personally assigned transactions still remain visible to the group, for example when the respective employee is ill. For support, a mechanism was created to always make the current user the responsible agent when the partner function is empty as soon as the employee starts processing the service request. This was implemented via a *hidden component* (see also Section 4.4) which is outlined as follows:

Agent group concept

▶ **Step 1**

Register the function module for the event **Set the current document to change mode** (see Listing 5.1).

▶ **Step 2**

Extend the function module responsible for the distribution of calls from IC WinClient (see Listing 5.2).

▶ **Step 3**

Create a function module that checks whether the partner function is filled with the responsible employee and fills it, if necessary (see Listing 5.3).

```
METHOD if_ccm_workspace~create .
* ZCL_HIDDEN_COMPONENT class
...
  ls_subscriber = 'ZWSP_HIDDEN'.
  ls_cb_fct    = 'Z_HIDDEN_CALLBACK'.
  ls_event     = 'OK_CODE'.
  CALL FUNCTION 'CIC_EVENT_SUBSCRIBE'
    EXPORTING
      event                 = ls_event
      subscriber            = ls_subscriber
      callback_function     = ls_cb_fct
      handle                = '1'
    EXCEPTIONS
      OTHERS                = 9.
  CALL FUNCTION 'CIC_OKCODE_SUBSCRIBE'
    EXPORTING
      okcode                = '10MAIN_TT'
      subscriber            = ls_subscriber
    EXCEPTIONS
      OTHERS                = 9.
...
ENDMETHOD.
```

Listing 5.1 Registering a Callback Function Module

```
FUNCTION z_hidden_callback.
*"----------------------------------------------------------
*"*"Local interface:
*"    ...
*"----------------------------------------------------------
```

```
  CASE event.
...
    WHEN 'OK_CODE'.
      CASE p1.
        WHEN '1OMAIN_TT'.
          CALL FUNCTION 'Z_SET_RESPONSIBLE_AGENT'.
      ENDCASE.
  ENDCASE.
...
ENDFUNCTION.
```

Listing 5.2 Callback Module

```
FUNCTION z_set_responsible_agent.
*"----------------------------------------------------
*"*"Local interface:
*"----------------------------------------------------
  DATA:
    lv_process_mode  TYPE crmt_mode,
    lv_partner_guid  TYPE bu_partner_guid,
    lv_bu_partner    TYPE bu_partner,
    lv_header_guid   TYPE crmt_object_guid,
    lt_header_guid   TYPE crmt_object_guid_tab,
    lt_partners      TYPE crmt_partner_external_wrkt,
    lv_bp_number     TYPE bu_partner.
    FIELD-SYMBOLS: <ls_partner> LIKE LINE OF
    lt_partners.
    CALL FUNCTION 'CRM_INTLAY_GET_PROCESS_MODE'
      IMPORTING
        ev_process_mode = ls_process_mode.
    CHECK ls_process_mode = 'B'.

  CALL FUNCTION 'CRM_INTLAY_GET_HEADER_GUID'
    IMPORTING
      ev_header_guid = ls_header_guid.
* Partner function 'Responsible employee' empty?
  INSERT ls_header_guid INTO TABLE lt_header_guid.
  CALL FUNCTION 'CRM_ORDER_READ'
    EXPORTING
      it_header_guid      = lt_header_guid
    IMPORTING
      et_partner          = lt_partners
```

```
      EXCEPTIONS
        OTHERS                    = 9.
    CHECK sy-subrc = 0.
    READ TABLE lt_partners ASSIGNING <ls_partner>
      WITH KEY partner_fct = gc_resp_user.
    CHECK <ls_partner>-partner_no IS INITIAL.
  * Nothing found => Set automatically!
    CALL FUNCTION 'BP_CENTRALPERSON_GET'
      EXPORTING
        iv_username           = sy-uname
      IMPORTING
        ev_bu_partner_guid    = ls_partner_guid
      EXCEPTIONS
        OTHERS                = 9.
    CHECK sy-subrc = 0.
    CALL FUNCTION 'BUPA_NUMBERS_READ'
      EXPORTING
        iv_partner_guid          = ls_partner_guid
      IMPORTING
        ev_partner               = ls_bu_partner
      EXCEPTIONS
        OTHERS                   = 9.
    CHECK sy-subrc = 0.
  * As soon as this employee (ls_bu_partner) is
  * found:
  * - Update partner function with CRM_ORDER_MAINTAIN
  * - Mark transaction as "changed"
  ...
    ENDIF.
```

Listing 5.3 Setting the Responsible Agent

Automated valida-
tions in every step
of the process Every type of forwarding is associated with certain steps that need to be carried out before the forwarding may take place. This is verified by the Interaction Center to make sure that a service request is completed by the front office, if possible, before it is forwarded to the back office. Additionally, a service employee can actively select service requests if he or she has the appropriate authorization. This can make sense, for example, if the employee is responsible for supporting one specific customer (*One face to the customer*) but the request has not yet been forwarded to the employee.

Software-Aided and -Supported Processing

There are several types of service requests, based on which further steps need to be performed. These steps are documented through activities associated with the service request, in which the working time required is recorded as well. The necessary steps in turn vary depending on the type of service request. For example, processing an internal service request requires fewer steps than processing that of an external customer, because internal requests can be processed in a less formal way. Likewise, service requests found to be incorrect can be closed directly without further processing steps.

Activities as process history

The company already faces a demand to solve as many problems as possible in the front office, in order to minimize processing times. Most customers have negotiated individual agreements (*Service Level Agreements*) defining the period within which a response or a solution must be provided. When recording a service request, the corresponding service level agreement is automatically determined based on the categorization, and the agreed service-level times are transferred into the service request. At the same time, SAP Business Workflows are started that control the timely processing of the service request. The current service employee is then notified on time when the service level time is about to expire.

Service Level Agreements

The service-level timeframes depend on several criteria, including the respective installation and the priority of the service request. The outage of a technical component must be rated differently from the customer's demand for further development; both, however, are valid service requests.

The status schema was designed to make the current processing status immediately transparent to every employee. The Interaction Center carries out numerous status changes automatically while showing its progress directly in the processing phase. For example, the completion of some associated activities results in an update of the service-request status.

Automatic status changes

Organization and Permissions

Master-data quality is one of the critical success factors for the service process. Only if it is maintained correctly can high service quality be achieved.

Due to the worldwide operation of the service organization in this case, it is necessary to capture and maintain the master data decentrally. For this purpose, the permissions for maintaining the master data are determined

Decentralized master data maintenance

based on the organization model. Using so-called *structural authorizations*, the organization model is validated, and the maintenance of customer master data and service level agreements is either permitted or refused. The most interesting aspect of these authorizations is that the maintenance of the organization model itself can be restricted to single branches within the organization, thus enabling the decentralized administration of master data.

Integration of Communication Channels

Integration of emails in service requests

Service requests usually reach the company via two channels: email or telephone. In both cases, the requests are recorded in the Interaction Center, where inbound emails can be opened directly: The email text is automatically included in the service request. Email attachments are enclosed with the service requests as Content Management documents, so that every service employee can access all data.

Linking the email automatically to the service request

For inbound emails, customer responses can be recognized as such. In this case, the system automatically determines the original service request and creates a follow-up activity for this request. The email text is copied there as well, and attachments are enclosed.

It is even possible to answer the requests directly from the Interaction Center. Documents attached to the internal responses by back office and development employees, like operating instructions or technical specifications, can be included in the response to the customer.

Internet Customer Self-Service

Many customers wanted to be able to enter their service requests themselves. For this purpose, the *SAP CRM Internet Customer Self-Service* (ICSS) was integrated, enabling a structured data entry by customer employees. All service requests entered this way can be processed by service employees immediately after their entry in the Interaction Center. The current processing status is transparent to customer employees in the ICSS, and the documentation attached to the service request can be downloaded directly; sending the documentation is no longer necessary.

Worklist at lower support levels

One drawback of IC WinClient in the implemented release for this project was the lack of an appropriate search functionality to adequately support back-office processes. The service employees had to be able to search for existing transactions using numerous criteria, because not every process takes place in the context of a customer interaction. They also needed to be able to simply revert to their personal worklists. If service requests could not be completed immediately and a new processing was required, the worklist could be used to easily find these service requests. The worklist also helps to find requests transferred by other departments. For this purpose, a new workspace was developed which permitted the execution of complex searches—a functionality which has always been available by default in IC WebClient (*agent inbox*) and, since SAP CRM Release 5.0, in IC WinClient.

During the course of developing the customer-specific workspace for the search, an analysis was run on response times that resulted when searches were performed with standard SAP methods. It turned out that many frequently run searches were based on combinations which led to very long response times. By changing to a separate table especially designed for the requirements of high-performing searches, response times could be significantly accelerated. With the SAP CRM Release 5.0 for the Interaction Center, this functionality is available by default as *Business Transaction Search*.

Business transaction search

5.2.4 Benefits of the Project Implementation

The original solution was released in 2002 and has been regularly enhanced. In the meantime, the user interface has been implemented in IC WebClient as well. So far, the solution has met all demands and is very robust and reliable.

For the customer, it brought the benefit of integrated service processing, which provided all persons involved in the service process with a unified interface that showed all relevant information in the customer context. Users had to be trained in one application only. In the course of the project, some legacy systems were replaced with the standard system, which was advantageous for operation and maintenance. Today, more than 5,000 users work with this solution at different sites all over the world.

One interface for all support levels

Much of the experience and impressions gained during this project was used to define desirable enhancements to the SAP CRM standard version, the majority of which are available with Releases 4.0 and 5.0.

5.3 Interaction Center Analytics for a Support Help Desk

5.3.1 Customer Objective

This section describes the reporting system which was built around the scenario presented in Section 5.2. We therefore recommend that you

Reporting

read the first parts of Section 5.2, where the customer processes are described.

In the analytical CRM, the company wants to find out, above all, who dealt with the transaction for how long, and what actions were taken by specific employees. In addition, certain action times are needed because they reflect the achievement of milestones that are important for a performance appraisal. Such milestones can be data entry, escalation to the back office, escalation to development, internal response from the back office, internal response from development, remedy, solution, acceptance or refusal of a solution, etc.

The project solution is the logical sequel to the Interaction Center Analytics in the area of service processes in mySAP CRM (see Chapter 3, Section 3.4.3). Although it is easily possible to establish a link to the interaction statistics presented there, this combination was deferred in the project we are describing.

5.3.2 Solution Description

The main purpose of reporting is to analyze which agent or which group ("who") performed which action ("what") at what time in the transaction.

Who changed something can be determined from the *business-partner change history*. For every document, this history records which business partner assigned the document at what time and which assignments have been canceled. One of the business partner roles is "responsible agent," and the history of this role provides an overview of how long and when a specific employee dealt with this transaction.

The status change history shows what has been changed. As with the business- partner change history, this history shows the times when a status was set. In this case, the employees almost exclusively work with follow-up documents, and when reaching a certain status on the follow-up document, the status of the service order is changed by a workflow. For example, the action **Solution accepted by the customer** means that the status **Provided and accepted by the customer** was set for the "Customer solution" activity.

The wait times for the customer are also mapped via document statuses. The wait time for further information, for example, is implemented in the status **Analysis, waiting for further information** on the **Analysis** activity document.

For this "who" and "what" information, three report categories are used for structuring the following sections:

1. Status and target achievement for individual service processes

2. Development of productivity over time

3. Detail analysis below the service process

Status and target achievement for individual service processes

The InfoProviders in this area contain one record per service request. Its characteristics describe the service process and provide information about the following areas (excerpt):

One record per service request

▶ **Service order**
Order number, external reference number, solution number in the knowledge database, priority, contract number, etc.

▶ **Problem**
Product, service type, component, etc.

▶ **Customer**
Customer number, name, country, contact person

▶ **Organization responsible for the customer**
Business partner number, name, country

▶ **Organization last responsible for the process**
Business partner number, name, country

▶ **Employee last responsible for the process**
Business partner number, name, country, contact data

▶ **Organization that created the process**
Business partner number, name, country

▶ **Status**
The last status of the process

▶ **Time information (year, quarter, month, week, and day) when**

  ▶ The process was created

  ▶ The process was last changed

  ▶ The process was solved

  ▶ Corrective action is due

  ▶ The solution is due

  ▶ The process was assigned an internal response from the back office or development

These key performance indicators describe the critical success factors at the service-process level. Figure 5.2 illustrates the evaluation range.

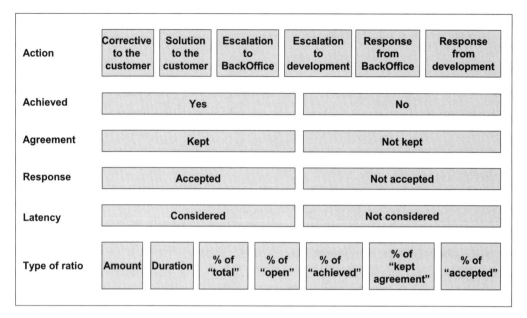

Action	Corrective to the customer	Solution to the customer	Escalation to BackOffice	Escalation to development	Response from BackOffice	Response from development
Achieved	Yes			No		
Agreement	Kept			Not kept		
Response	Accepted			Not accepted		
Latency	Considered			Not considered		
Type of ratio	Amount	Duration	% of "total"	% of "open"	% of "achieved"	% of "kept agreement"	% of "accepted"

Figure 5.2 Key Performance Indicators at Service Process Level

A key performance indicator results from the combination of selection options in individual rows, as you can see in Figure 5.3. In taking wait times into account, you want to be able to clearly tell if potential delays can be attributed to the customer. Similar to SAP Support, the company can assign the process to the customer if it needs to wait for further information.

Development of performance over time

For the development of performance over time, the same key performance indicators are measured as in the evaluation area **Status and target achievement for individual service processes**. The difference is that the value of a specific key performance indicator is saved several times for one process. For this reason, the term "snapshots" was introduced in the project: It describes a certain period and reflects the status of the company as it presented itself during this period.

In the solution outlined here, it was decided to save weekly and monthly snapshots in order to understand at a later stage how each key performance indicator turned out in a specific week or a specific month or at the end of a specific week or a specific month.

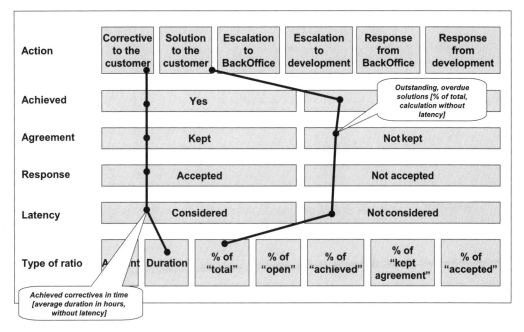

Figure 5.3 Examples of Key Performance Indicators

Technically, this means that the InfoProvider no longer just stores one record per service process but one record per snapshot period. Only those periods are relevant in which the service process is open, given that there are no more changes after it has been closed. Figure 5.4 illustrates this with an example.

Service transaction	Action	Date	Remaining time for corrective [agreement, days]	Remaining time for solution [agreement, days]	Open [amount]	Corrective, outstanding [amount]	Corrective, achieved in time [amount]	Solution, outstanding [amount]	Solution, achieved in time [amount]
100	Create	03/15/05	10	20	1	1	0	1	0
100	Analysis	03/16/05	9	19	1	1	0	1	0
100	Escalation to BackOffice	03/16/05	Snapshot Week 11	19	1	1	0	1	0
100	Analysis in BackOffice	03/17/05		18	1	1	0	1	0
100	Corrective to FrontOffice	03/25/05	Snapshot Week 12	10	1	1	0	1	0
100	Corrective to customer	03/28/05	-3	7	1	0	0	1	0
100	Solution to FrontOffice	03/30/05	-3	5	1	0	0	1	0
100	Solution to customer	03/31/05	-3	4	1	0	0	0	1
100	Transaction complete		0		0	0	0	0	1

Snapshots April 04 and Week 13 — Snapshot March 04

Figure 5.4 Example of a Service Processing and the Records Relevant for Snapshots

In the **Status and target achievement for individual service processes** evaluation area, only the last record of 04/01/05 is saved and analyzed, while snapshot reports include five records:

▶ The record of 3/17/05 with the last status in calendar week 11

▶ The record of 3/25/2005 with the last status in calendar week 12

▶ The record of 3/31/05 with the last status of March 2005

▶ The record of 4/1/2005 with the last status in calendar week 13

▶ The record of 4/1/2005 with the last status of April 2005

Historical evaluations Historical evaluations as shown in Figure 5.5 then present the sum of the individual snapshot records, where the snapshot month or the snapshot week are used as a drilldown characteristic.

Detail Analysis Below the Service Process

What is special about reports from **Status and target achievement for individual service processes** and **Development of performance over time** is that the underlying InfoProviders aggregate the information to the level of a service process.

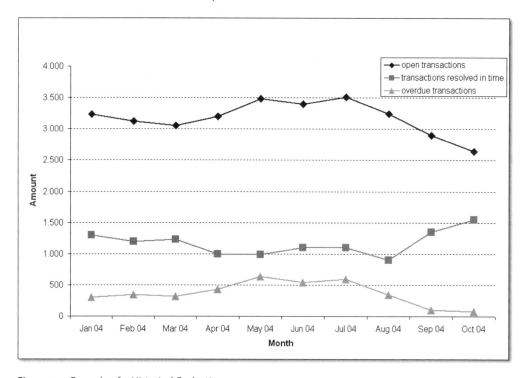

Figure 5.5 Example of a Historical Evaluation

This is the main difference of the report **Detail analysis below the service process**: The detail analysis deals with evaluating the individual change documents. The benefit is that it is possible to tell exactly who did what at what time with the document.

Who did what at what time with the process?

Figure 5.6 shows, for example, that the document 0000252827 was entered on July 6, 2004 at 1:27:56 p.m. by the front office in Brazil. Shortly afterwards, it was forwarded to the back office where it was processed for 10 days. Then it went back to the front office, where the response to the customer was prepared using the response from the back office. The customer accepted the response on August 9, 2004, and the transaction could be closed on August 10.

Service process	Organization	Status	Date of change	Time of change
0000252827	FrontOffice Brazil	Recorded	07.06.04	1:27:56 PM
	BackOffice Brazil	Recorded	07.06.04	1:34:42 PM
		Analysis	07.06.04	2:24:34 PM
	FrontOffice Brazil	Solution provided	07.16.04	2:53:23 PM
		Solution accepted	08.09.04	5:13:02 PM
		Wrap-up	08.10.04	2:45:52 PM
		Process completed	08.10.04	2:47:09 PM

Figure 5.6 Example of a Change History

Based on such a change history, a multitude of evaluations can be carried out. This always means counting certain events. For example, when evaluating the amount of work in the organization X, you will always count the following aspects (see Figure 5.7):

Counting events

▶ **Service processes created: How many processes were created by the organization X?**
For this figure, the status "new" is counted, provided that there is no predecessor organization.

▶ **Service processes transferred: How many processes were transferred by the organization X?**
This corresponds to the number of business partner changes in which the predecessor organization is set and the current organization is the organization X.

▶ **Service processes forwarded: How many processes were forwarded by the organization X?**
This is the number of business partner changes in which the organization X is the predecessor organization.

Week	Service processes created	Service processes adopted	Service processes forwarded
46,2002	3	2	0
47,2002	1	0	1
48,2002	0	11	16
49,2002	1	15	5
50,2002	3	4	2
51,2002	4	3	2
52,2002	1	7	8
01,2003	1	1	1
02,2003	9	23	3
03,2003	0	9	4
04,2003	12	14	4
05,2003	3	44	5
06,2003	2	25	14
07,2003	24	17	1
08,2003	8	30	16
09,2003	17	6	58
10,2003	24	87	83
11,2003	36	84	122
12,2003	36	132	47
13,2003	48	32	154
14,2003	7	4	235
15,2003	61	116	224
16,2003	36	64	55
17,2003	6	56	22
18,2003	24	2	103
19,2003	20	69	57
20,2003	17	119	48

Figure 5.7 Report of the Amount of Work

Some examples of evaluations based on the change history:

▶ **Processing time per organizational unit and employee**
These reports show, for example, how long the front office, how long the back office, and how long a specific employee were responsible for the process.

▶ **Activity overviews**
In this case, documents are counted in order to tell how often the process was escalated (corresponds to the number of escalation activities), how often a solution was found in the knowledge database (corresponds to the number of knowledge-database activities), and how often external partners worked on the solution (number of activities of the type **External escalation**).

▶ **Status overviews**
This reflects the duration of the individual status. For example, you can see the wait times, the duration of the analysis and the number of solutions (corresponds to the number of solution activities with the status **Solution provided**).

▶ Response quality
Ratio of refused and accepted, for remedy, solution, internal responses.

SAP CRM 5.0 Content for Service Processes

The extractors of the change history as described in the last section are largely delivered with SAP CRM Release 5.0. They record status tracking ("How long did a document remain in a specific status?"), process tracking ("How long was a business partner responsible for the document?"), and record tracking data ("How long did a specific document field—for example, **Priority**—have a specific value?").

BW content on the standard system

5.3.3 Benefits of the Project Implementation

The reporting described here is implemented globally by the company to control the service organization with more than 5,000 employees. Four hundred analysts worldwide use the system most intensely. They prepare daily, weekly, monthly, quarterly and annual evaluations: detailed ones for the individual team leaders, but also summarized ones for the company's Executive Board. Additionally, service employees can retrieve important evaluations themselves via the SAP Enterprise Portal.

5.4 Consumer Care Based on IC WebClient

5.4.1 Customer and Problem

This example deals with the introduction of IC WebClient in SAP CRM Release 4.0 at a leading manufacturer in the food industry. The product range of the manufacturer also included pet food. The idea was to enter, edit, and analyze all consumer-care interactions of all areas in a central system, for example complaints, info mail, or targeted marketing campaigns.

Interactions with the consumer

One challenge was that different call centers are assigned to different countries that essentially sell the same products. In each country, the individual teams can in turn be organized by brands. Besides the call centers, there are several home offices that are integrated in the consumer interaction as well. Additionally, the consumer has numerous possibilities to get in touch with the company, such as direct contact via the telephone, email, forms on Web sites, and letter or fax. Moreover, the company is also interested in addressing the consumer individually, e.g. via

Complex call center structure

email or letter or via automated personal info mail. For this purpose, the company uses numerous templates.

Manifold consumer questions Because of the variety of possible consumer questions, companies have to maintain a knowledge/solution database that needs to be directly connected to an Interaction Center. Additionally, it must be possible to link historical interactions (*calls*) to current ones and to merge similar interactions in *cases*.

5.4.2 Project Description

Remote access and layout Because employees work in different locations and there are so many kinds of consumer interactions, IC WebClient is well-suited to perform these tasks. This ensures location-independent access as well as a flexible and consistently ergonomic user interface. Furthermore, a layout adapted to the individual company guidelines can be supported to a certain extent.

Product-specific email addresses The broad range of products and the resulting agent groups were accounted for by a correspondingly designed organizational management. Every agent group was assigned to an organizational unit that technically represents a *queue*, i.e. was assigned to a unique email address (see Figure 5.8), for example:

▶ *dogfood@company.com*

▶ *catfood@company.com*

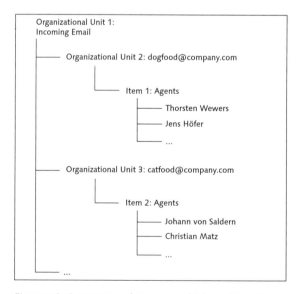

Figure 5.8 Organizational Structure of Inbound Email

Another possibility is dividing these structures by countries or regions. This ensures the correct delivery of an email with regard to its contents. This mapping is carried out by an *inbound workflow* which receives inbound emails, determines the relevant agent group, and places the email as a work item in the agents' worklist. At the same time, this organization forms the basis for the forwarding of entered interactions and their escalation when the defined processing time is exceeded.

The worklist is therefore accessed via the agent inbox, which provides various filter criteria and information about the interaction status, the current agent, links to other interactions, and other aspects. (see Figure 5.9).

Agent inbox as a worklist

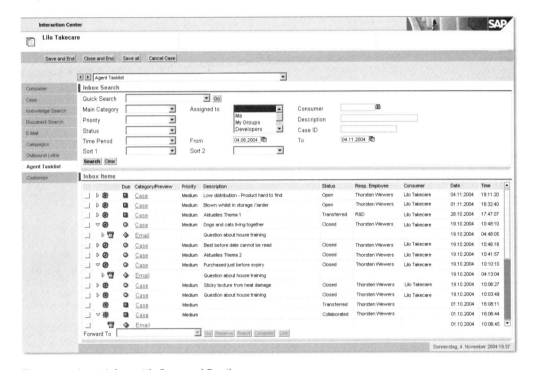

Figure 5.9 Agent Inbox with Cases and Emails

Inbound communication is obviously focused on the email channel, which also includes the requests submitted via forms on various Web pages.

Focus on email

After selecting an interaction to be processed, the consumer is identified in the next step. If the inbound channel is email or form, the system assists you by, for example, initializing the search fields with values. The agent also is provided with an overview of all previous interactions of the consumer as well as of the children and pets living in the household, if this data was recorded during other interactions (see Figure 5.10).

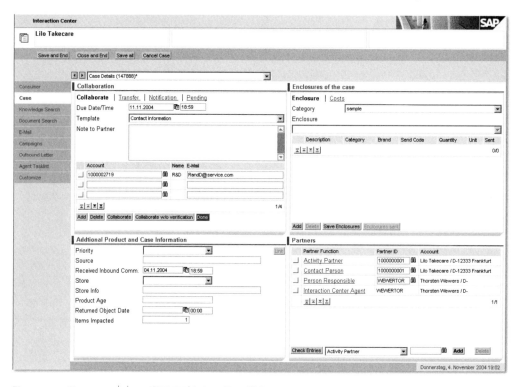

Figure 5.10 Consumer Information and Interaction History

Brand preferences of the consumer

You also can specify the preferred communication channels and brands of the consumer. This enables the agent to address the consumer in a very personal way (see Figure 5.11). This information also helps to create purposeful marketing campaigns.

Interaction data

Another significant part of the solution is the processing of the actual contact. Relevant details are recorded, for example the reason for the interaction, the respective product or the problem (see Figures 5.12 and 5.13).

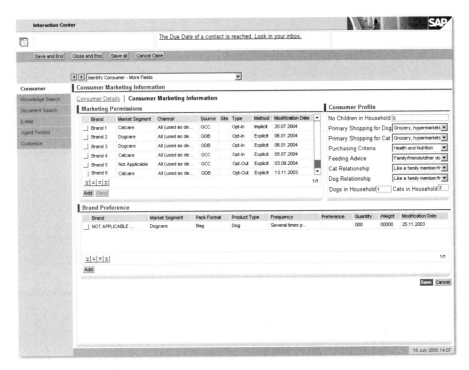

Figure 5.11 Entry of Brand Preferences and Marketing Permissions

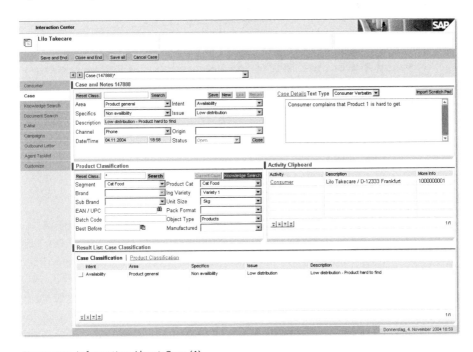

Figure 5.12 Information About Case (1)

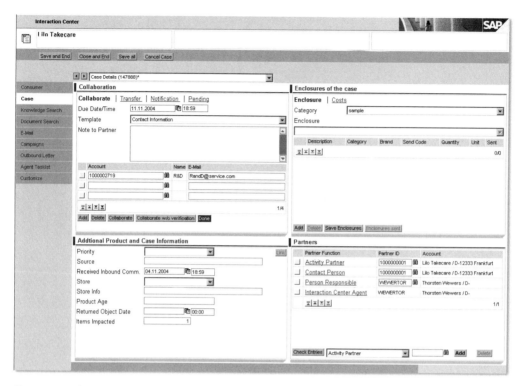

Figure 5.13 Information About Case (2)

5.4.3 Solution Outline

Brand Preference, Marketing Permission and Pet Information

Due to the demand of addressing the consumer personally and suppressing unwanted marketing actions, it was necessary to keep the following consumer-specific data ready in the system:

▶ Brand Preferences

▶ Marketing Permissions

▶ Information about children and pets living in the household

Pets Technically, the pets were stored as individual objects (*iObjects*). To be able to create pets via the user interface, it was necessary to generate individual objects in the background. Marketing permissions and brand preferences are business-partner extensions which were created using Easy Enhancement Workbench or as marketing attributes. To enable IC WebClient to access this extension, the GenIL implementation of the business partner was specially extended. For this purpose, IC WebClient starts the GenIL application ZALL (instead of ALL), which is specified in the framework profile and contains the component ZBP (instead of BP). This GenIL component is implemented by the ZCL_CRM_BUIL class, a subclass of CL_CRM_BUIL in which accordingly extended methods read, maintain, and store the marketing attributes in the database. Listing 5.4 shows example source code.

```
METHOD get_object .
  CONSTANTS: true TYPE crmt_boolean VALUE 'X'.
* Call super method
  cl_buil_header=>get_object( iv_cont_obj =
    iv_cont_obj ).
* Additional header fields
  get_addt_header_fields( iv_cont_obj = iv_cont_obj ).
* Read additional relationships, if necessary
  IF iv_cont_obj->check_rels_requested( ) = true.
*    Marketing attributes
    READ TABLE it_request_objects
      TRANSPORTING NO FIELDS
      WITH KEY object_name =
        zcl_crm_buil=>mktg_info_obj.
    IF sy-subrc = 0.
      get_marketing_info( iv_cont_obj = iv_cont_obj ).
    ENDIF.
*    Brand preferences
    READ TABLE it_request_objects
      TRANSPORTING NO FIELDS
      WITH KEY object_name =
        zcl_crm_buil=>brand_pref_obj.
    IF sy-subrc = 0.
      get_brand_preferences( iv_cont_obj =
        iv_cont_obj ).
    ENDIF.
*    Marketing permissions
    READ TABLE it_request_objects
      TRANSPORTING NO FIELDS
      WITH KEY object_name =
        zcl_crm_buil=>marketing_perm_obj.
    IF sy-subrc = 0.
      get_marketing_permissions( iv_cont_obj =
        iv_cont_obj ).
    ENDIF.
```

```
*    Pets
     get_pets( iv_cont_obj = iv_cont_obj ).
   ENDIF.
ENDMETHOD.

METHOD get_marketing_info .
  INCLUDE z_constants.
  DATA: lr_cont_obj_child TYPE REF TO
          if_genil_container_object,
        lr_cont_obj_list  TYPE REF TO
          if_genil_container_objectlist,
        lv_guid           TYPE crmt_object_guid,
        ls_attr           TYPE st_consmktginf,
        lr_attr_props     TYPE REF TO
          if_genil_obj_attr_properties,
        ls_mktbp_wrk      TYPE crmt_mktbp_wrk,
        lt_return         TYPE STANDARD TABLE OF
          bapiret2,
        ls_charval        LIKE LINE OF
          ls_mktbp_wrk-charvalues,
        ls_key            TYPE lty_mktg_info_key.
  FIELD-SYMBOLS: <field> TYPE ANY.
  CALL METHOD iv_cont_obj->get_key
    IMPORTING
      es_key = lv_guid.
        lr_cont_obj_list = iv_cont_obj->
                     get_relation( iv_relation_name =
                     zcl_crm_buil=>mktg_info_rel
                     iv_as_copy       = abap_true ).
  CHECK lr_cont_obj_list IS BOUND.
  lr_cont_obj_child = lr_cont_obj_list->get_first( ).
  CHECK lr_cont_obj_child IS BOUND.
  CALL FUNCTION 'CRM_MKTBP_READ_OW'
    EXPORTING
      iv_bp_guid              = lv_guid
      iv_profile_template_id =
        gc_gcc_mktbp_profile-consumer
    IMPORTING
      es_mktbp_wrk            = ls_mktbp_wrk
    TABLES
```

```
      et_return                = lt_return.
   CLEAR ls_attr.
   LOOP AT ls_mktbp_wrk-charvalues INTO ls_charval.
     UNASSIGN <field>.
     ASSIGN COMPONENT ls_charval-atname OF STRUCTURE
       ls_attr TO <field>.
     IF <field> IS ASSIGNED.
       <field> = ls_charval-atwrt.
     ENDIF.
   ENDLOOP.
* Set key
   ls_key-guid = lv_guid.
   ls_key-profile = ls_mktbp_wrk-profile_template_id.
   TRY.
     lr_cont_obj_child->set_key( ls_key ).
     CATCH cx_root.
   ENDTRY.
* Set attributes
   ls_attr-bp_guid = lv_guid.
   lr_cont_obj_child->set_attributes( ls_attr ).
   lr_attr_props =
     lr_cont_obj_child->get_attr_props_obj( ).
   CALL METHOD lr_attr_props->set_all_properties
     EXPORTING
       iv_value =
         if_genil_obj_attr_properties=>changeable.
ENDMETHOD.

METHOD maintain_marketing_info .

   INCLUDE z_constants.
   INCLUDE crm_direct.
   DATA: ls_attr      TYPE st_consmktginf,
         ls_mktbp     TYPE crmt_mktbp_wrk,
         lt_name_tab  TYPE crmt_attr_name_tab,
         lr_props_obj TYPE REF TO
           if_genil_obj_attr_properties,
         lt_return    TYPE STANDARD TABLE OF bapiret2,
         ls_object    LIKE LINE OF ct_changed_object,
         lv_guid      TYPE crmt_object_guid,
```

```abap
            ls_atname       TYPE atnam,
            ls_val          LIKE LINE OF ls_mktbp-charvalues,
            ls_key          TYPE lty_mktg_info_key,
            lr_parent       TYPE REF TO
              if_genil_container_object.
      FIELD-SYMBOLS: <field> TYPE ANY,
                     <val>   LIKE LINE OF
                               ls_mktbp-charvalues.
* Get values
    iv_cont_obj->get_attributes( IMPORTING
      es_attributes = ls_attr ).
* Get BP GUID
    lr_parent = iv_cont_obj->get_parent( ).
    CALL METHOD lr_parent->get_key
      IMPORTING
        es_key = lv_guid.
    CALL FUNCTION 'CRM_MKTBP_READ_OW'
      EXPORTING
        iv_bp_guid            = lv_guid
        iv_profile_template_id =
          gc_gcc_mktbp_profile-consumer
      IMPORTING
        es_mktbp_wrk          = ls_mktbp_wrk
      TABLES
        et_return             = lt_return.
* Found something?
    READ TABLE lt_return TRANSPORTING NO FIELDS
      WITH KEY id     = 'CRM_MKTBP'
               number = '012'.
    IF sy-subrc = 0.
*     Record does not exist => Create first
      ls_mktbp-mode = gc_mode-create.
      ls_mktbp-guid = lv_guid.
      ls_mktbp-profile_template_id =
        gc_gcc_mktbp_profile-consumer.
    ELSE.
*     Record exists: Maintain!
      ls_mktbp-mode = gc_mode-change.
    ENDIF.
    lr_props_obj = iv_cont_obj->get_attr_props_obj( ).
```

```
  CALL METHOD lr_props_obj->get_name_tab_4_property
    EXPORTING
      iv_property =
        if_genil_obj_attr_properties=>modified
    IMPORTING
      et_names    = lt_name_tab.
  LOOP AT lt_name_tab INTO ls_atname.
    UNASSIGN <field>.
    ASSIGN COMPONENT ls_atname
      OF STRUCTURE ls_attr
      TO <field>.
    IF <field> IS ASSIGNED.
      READ TABLE ls_mktbp-charvalues ASSIGNING <val>
        WITH KEY atname = ls_atname.
      IF sy-subrc = 0.
*       Field exists in work space
        <val>-atwrt = <field>.
      ELSE.
*       Field does not exist in work space
        ls_val-atname = ls_atname.
        ls_val-atwrt = <field>.
        APPEND ls_val TO ls_mktbp-charvalues.
      ENDIF.
    ENDIF.
  ENDLOOP.
  CALL FUNCTION 'CRM_MKTBP_MAINTAIN_OW'
    EXPORTING
      is_mktbp_wrk = ls_mktbp
    TABLES
      et_return    = lt_return.
  READ TABLE lt_return TRANSPORTING NO FIELDS
    WITH KEY type = 'E'.
  IF sy-subrc <> 0.
*   Set container key
    ls_key-guid = lv_guid.
    ls_key-profile = ls_mktbp-profile_template_id.
    TRY.
        iv_cont_obj->set_key( ls_key ).
      CATCH cx_root.
    ENDTRY.
```

```
*       Attach to table with changed objects
        ls_object-object_id =
          cl_crm_genil_container_tools=>
          build_object_id( ls_key ).
        ls_object-object_name = iv_cont_obj->get_name( ).
        APPEND ls_object TO ct_changed_object.
      ENDIF.
ENDMETHOD.
```

Listing 5.4 GenIL Extensions for the CRM Business Partner (Extracts)

Integration of a Third-Party Solution Database

Consistent responses due to solution database

To ensure that the agent could efficiently support the consumer, it was necessary to integrate the company solution database directly with IC WebClient. The company already deployed a non-SAP solution database, and for organizational reasons it was not possible at the time of the project to migrate to the SAP solution database.

COM4ABAP and SAP .NET Connector

The third-party solution database only provided a COM component and therefore needed to be integrated via the COM4ABAP interface. In future projects, this interface can be replaced with the SAP .NET Connector, the successor of COM4ABAP.

In the solution, only the *interaction record* is transferred to the third-party software. The mapping of this number (*IncidentID*) to corresponding solutions takes place entirely within the solution database. At a later stage, the mapped solutions can be transferred to the CRM system at any time for further processing, for example for letter/email outbound. On the client side, the tool is integrated as a URL using its web interface. Because of its consequent Web architecture, this is the strong point of IC WebClient with regard to the integration of third-party applications (see Figure 5.14).

Outbound Templates for Emails and Letters

Standardized but individual responses

Templates offer one method of providing the consumer with standardized but still individual responses. Enhanced with interaction-specific details such as concrete solutions, they often form the basis and the conclusion of an interaction with a consumer. Additionally, they make the agents' work more efficient.

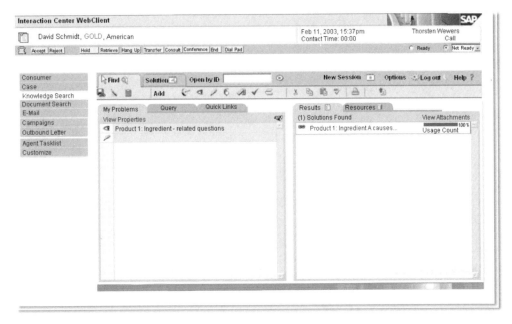

Figure 5.14 Third-Party Solution Database

In this case, email templates or parts of a response email such as the salutation, as well as Microsoft Word templates were implemented. In order to ensure a permanent extensibility of the system, these templates can be customized. In the case of email templates, this is done through SAP standard texts. Additionally, there is a project-specific customizing that includes the maintenance of Microsoft Word templates (path specifications), where the templates themselves are stored on a server.

All templates can contain any number of placeholders (variables) in the form of xPaths (see Figure 5.15, Figure 5.16, and Listing 5.5) which are replaced with the specific interaction data at runtime. For maintaining the placeholders, there is a project-specific customizing as well. The Microsoft Word templates are completed via client-side JavaScript. Another requirement was the implementation of spell-checking for outbound emails. This was accomplished via client-side JavaScript, which in turn uses the Microsoft Office spell check.

Variable replacement in the text

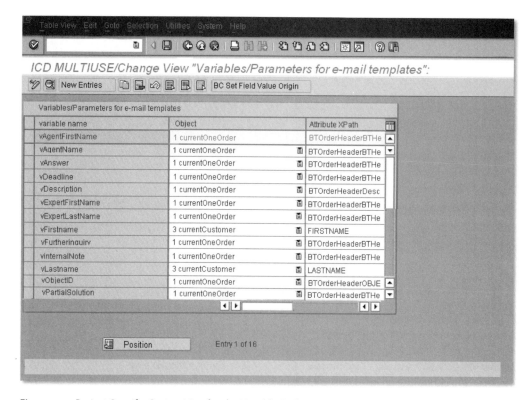

Figure 5.15 Project-Specific Customizing for the Variable Definition

variable name			AgentFirstName	
Variables/Parameters for e-mail templates				
Object		1 currentOneOrder		
Attribute XPath		BTOrderheaderBTHeaderPartnerSet/BTPartner_ICAGENT/BuisnessPartnerF_		
Text Table				
Key Field				
Value Field				
Language Field				

Figure 5.16 Definition of a Variable

```
LOOP AT lt_outbound_par INTO ls_outbound_par.
  CLEAR ls_parameters.
  lv_par_xpath = ls_outbound_par-attribute_xpath.
  ls_parameters-name = ls_outbound_par-parameter_name.
  TRY.
      ls_parameters-value =
        ir_cucobdc->get_xpath_property_as_string(
          iv_xpath = lv_par_xpath ).
```

```
      CATCH cx_crm_bdc_xpath_error
            cx_crm_bdc_no_data
            cx_root.
    ENDTRY.
    IF ls_parameters-value IS NOT INITIAL.
      IF ls_outbound_par-text_table
        IS NOT INITIAL AND
        ls_outbound_par-text_tab_keyfld
        IS NOT INITIAL AND
        ls_outbound_par-text_tab_valfld IS NOT INITIAL.
      CONCATENATE ls_outbound_par-text_tab_keyfld
        ' = ''' ls_parameters-value ''''
        INTO where_clause.

      IF ls_outbound_par-text_tab_langfld
         IS NOT INITIAL.
        CONCATENATE where_clause ' AND '
          INTO where_clause SEPARATED BY space.
        CONCATENATE where_clause
          ls_outbound_par-text_tab_langfld
            INTO where_clause SEPARATED BY space.
        CONCATENATE where_clause ' = ''' sy-langu ''''
          INTO where_clause.
      ENDIF.

        SELECT SINGLE (ls_outbound_par-text_tab_valfld)
          FROM (ls_outbound_par-text_table)
          INTO lv_param_new
          WHERE (where_clause).

        IF sy-subrc = 0.
          ls_parameters-value = lv_param_new.
        ELSE.
          ls_parameters-value = ' '.
        ENDIF.
      ENDIF.
      APPEND ls_parameters TO et_parameters.
    ELSE.
      APPEND ls_parameters TO et_parameters.
    ENDIF.
ENDLOOP.
```

Listing 5.5 Replacement of a Variable at Runtime

5.4.4 Benefits of the Project Implementation

Process unification
The customer's approach was to unify the *consumer-care* process throughout the corporate group and worldwide. For this purpose, a worldwide applicable process was defined with the international subsidiaries. The solution first went live in Germany and was then rolled out gradually. The objective of a harmonized consumer care process has thus been achieved.

Consistent information for consumers
With the knowledge database described, all users of the system can be provided with the same information, so that the consumer receives a consistent picture of the company. The database can even account for local characteristics and translations.

Integration of non-CRM users
For the first time, the implemented process now allows for the full integration of non-employees, like veterinarians, via the email functions described.

Data collection for marketing campaigns
One critical benefit of the solution is that information is collected during consumer-care processes, provided that the consumer agrees to the data collection. This information offers marketing advantages because the marketing permissions and brand preferences play significant roles in the creation of target groups for marketing campaigns. This means, in effect, that after-sales activity generates important input for the sales process, and thus improves sales.

5.5 Employee Interaction Center Based on IC WinClient

5.5.1 Customer and Problem

Business Process Outsourcing
When transferring business transactions to a service provider, it is crucial that the communication between the provider and its customers be efficient and timely. For this reason, a Norwegian company specializing in HR outsourcing was looking for an application with which it could build an employee interaction center that would optimally support communication with customers and enable quick access to all data needed to process customer requests.

5.5.2 Project Description

Application management through the customer
Because of its own high level of SAP expertise, the company in September 2003 decided in favor of mySAP CRM, specifically IC WinClient Release 3.1. A crucial element in this choice was the company's decision

that system support would remain in its hands once implementation was successful. Meeting this condition is simplified by having a homogeneous SAP system landscape.

Another reason for implementing mySAP CRM was the simple integration with SAP R/3, given that the employee data was already available in that system. However, there was one challenge to overcome: For most customers, a separate client was used in the backend, but all customer requests were to be processed in a single SAP CRM client. This scenario had never been implemented up to that point.

Integration with SAP R/3

There were other criteria against which mySAP CRM could score. For example, it was a benefit of mySAP CRM Interaction Center that emails can be received and immediately forwarded to the relevant agents, an important functionality in this case, since most of the customer requests are sent to the company via email. At the same time, requests coming in via telephone could be processed in the same user interface.

Important channel: email

5.5.3 Solution Outline

The central object for processing customer messages is the *service request*. Although a service request can be submitted per email or telephone, it is usually answered via email. The requests apply to all HR aspects and can range from address changes over payroll-related questions to the demand for the development of a new settlement variant. Support requests can be created by customer employees as well as from in-house employees.

From change of address to the payroll

Comprehensive – but Still Compact

During the first days of the implementation phase, it already became clear that mySAP CRM Interaction Center was the adequate application. One of the requirements was that all support employees should use the same interface, irrespective of their individual field of application, either front office or back office. The interface should be easy to use in order to keep the training and familiarization phases short, but at the same time it should be able to provide all desired functions.

Simple operation

Also crucial in deploying mySAP CRM Interaction Center was that all support employees should always have access to all information relevant to a support request. This included in particular all inbound and outbound emails and all internal documents created in the course of processing requests. These can, in fact, be displayed directly from the support request.

Integration of all information in one interface

Automatic linking of emails to support requests

Inbound emails are directed by the CRM system to those support employees who are familiar with the transactions of the respective customer. The emails are processed in the agent inbox, and the system detects automatically if the email is a response to an existing support request or if a new request needs to be created. Likewise, email attachments are stored directly in the content management of the service request.

Integration of multiple backends

The data of customer employees who are looked after by the medium-sized Norwegian company is available in SAP R/3 HR, where a separate client is used for every customer. This is necessary because the same employee number is used with several customers and is partially provided by external proprietary systems. In order to use this data in SAP CRM, the interface provided by the SAP standard system for integrating HR data was extended to include support for multiple backends. This could be achieved with minimum effort, and the HR employee data of the various clients is all available in one single client of the CRM system. It is even possible to determine the employee data using the employee number. Meanwhile, the SAP standard system supports multiple backends as well (see Figure 5.17). In the SAP Employee Interaction Center, there is also the possibility of using several CRM clients for storing employee data of different companies and accessing it via the client switch functionality (see Section 2.2.2).

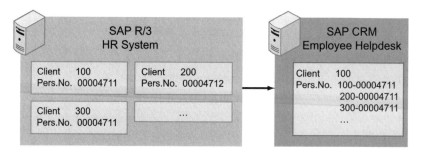

Figure 5.17 Integration of Multiple Back-End HR Systems Under SAP CRM 3.1

Worklist

However, one drawback of mySAP CRM Interaction Center became obvious fairly quickly: an inadequate ability to search for and retrieve a previously processed request using multiple criteria, especially when the customer or employee was not yet known at the time of the search. For this very important functionality, a new workspace was developed that enables searching for multiple criteria in a worklist.

As in all service areas, timely processing is critical for the success of HR processes. To ensure that the times negotiated with the customers in the *Service Level Agreements* are observed, the SAP Business Workflow is used to notify the employees before reaching the time limit. These time limits can be maintained for each customer and are dependent on the priority of the support request.

Service Level Agreements

Quick Access to Data

Besides the actual service, an appropriate reporting system is crucial for the acceptance and the success of an application. Typically, SAP BW is used for this purpose in SAP projects, but this was not planned for the first implementation phase. Instead, a simple reporting method was implemented directly in mySAP CRM, allowing for quick access to the most important information. Thus, the various departments can always get an overview of the pending and completed tasks, for example, or add staff to those areas with the highest demand. At the same time, it is possible to check regularly whether the times are observed in accordance with the service level agreements.

Reporting

5.5.4 Benefits of the Project Implementation

To the extent described so far, the solution went online at the beginning of March 2004 after a project timeframe of only three months. The company first started with few customers so that the service employees could gain experience in using mySAP CRM Interaction Center. Because the solution turned out to be very successful and robust, the operation was extended to all customers. No difficulties have occurred since then.

Three months project duration only

The efficient cooperation between the employees of the project team was a significant factor in minimizing the implementation time. Concurrently, the company was able to operate the SAP CRM system independently. Presently, the user company intends to migrate to IC WebClient to be able to access extended functions like the Case Management or the service-ticket scenario.

Transferring the knowledge to the customer

This project proved anew that mySAP CRM is suitable for midsized companies. The implementation effort can be kept low if the desired functionalities and results are defined at an early stage. Also decisive for the success of the project was the makeup of the project team, consisting of external consultants as well as those in-house employees who should technically and effectively maintain the CRM system. The required expertise could be built up at an early stage so that a largely independent system operation already would be possible during the piloting phase.

5.6 Sales Advisory Services for Supporting the Sales Process

5.6.1 Customer and Problem

Supporting the sales process

The following example refers to an implementation project in a large software company. The entrepreneurial focus of the corporate group is to develop and globally sell standard software for companies. To fulfill objectives such as increasing market shares in the sector of medium-sized companies, the corporate group not only focuses on development innovations but also on a continuous improvement of the sales processes. To this end, there is an in-house *support line* for questions from the sales employees regarding their sales activities. The intention of this support is to provide a contact point for quickly and effectively collecting detailed information.

Research

In general, in the course of a sales process there is a basic need for information closely related to the current negotiations with the customer or prospect. Sales employees must be able to quickly find the information they need or want. The availability of this information is of vital importance in convincing the customer to move forward with the deal.

The quality of the information can vary markedly: It can be very detailed knowledge about the own products, or it could be comparisons with corresponding competitive products, or it could be details about corporate policies. Would you go with a provider who implements a product for the first time in your industry? Or, would you prefer the competitor who can prove some experience in your industry? In short: A successful sales activity can significantly depend on the knowledge of the negotiating partner.

5.6.2 Project Description

Replacement of various legacy applications

Because of the fast-increasing number of people using this support option and the growing process complexity for support employees, process restructuring and IT support became necessary in order to ensure efficiency. The previous solution was a conglomerate of different applications, for example Microsoft Excel, Microsoft Access, and an HTML entry form on the company intranet. The decision to replace this solution with mySAP CRM Interaction Center (Release 4.0) was easy. For one thing, all processes existing so far can be integrated into one single application. For another, mySAP CRM had already been used for customer management and SAP Business Information Warehouse had been implemented for analyzing business transactions.

The central object of this process is the request for information, the *call* of a sales employee. This should always be transferred via email, via entry form on the intranet, or per telephone. After receiving the call, the sales support employees start their processing activities. They all should employ the same user-friendly interface, irrespective of their individual task area. If the support employees cannot respond to the call with the information available to them, it will be transferred to employees in the relevant user departments. A crucial criterion in this context was that the functionality would be very restricted for employees from the user departments. They were to work with the same interface as the support employees. They were to see all the information about the call but process it only in specific restricted areas. Finally, the call was to be revised by sales support employees, and the gathered information sent back to the inquiring sales employee. Parallel to this process, the answered questions should be collected in a database and provided via the intranet and the interaction center to the inquiring employees, as well as to the employees of the sales support and the user departments for information research.

Multilevel support process

The basic requirement for achieving a smooth flow for this process is a well-defined restriction of the request to specific subjects and specialist areas. This restriction is effected by means of a classification of the request according to specific criteria. If the request is classified, the sales-support employee can use this classification to obtain needed data or at least identify the user department that dispenses that data. This prerequisite leads to another interaction center requirement: In an administrative interface, it must be possible to create and maintain the available classification characteristics as well as a database with the user-department employees related to this classification.

Call classification

5.6.3 Solution Outline

First, the decision needed to be made in which form the previously implemented entry form on the intranet can be integrated in IC Web-Client. There were two obvious concepts: First, creation of a separate user profile for the role of the inquirers in IC WebClient; second, an independent BSP application built in SAP CRM. The second option was eventually chosen (see Figure 5.18).

Call entered by the sales employee

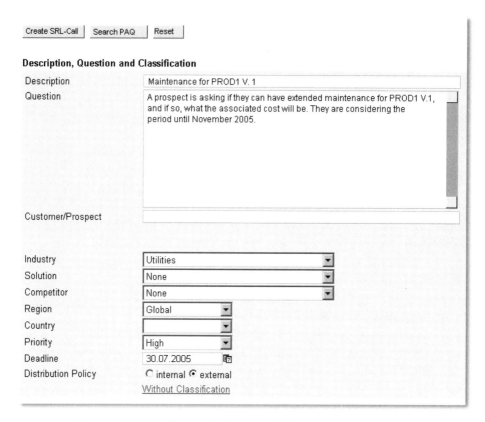

Figure 5.18 BSP Application for Entering a Call

This procedure has several advantages: A crucial one is the performance. For a simple entry form, the inquirer does not need to start up the entire IC WebClient including its framework. Another advantage was that the layout of this entry form was not bound to the overall layout of IC Web-Client. Thus, a form similar to the one previously used was implemented, and, as a result, the inquirer does not need to adapt himself to a completely new form. The essential difference compared to the previous implementation is that all data transferred to the form now already exists in the CRM system and that a CRM business transaction of the transaction type used in IC WebClient is created immediately when the form is sent. This business transaction is exactly the same as an incoming information request in IC WebClient—the call.

Based on the knowledge about the Business Object Layer (BOL), the most obvious solution is to create the transaction in the BSP application using BOL functions. This can be achieved, for example, with the source code shown in Listing 5.6.

```
*  1. Create BOL instance
   lr_core = cl_crm_bol_core=>get_instance( ).
   TRY.
        lr_core->start_up( 'ALL' ).
      CATCH cx_crm_genil_general_error.
   ENDTRY.
*  2. Create transaction context
   lr_transaction = lr_core->begin_transaction( ).
*  3. Get factory for 'BTOrder'
   lv_factory =
      lr_core->get_entity_factory( 'BTOrder' ).

*  4. Set parameter
   ls_params-name = 'PROCESS_TYPE'.
   ls_params-value = gc_srl_process_
type. " Transaction type
   APPEND ls_params TO lt_params.
*  5. Create BTOrder
   lr_order = lv_factory->create( lt_params ).
   ...
*  6. Send all changes to BO layer
   lr_core->modify( ).
*  7. Get transaction
   lr_transaction = lr_core->get_transaction( ).
*  8. Save and commit work
   lv_save_success = lr_transaction->save( ).
   IF lv_save_success = abap_true.
      lr_transaction->commit( ).
   ENDIF.
```

Listing 5.6 Creating a CRM Business Transaction Using BOL Functions

At first, an instance of the data model is generated, and in the next step an entity of the relevant type is created within the data model. Then, you are able to set various data in the BTOrder object (not shown here). As the last step, the created entity is saved and the CRM business transaction is created. After this procedure, the call is immediately displayed in the worklist (agent inbox) of the sales support employees (agents) and contains all data entered, as well as all business partner information available in the CRM system that refers to the inquirer.

Integration in the worklist

The BSP application thus created can smoothly be integrated in the company intranet via a URL. Although the existing process structure was maintained, the functionality of the entry form was significantly increased. For example, a solution-database search was integrated in this process. In the new support line process, a call can only be initiated if the solution database has been searched. Considering that this solution database is continuously growing because the majority of answered questions are continuously added, it is possible to forecast a workload reduction for the agents.

As already mentioned, one of the decisive points in the entire process is a suitable classification of the desired information. The presented BSP application for entering the call already provides a classification option using three main criteria. As a general rule, however, the inquirers do not use this classification option to its full extent. Therefore, the majority of the work needs to be done by the agents. For the technical implementation, we first had to find out how many different classification criteria are necessary in order to support the work process of the agents. At the same time, we had to bear in mind that the employees from the user departments (experts) also had to be integrated in this classification schema. We had to consider that the classification possibilities are much finer for experts than those for a call, given that the specialized knowledge of an expert can be defined much more exactly than the subject of an information request.

This called for a classification structure with multiple levels and dependencies. Depending on the entry selected at the top classification level, only specific characteristics could be selected at the subordinate classification level. The standard functions of SAP CRM Release 4.0 do not provide the option of a dependent classification. This function, the *Category Modeler,* was introduced in the standard version with mySAP CRM Edition 2004. The example of the classification is still discussed here because it also allows for non-hierarchical structures, which are always required by the Category Modeler up to mySAP CRM 2004 Edition.

The individual classification levels and their characteristics can be maintained in the Customizing of SAP CRM under **Catalogs, Code groups and Codes** (see Figure 5.19). In the project described, several code groups were created in a catalog, and these corresponded to the various classification levels. The possible characteristics of a level were defined as code within the code group. Thus, a multilevel classification system could be created easily by establishing relationships between the different code groups. This is the same approach taken by the Category Modeler. Knowing up front about its design-to-be helped us in our own design decision.

Dialog Structure		Catalog	A1			
▽ ☐ Code groups		Code Group	YSIND			
☐ Codes		Catalog Text	Activities: Reason			
		Short text	SAS: Industry			

Codes

Co...	Descript.	U	Created By	On
Z002	Automotive	☑		30.11.2004
Z003	Banking	☑		30.11.2004
Z004	Chemicals	☑		30.11.2004
Z005	Consumer Products	☑		30.11.2004
Z006	Defense & Security	☑		30.11.2004
Z007	Engineering, Construction & Operations	☐		30.11.2004
Z008	Financial Service Providers	☑		30.11.2004
Z009	Healthcare	☐		30.11.2004
Z010	High Tech	☑		30.11.2004
Z011	Higher Education & Research	☐		30.11.2004
Z012	Industrial Machinery & Components	☑		30.11.2004
Z013	Insurance	☑		30.11.2004
Z014	Life Sciences	☑		30.11.2004
Z015	Logistic Service Providers	☐		30.11.2004
Z016	Media	☐		30.11.2004
Z017	Mill Products	☑		30.11.2004
Z018	Mining	☐		30.11.2004
Z019	None	☑		30.11.2004
Z020	Oil & Gas	☐		30.11.2004
Z021	Pharmaceuticals	☑		30.11.2004
Z022	Postal Services	☑		30.11.2004
Z023	Professional Services	☐		30.11.2004
Z024	Public Sector	☐		30.11.2004
Z025	Railways	☐		30.11.2004
Z026	Retail	☐		30.11.2004
Z027	Service Providers	☑		30.11.2004
Z028	Telecommunication	☑		30.11.2004

Figure 5.19 Customizing View for Maintaining the Code Groups of a Specific Catalog

For implementing the dependencies among the individual levels, a table of the parent-child relationships was created. This table contains the information about the possible characteristics of the classification level dependent on the selected characteristic of the superior classification level. In IC WebClient, the different classification levels are rendered in the form of dropdown listboxes. In the case of dependent classification levels, only the dropdown listbox of the highest level is enabled at first, and one of the characteristics can be selected. As soon as the user has specified this characteristic, the next dropdown listbox is populated with entries according to the parent-child relationship table and is then activated.

Listing 5.7 presents a possible implementation in the layout.

```
<%  IF controller->gt_product IS NOT INITIAL.
        lv_dd_product_disabled = 'FALSE'.
    ENDIF. %>
<crmic:gridLayoutCell columnIndex="2" rowIndex="1"
<crmic:dropdownListBox
            id    = "dd_solution"
            width = "100%"
            table = "<%=controller->gt_solution %>"
            nameOfKeyColumn = "CONC_KEY"
            nameOfValueColumn = "CODE_DESCR"
            selection = "//Classification/Solution"
            onSelect = "dummy" />
</crmic:gridLayoutCell>
<crmic:gridLayoutCell columnIndex="2" rowIndex="2"
<crmic:dropdownListBox
      id    = "dd_product"
      width = "100%"
      table = "<%=controller->gt_product %>"
      nameOfKeyColumn = "CONC_KEY"
      nameOfValueColumn = "CODE_DESCR"
      selection="//Classification/Product"
      disabled ="<%=lv_dd_product_disabled%>" />
</crmic:gridLayoutCell>
```

Listing 5.7 Layout With Dropdown Boxes for Classification

When selecting the top dropdown box, the DUMMY event is triggered, which only causes a server roundtrip. This refreshes the active view. Figure 5.20 shows an example with activated and deactivated dropdown boxes: The dropdown box **I-Type** is populated dynamically depending on the choice of **Main-I-Type**. The same applies to the **Product** dropdown box. This box is still deactivated because no entry has been selected in the **Solution** dropdown box.

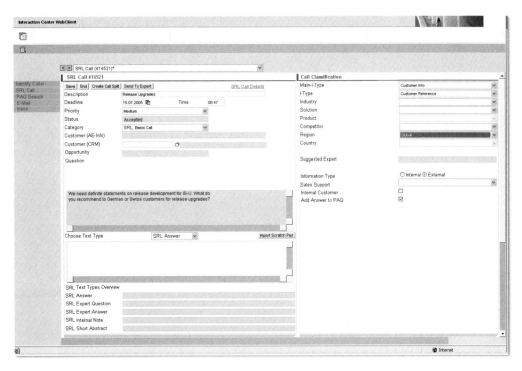

Figure 5.20 Call Classification

The corresponding method of the controller class checks whether the user has selected a value of the upper dropdown box. Accordingly, the possible characteristics are read into the table underlying the second dropdown box, which is then activated in the view (see Listing 5.8).

```
lv_code_val =
  typed_context->subjectsetf->get_classification_code(
    attribute_path = 'Solution'
    codegroup = gc_srl_codegrp-solution ).
IF lv_code_val IS NOT INITIAL.
  lv_code = lv_code_val.
  gt_product =
    zcl_crm_ic_srl_service=>get_codes_for_codegrp(
      iv_parentcodegroup = gc_srl_codegrp-solution
      iv_parentcode      = lv_code
      iv_childcodegroup  = gc_srl_codegrp-product ).
ENDIF.
```

Listing 5.8 Event Handler for the Selection from a Dropdown Box

The called method reads the code and code groups from Customizing and filters the results using the parent-child relationship entries of its own table (see Listing 5.9).

```
. . .
CALL FUNCTION 'CRM_GET_CODES_FROM_CODEGROUP'
  EXPORTING
    iv_catalog   = lv_catalog
    iv_codegroup = iv_childcodegroup
  IMPORTING
    et_codes     = rt_codes.

IF iv_parentcodegroup IS INITIAL
  OR iv_parentcode IS INITIAL.
    EXIT.
ENDIF.

APPEND '(''I'')' TO ftab.
APPEND '(''EQ'')' TO ftab.
APPEND 'childcode' TO ftab.
ls_codes_rng-sign = 'I'.
ls_codes_rng-option = 'EQ'.

SELECT childcode AS low
       INTO CORRESPONDING FIELDS OF ls_codes_rng
       FROM zsrl_classify
       WHERE parentcodegroup = iv_parentcodegroup
       AND parentcode = iv_parentcode.
  APPEND ls_codes_rng TO lt_codes_rng.
ENDSELECT.

DELETE rt_codes WHERE code_id NOT IN lt_codes_rng.
. . .
```

Listing 5.9 Read the Code of a Level in Dependency of the Code Selected at the Superior Level

Expert selection using call classification

In the case of calls, this results in a classification with as many as two levels. The same principle was applied to the selection of possible experts, with the difference that an expert can be classified using up to four levels in certain areas.

It would have been possible to send the entire classification to the client when the page is first built in order to implement the dependencies of the dropdown listboxes using JavaScript, but the effort seemed too great because the project had already planned migrating to mySAP CRM Edition 2004, where such a functionality is available in the standard version.

In this context, the required maintenance interfaces can easily be integrated due to the great flexibility of IC WebClient. To this end, a separate IC WebClient user profile was first created. This restricts the number of users who can access the maintenance interfaces. This IC WebClient profile contains the required maintenance views as new links in the navigation bar. Depending on the scope of data to be processed, these new views and view sets can be bound to the data model of IC WebClient via context and context-node classes, or the data processing is carried out directly using suitable methods and function modules in the controller class. The example shows a maintenance interface for experts and the associated classification characteristics (see Figure 5.21).

Maintenance of the classification model also in IC WebClient

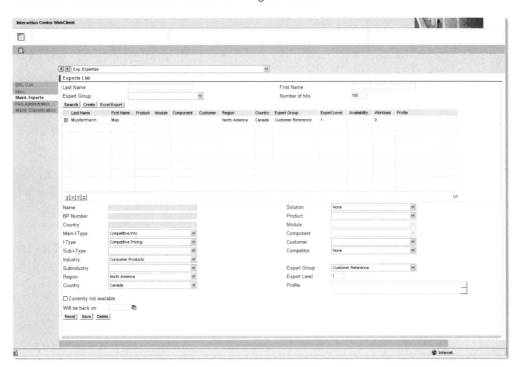

Figure 5.21 View for Maintaining the Expert Table

5.6.4 Benefits of the Project Implementation

Data integration in the CRM system

If you compare the solution implemented in IC WebClient to the solution used previously, you can immediately find many advantages: The crucial benefit is that in IC WebClient all processes necessary for completely processing a call can be run in the same interface. In this regard, it should be mentioned that today all data are available in the CRM system. The solution used beforehand was based on different applications installed on different application servers, and at the same time demanded locally installed applications. IC WebClient, however, can be used on every computer with an installation of Microsoft Internet Explorer. Additionally, CTI was introduced in order to further automate telephony processes.

Unification of the classification

Another benefit is the consolidation of the used classification. The fact that all used classification characteristics are stored and maintained in IC WebClient in a central place makes the system considerably less error-prone. The work process carried out beforehand allows a different classification of call and expert. Even provided that the response quality is not affected, the informational value in the subsequent analysis of the process data will be limited. Especially with regard to the analysis, another benefit is that all data are transported via one interface only: from the SAP CRM to the SAP BW system. Therefore, complex loading processes from several systems, format conversions and mapping processes among the data are avoided. It is worth mentioning that substantial data related to employees, customers, and business opportunities naturally exists in CRM and is thus ready for analysis together with the process data.

The positive experience with IC WebClient in the company led to the result that meanwhile IC WebClient is also introduced in the externally operated call centers of product marketing.

5.7 Integration of a Third-Party Telephony Bar in IC WinClient

5.7.1 Customer and Problem

Large interaction volume

In this example, the customer is a large logistics service company. For communicating with its customers, the company operates several interaction centers located in five different sites that employ about 400 agents altogether. These process about six million interactions per year (24,000 per day), five million of which come in per telephone, the rest being emails and faxes.

5.7.2 Project Description

The main objective of the overall project was to significantly increase the efficiency of the company. SAP software was to be introduced in almost all areas to replace and unify the previous conglomeration of different legacy systems. For this purpose, SAP CRM, SAP BW, and various R/3 modules like FI, CO, or HR were implemented. The overall project was and still is carried out by the in-house IT department of the company as well as several external consultants.

SAP software for almost all company areas

For the CRM area, the intention was to simplify and optimize the processing of customer requests while maintaining the implementation of the previous contact-center solution. That solution already had proved its worth when processing the large number of inbound interactions.

Thus, one of the central requirements was the integration of the established contact-center solution in IC WinClient in order to unite both applications in one interface and enable the interaction between them (see Figure 5.22). At the same time, the solution integrates the SAP Business Workflow for receiving emails and faxes on the CRM server with the routing capabilities of the contact-center software.

Integration of the existing contact-center solution in IC WinClient

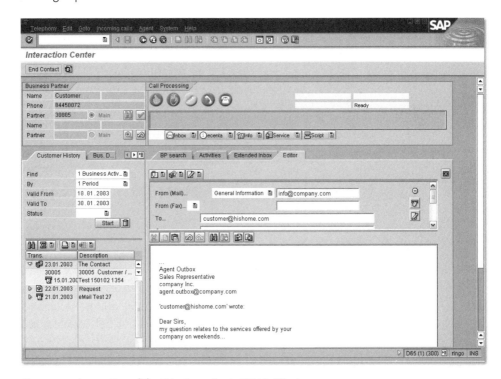

Figure 5.22 Integration of the Telephony Bar in IC WinClient

Push mode also for email and fax via client-side integration

For this integration, the developer of the contact-center solution created an ActiveX component of its client application within the project, containing all control elements for controlling the application. This ActiveX component could now be completely integrated as a new element in the interaction center interface, and thus telephone interactions could be processed directly in the CRM just like emails or faxes. The distribution of inbound emails or faxes to a call-center agent is carried out in the same way as with inbound phone calls (push mode). Should the routing server be down, inbound emails and faxes are automatically placed in the agent inbox of IC WinClient.

5.7.3 Solution Outline

The integration consists of two parts: On the client side, the new interface component is integrated; on the server side, inbound emails and faxes are transferred to the server of the contact-center solution which then carries out the queuing and routing to the agents (see Figure 5.23).

Client-side integration of a CTI software

For integrating a new visible component in IC WinClient, a function group is required in which the subscreen to contain the ActiveX component is defined. Additionally, this is where its creation and the initialization of the objects takes place (see Listing 5.10). In customizing, this function group can be defined as customer-specific component to be used in the IC framework.

```
MODULE init_0100 OUTPUT.
  IF gv_container_actx IS INITIAL.
    CREATE OBJECT gv_container_actx
      EXPORTING container_name = 'ACTIVEX'.
    CREATE OBJECT gv_control_actx
      EXPORTING parent = gv_container_actx.
    CALL METHOD gv_control_actx->initialize
      EXCEPTIONS
        OTHERS = 1.
    IF sy-subrc <> 0.
      MESSAGE e010(zcrm_mcc).
    ENDIF.
  ENDIF.
ENDMODULE.                    " init_0100  OUTPUT
```

Listing 5.10 Integration of the ActiveX Component

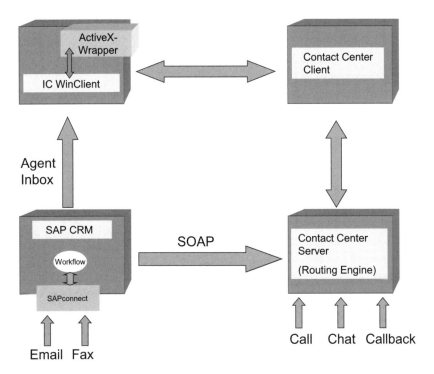

Figure 5.23 Architecture of the Integrated Solution

For the ActiveX component itself, a wrapper class is required, and this— **Like an SAP Enjoy** like the SAP screen elements—is derived from the CL_GUI_CONTROL **Control** class. The procedure does not differ from the integration of SAP Enjoy Controls. Via the *Windows ProgID*, the object is created in the constructor of the class; then, the events are to be registered (see Listing 5.11). Appropriate handling methods for different events are also defined in the class.

```
METHOD register_events .
  DATA: event TYPE cntl_simple_event.
  event-appl_event = 'X'.
* Check handle
  IF h_control IS INITIAL.
    RAISE cntl_error.
  ENDIF.
* Register for event 'new_contact'
  event-eventid = event_new_contact.
  CALL METHOD control_register_event
    EXPORTING
```

```
      event                          = event
        EXCEPTIONS
          event_already_registered = 1
          error_event_control      = 2.
      IF sy-subrc <> 0.
        RAISE error_regist_event.
      ENDIF.
      SET HANDLER on_new_contact ACTIVATION 'X'.
    ...
    ENDMETHOD.
```

Listing 5.11 Method of the Wrapper Class for Registering the Event

Handling client events At runtime, the DISPATCH method is called for all registered events, in which parameters of the event, if any, can be retrieved. Thus, the ActiveX component can transfer data to the CRM system (see Listing 5.12).

```
METHOD dispatch .
  CASE eventid.
* Process event 'new_contact'
    WHEN event_new_contact.
      DATA lv_newinfo TYPE string.
      CALL METHOD get_event_parameter
        EXPORTING
          queue_only   = ' '
          parameter_id = 0
        IMPORTING
          parameter    = lv_newinfo.
      RAISE EVENT new_contact
        EXPORTING info = lv_newinfo.
  ...
ENDMETHOD.
```

Listing 5.12 Method of Wrapper Class for Distributing the Event

Hidden component For the event-handling in the interaction center, a hidden customer-specific component was implemented, which was also defined in customizing and then used in the interaction-center framework. Every inbound interaction contains additional information, in other words *call-attached data*, which triggers further processing.

Automatic search for business partners Business partners are searched automatically and may be confirmed, emails or faxes are displayed, and the corresponding business transaction created beforehand is automatically opened for processing. It is even possible to transfer inbound phone calls to a second employee, including the correct transfer of the created business transaction. Listing 5.13 shows a part of the event-handler method of the hidden component.

In contrast to the SAP standard solution, the push principle, which is usually only used in telephony, was implemented also for emails and faxes.

Push mode also for email and fax

```
METHOD if_ccm_cmpwsp_cic_ev_handler~handle_event .
  CASE event.
    WHEN 'MCC_INCOMING_CAD'.
* Read Call-attached data
* Event parameters:
* P1--medium
* P2--number (ANI)
* P3--ticket number (CRM process)
* P4--GUID (CRM process)
* Try first to find the BP using the ticket number
* If the GUID is initial, try using telephone number

* Save GUID
      lv_guid = p4.
      CALL METHOD me->set_guid
        EXPORTING
          iv_guid = lv_guid.
* Save ticket number
      lv_ticket_no = p3.
      CALL METHOD me->set_ticket_number
        EXPORTING
          iv_ticket_no = lv_ticket_no.
      IF lv_guid IS NOT INITIAL
         OR lv_ticket_no IS NOT INITIAL.
* BP search
        CALL METHOD me->execute_1o_document.
        IF media_type = co_media_bo_task.
* Read category of activity header
          lz_guid = lv_guid.
          INSERT lz_guid INTO TABLE lt_guid
          CALL FUNCTION 'CRM_ORDER_READ'
            EXPORTING
              it_header_guid       = lt_guid
            IMPORTING
```

```
                    et_activity_h          = lt_activity_h
                EXCEPTIONS
                    OTHERS                 = 1.
                READ TABLE lt_activity_h
                INTO lv_activity_h INDEX 1.

* Open email/fax (back office) ...
                IF lc_email_edit IS INITIAL OR
                    ls_global_set-comm_type <> 'INT'.
*   ... in new window (and then also in editor)
                    CALL METHOD me->open_email_viewer.
                    CALL METHOD me->open_email_editor.
                ELSE.
*   ... in extended editor
                    CALL METHOD me->open_email_editor.
                ENDIF.
            ENDIF.
        ELSE.

* Tel. no. (ANI)
            lv_remote_no = p2.
            IF lv_remote_no IS NOT INITIAL.
              CALL METHOD me->set_remote_number
                EXPORTING
                    iv_remote_no = lv_remote_no.
* Search BP per ANI
                CALL METHOD me->do_bpsearch_via_ani
                    EXPORTING
                        iv_remote_no = lv_remote_no.
            ENDIF.
        ENDIF.
  ...
    ENDCASE.
ENDMETHOD.
```

Listing 5.13 Event Handler Method of the Hidden Component

Agent inbox For the server-side integration of inbound emails and faxes, the standard workflow of the inbound communication was extended. Instead of providing work items in the agent inbox, the ID of the created business transaction (ticket number) is transferred to the routing server. For this purpose, special RFC functions were provided which can address the server via SOAP (*Simple Object Access Protocol*). Thus, the emails and faxes coming into the CRM system are placed into the routing server queue which can distribute them in the call center just like it does with inbound phone calls (*universal queue*).

5.7.4 Benefits of the Project Implementation

This project succeeded in combining the well-established telephony solution, including its powerful routing functionality, with the interaction center. In this context, the seamless integration in the business transaction workspace and the automatic business-partner search and confirmation are worthy of special mention.

Seamless integration in the business transaction workspace

The call center employees only have one interface for all interaction channels and at the same time can use all benefits of the CRM system, which simplifies their work considerably and was widely accepted thanks to the intuitive user interface.

One interface for all interaction channels

It should be pointed out that the previously described integration of a telephony bar in IC WinClient can also be carried out for IC WebClient in a slightly modified way. In this case, the integration is performed, for example, using a Java applet that interacts with the IC WebClient views per JavaScript and thus triggers server roundtrips and other actions. Such an integration already has been carried out in a project.

Procedure also suitable for IC WebClient

6 Summary and Future Outlook

The extension options and project examples described in this book show that mySAP CRM Interaction Center enables you to flexibly implement specific demands on business software and at the same time benefit from the standard SAP functionality.

Even in standard Customizing, a multitude of customizations of the standard business scenarios and transactions described in Chapter 2 can be carried out based on the mySAP CRM Interaction Center concept, also discussed in that chapter. This was illustrated in Chapter 3, when we presented technical principles for the areas, framework, basic functions, process and master data integration, integration of communication channels, and supporting functions of IC WinClient and IC WebClient—as well as for the processes of Interaction Center Management.

Additional customization and extension options come into play, provided by the open architecture of mySAP CRM Interaction Center and the underlying integration and technology platform, SAP NetWeaver. Selected customization and extension options were discussed in detail in Chapter 4. Besides a technical presentation of customization and extension options, it is helpful to place them in a business context using real-life sample projects. Chapter 5 contained descriptions of selected sample projects.

Open architecture

All projects presented stand out because they use standard functionality extensively and in specific ways use the potential provided by the extension concept of mySAP CRM Interaction Center. At the same time, they are good examples of successful project work because—using an appropriate combination of standard functionality and project customization—a specific implementation can be crucial for achieving the business goals associated with the project. The multitude of the ROI (*Return on Investment*) studies related to mySAP CRM Interaction Center published on the SAP Web page (*http://www.sap.com*) prove that business objectives can be achieved in a particularly successful way with mySAP CRM Interaction Center.

Successful interaction center projects

The potential of mySAP CRM Interaction Center results from combining technical possibilities to form economically usable functions. This successful concept will certainly gain strength in future. Even today, mySAP CRM Interaction Center benefits from the continuous enhancement of SAP NetWeaver, for instance in the area of knowledge-based search. In

Benefit from technical innovations

the future, additional possibilities for mySAP CRM Interaction Center will arise from innovations in SAP NetWeaver. Customers of mySAP CRM Interaction Center already experienced this as a smooth and unproblematic transition to the integration and technology platform of the future.

Further gain in flexibility and agility through ESA
Today, mySAP CRM Interaction Center provides ways to quickly and flexibly integrate in (partial) processes and to access processes available in other systems. Thanks to *Enterprise Services Architecture* (ESA), these capabilities will even be enhanced in the future. Considering this perspective, we can expect an increase in business flexibility, and agility for interaction centers. ESA enables companies to flexibly and quickly adapt their value chains to a changing business environment by incremental changes in the IT landscape. For interaction centers, this might mean, for instance, that interactive services for an acquired company part can be quickly and flexibly provided based on its existing processes or processes mapped in its IT landscape. The scope for design also will be extended because the downstream processes or those integrated in the interaction center themselves consist of combinations of enterprise services, and can thus be integrated flexibly in a heterogeneous IT landscape to the level of a single process component.

The future of mySAP CRM Interaction Center will consequently be determined by a further enhancement of customization and extension options. The core intention of this book was to show that, even today, companies with mySAP CRM Interaction Center can use a broad range of customization and extension options. Thus, with mySAP CRM Interaction Center the future has already begun.

A   The Authors

Dr. Thorsten Wewers is a member of the board of directors at ecenta AG, a medium-sized SAP consulting firm with offices in Walldorf, Germany, and in Singapore and the Americas. As a consultant Thorsten has led multiple international projects in the SAP Interaction Center area.

Prior to co-founding ecenta AG in 2000, he worked for two years in Business Process Technology product management at SAP, where he was responsible for SAP Business Workflow applications in SAP CRM. In 1998, he received a doctorate from Prof. Dr. Dr. h. c. mult. Peter Mertens at the University of Erlangen-Nuremberg, Germany, for his thesis on Inter-Enterprise Workflow Management.

Dr. Tim Bolte has been working in the Interaction Center area at SAP since 1999. He is responsible for SAP Interaction Center product management.

Prior to joining SAP, Tim worked as a consultant from 1997 until 1999. During that time, he advised several companies in establishing and reorganizing their call centers with a focus on business processes and workforce management in call centers. Tim received his doctorate in 2002 from Prof. Dr. Gösta B. Ihde at the University of Mannheim, Germany, for his thesis on CRM and Call Centers.

Index

**Detailed guidance
on RFC programming**

**Object-oriented access with
BAPIs, Active X, and JCo**

**Advanced techniques: tRFC,
qRFC, and parallel processing**

380 pp., 2004, US$ 69.95
ISBN 1-59229-034-5

SAP Interface Programming

www.sap-press.com

J. Meiners, W. Nüßer

SAP Interface Programming

A comprehensive reference for RFC, BAPI, and JCo
programming

With a strong focus on the RFC Library, this book
gives beginners a first-hand introduction to basic
concepts, and highlights key tools in the ABAP
Workbench. Actual programming examples help to
illustrate client-server architecture, and show you
how to assess the appropriate tools for error diag-
nosis, troubleshooting and more. Experienced SAP
developers can dive right into comprehensive
chapters on programming the RFC interface, and
advanced techniques such as tRFC, qRFC, and
parallel processing. Extensive coverage of BAPIs,
ActiveX, JCo and highly-detailed programming
examples serve to round out this exceptional
resource.

>> www.sap-press.de/906

The official guidebook to SAP CRM 4.0

462 pp., 2004, 59,95 Euro
ISBN 1-59229-029-9

mySAP CRM

www.sap-press.com

R. Buck-Emden, P. Zencke

mySAP CRM

The Official Guidebook to SAP CRM 4.0

Discover all of the most critical functionality, new enhancements, and best practices to maximize the potential of mySAP CRM.

Learn the essential principles of mySAP CRM as well as detailed techniques for employing this powerful SAP solution. Practical examples highlight important functional aspects and guide you through the complete Customer Interaction Cycle. Plus, you'll also discover the ins and outs of key functional areas and benefit from expert advice illustrated throughout with mySAP CRM business scenarios. A fully updated presentation of the implementation methodology, as well as the technical fundamentals of SAP CRM 4.0, on the basis of SAP NetWeaver, serve to round out this formidable resource.

Interested in reading more?

Please visit our Web site for all
new book releases from SAP PRESS.

www.sap-press.com